IT'S CRIMINAL

IT'S CRIMINAL

THE TRUE CONFESSIONS OF
A JET SET MASTER CRIMINAL

JAMES CROSBIE

with Stephen Richards

JOHN BLAKE

Published by John Blake Publishing Ltd,
3, Bramber Court, 2 Bramber Road,
London W14 9PB, England

www.blake.co.uk

First published in hardback in 2004

ISBN 1844540596

British Library Cataloguing-in-Publication Data:

A catalogue record for this book is available from the British Library.

Design by www.envydesign.co.uk

Printed in Great Britain by Creative Print and Design (Wales)

1 3 5 7 9 10 8 6 4 2

Papers used by John Blake Publishing are natural, recyclable products
made from wood grown in sustainable forests. The manufacturing processes
conform to the environmental regulations of the country of origin.

For Marlene, my wife.
Thank you for your devotion and loyalty.
Iceland can wait.

Contents

Introduction

CROSBIE!
WHERE IS HE NOW?

The headline leaped out at me from the pages of the *Scottish Daily Record* in the reading room of the Falkirk Public Library. It was July 1974. My head jerked back in surprise and, out of reflex movement rather than reasoned intent, I quickly folded the crackling pages over and stared around at the library's other visitors.

Had anyone noticed my panicked reaction? Was there a curious eye peering suspiciously in my direction? No. All was peaceful. Everyone just continued to read or study quietly to themselves, simply minding their own business. Gradually, I brought my breathing under control and, careful not to rustle the paper too much, I teased the pages open again and read beyond the headline.

BANK ROBBER SPOTTED IN CYPRUS. Apparently, the police were considering sending a squad of detectives to scour the beaches for me in that sunny land. It seemed to me that they would need a lot of cops if they were going to send squads of them to all the places I had been 'spotted' in so far: the Middle East, West Africa and various European countries including, of course, the Costa del Sol in sunny Spain. And how I wished I really was in one of those far-flung places – the further flung the better! Instead, here I was in Falkirk, not twenty miles away from the scene of my most recent bank raid.

I weighed up my situation; out of jail through a trick by a wily Glasgow lawyer, my real money out of reach, my current cash reserve down to a last few hundred quid with my hotel bill quickly reducing that to zero, no-one to turn to for help, looking at a lifetime in prison if I didn't get myself out of this predicament and – last but not least – every cop in Britain scouring the country for me. There was no question: I had to do something, and do it fast, if I was going to flee the country and head for Brazil or, more specifically, Rio de Janeiro, to meet up with Biggsy and find out how to beat the extradition laws and hopefully live happily ever after. There was only one way I was going to be able to do that. I needed money – lots of it – and I needed it now!

There was only one thing for it. I would have to go and rob another bank.

Jesus, when I thought back about it, life was a lot simpler when I was only stripping lead from the local factory rooftops.

Chapter One

The Power of Money

I was born on 15 January 1937, the middle of three sons: Thomas Anthony, my big brother and William Ireland, my wee brother. I don't know if I was born in a hospital or at home, but I do remember my young brother being born at home. As far as homes go, it wasn't much: a single room and kitchen with a shared toilet on the ground floor of a grey, austere-looking sandstone tenement house at 47 Palermo Street in the heavily-industrialised district of Springburn, Glasgow.

My mother came from Greenock, on the Clyde coast. I never knew my maternal grandparents: when they died, she and her big sister travelled to Glasgow and became laundry maids in Stobhill Hospital. It was there, I suppose, that she met my father who lived in Springburn, a 15-minute walk from Stobhill. After they married, they moved to 47 Palermo Street, next door to my father's family.

So there I was, brought up in a room and kitchen along with my two brothers, where we slept in a recess bed, all three of us together. Just through the wall, my mother and father slept in a similar recess bed in the kitchen. In those days and right up until the mid-1960s when they started tearing down the sandstone tenements, the kitchen in Glasgow tenement houses was the centre of family activity. A black, gleaming cooking range with its open coal fire, three-ring gas fitting and oven and, in those pre-television days, a wooden-framed wireless formed the core of our domestic universe. As young children, we played under the table around the feet of our parents who would sit listening to the programmes on the wireless. As we became older, we spent our time playing board games like ludo, snakes and ladders, dominoes and draughts. And when my father took the fancy for it, he would entertain us by playing the accordion. I had a better-than-average upbringing.

My father, a hard-working tradesman, was a fitter who served his apprenticeship with the famous North British Locomotive Company of Springburn. He was fairly strict with us and I can recall getting skelped – hit – on the legs as a chastisement. Our values were based on being an honest, working-class family and our neighbours were the same. I grew up in a world of hessian rubbish-bag tents, football in the streets and jeely pieces (jam sandwiches) tossed out of kitchen windows to screaming demands of 'throw us a piece, maw!'

My schooling began at Saint Aloysius infant school in Elmvale Street, Springburn and it was while there that I got my first taste of the power of money. Yes – even at the tender age of five or six, I recognised the powerful influence of hard cash. In those days, our pocket money was sixpence; as you can imagine, that didn't last long. Somehow or other, I came into possession of a shiny half-crown piece and all I wanted to do was spend it. And spend it I did! My pals and I headed for the ice-cream shop and small bowls of ice cream smothered in red strawberry sauce with a crisp wafer stuck edgewise into it. I don't remember what they cost, but we had them for about three days in a row. That was my first lesson in the power of money and I never forgot it: I was suddenly popular.

I can't remember exactly when I started to steal, but I do remember being aware of the fact that if I wanted to enjoy myself, I needed money to do it. It was during WWII and every child in the class had to pay threepence a week – for a daily bottle of milk. The teacher would collect these coins in an empty pencil box which she would leave by the side of her desk.

At the end of classes, our teacher would march us out of the classroom and along the corridor to the school gates into the care of our mothers, or send us off up the road for home. I soon learned to hang back until teacher was out of the door attending to one of my classmates, usually one of the girls who was crying for some reason or another and quickly snatch a handful of threepenny bits from the pencil box. The handful of small brass coins wasn't a lot, but it was a lot more than anyone else had – this was at a time when rationing was still in force. I spent it on daft things like chalk for drawing on pavements and once even on a tobacco pouch so I could use it as a purse. I have fond memories of going up and down Springburn Road buying ice lollies for my pals, sucking the last vestiges of flavour from the stick, then wiping my sleeve across my satisfied, stained lips.

In those early days at Saint Aloysius, I was too young to really understand about stealing. I just knew that it was better to have money than to have none. It didn't take long before some others and I naturally formed into a wee gang; among other childish shoplifting forays, we would run into a little fruit shop at the foot of Balgrayhill Road to grab an apple, or even a carrot if that was all we could get our hands on and run away. The old woman used to race out from behind the counter and chase us up Springburn Road for about twenty-five or thirty yards, or until we tossed the loot away and she would stop to pick it up.

I soon devised a plan. I got one of the gang to walk right into the fruit shop and, without any attempt to hide his actions, boldly grab a huge turnip. I can still see it today: John Flynn, my pal who lived up the road from me, was the turnip-lifter. Sure as anything, the shopkeeper raced out after him, leaving my pals and me to take advantage of the diversion and pounce on whatever we fancied. We raced into the shop, grabbing at anything that looked edible and we were out just as fast with our ill-gotten gains, heading in the opposite direction while the misguided shopkeeper bent triumphantly to recover the 'stolen' turnip. We thought it was great! This worked a further two or three times before she rumbled us. How we young toerags must have tormented that poor shopkeeper.

My memory of life in those early days is just a blur of climbing walls and railings, playing in the rubbish tips and fighting with the Proddies from Elmvale Street Public School. Public schools in Glasgow were not, as one might suppose, expensive seats of learning where you picked up an upper-crust accent. In working-class Springburn, there were only two types of school – Catholic and Protestant. Although I swung my schoolbag at the heads of attacking 'Proddy dogs' from Elmvale Public when we clashed every day at 3.00 pm, I never felt superior or inferior or any different from them. It was just the way it was and, as far as I know, the way it still is. Catholic cats and Proddy dogs.

Religion was very important in my family. My granny and grandpa had a miniature altar with candles and my father was a good practising Catholic who never missed a Sunday mass – nor allowed any member of the family to miss it either. And he always attended chapel on holidays of obligation, going to mass at six or seven o'clock in the morning before heading on to work.

I suppose the Crosbies of Palermo Street were actually fairly well off, relatively speaking. I can remember one day raking through a drawer and finding what at first sight appeared to be a huge and very valuable banknote. My heart leaped with excitement – I think I had already started spending it in my mind. Then I took a closer look. It turned out to be a very fancy scrolled certificate stating that John Crosbie, my father, had satisfactorily served five years with the North British Locomotive Company. It is still the only certificate of a completed apprenticeship that I have ever seen.

My early years were spent in a very austere world. Oh, we

had a comfortable enough house when you consider all the slums that abounded in working-class Glasgow. There was always a fire and bread to toast on it. But there was only a cold-water tap in the house and the toilet was outside in the close to be shared by the occupants of one of the other houses on the ground floor. The third house on the ground floor, my granny's, was bigger than the other two. My granny's house was considered to be a 'foreman's' house because it had an extra bedroom and the luxury of an inside bathroom with hot water as well as a huge cast-iron bath – although I never once had a bath in it. I wonder why! You would think that it would be handy for the grandchildren to nip across the close to their granny's for a bath, but no. We were actually bathed in a large, two-handled zinc bath that had to be filled with kettles of boiling water and the one filling of water had to do the three of us. My father, like most other working-class men in Springburn, made his way to the public baths in Kay Street every Friday night or Saturday morning for his weekly douse. I wonder why he didn't use his mother's bathroom. It's strange when I think about it now.

I was always in and out of my granny's house. She used to send me on errands and get me to beat her bass mat – the heavy mat just inside her front door. I would take it out and whack it off the side of the tenement. Clouds of dust flew everywhere as I tried to figure out which way the wind was blowing. I got twopence for this twice- or thrice-weekly chore. Then, with running messages for neighbours, especially when I was sent on the hunt for a pound of under-the-counter sugar, I could earn as much as two bob a week and most of it went on ice lollies.

Most of the time, however, we kids were always skint. We knew about money, or at least I did, but unless we actually had a birthday present, or had accumulated a few coppers one way or another, we just amused ourselves climbing dykes and raking rubbish heaps, which we called middens or midgies. In every district, or perhaps every couple of blocks, there was always a lucky midgie which seemed to contain a much better quality of rubbish. Usually the middens behind shops were lucky. We would rake through the individual bins with our bare hands, even climb right in behind them for things that had been thrown too far in or had fallen down the back. We would eagerly grab a likely-looking object, sometimes finding old clothes and stuff which we promptly pulled on and proudly paraded about in until someone told our mothers and we were suddenly grabbed by the ear, had the offending article removed, marched back to the house for a good scrub with red carbolic soap (which my mother insisted in using right up until her death in 1994) and had our hair combed out for nits.

At the age of nine, I moved on up to the 'big school' – Saint Aloysius Primary. Mostly I would play truant, or plunk it, as we used to say. I used to keep my dinner money and spend it on sweets, ice blues (still a favourite) and wulks (whelks) for threepence a bag from a barrow in Wellfield Street. The wulks were sold in a twisted cone of ordinary newspaper with a tiny pin thrown in so we could hawk out the snotters – at least that's what we kids called the dead molluscs inside the shells – and eat them.

It was about this time that I learned to ride a bike. I remember it was Ronnie Gribben from round the corner in Ayr Street who had the bike – about the only one in the street. I think all the kids around us learned to ride on Ronnie's bike. I can still remember that day in Flemington Street when I managed to keep my balance without anyone holding on to the saddle. It was a wonderful feeling. Bikes were destined to play a big part in my life in the years ahead. As a matter of fact, my father was a very well-known racing cyclist in his day, gaining fleeting fame and his picture in the papers as the first man to climb Balmano Brae, the steepest hill in Glasgow, using a standard 72-inch fixed gear.

My time at the big school passed pretty uneventfully. I don't remember getting into any real trouble other than having my teacher, Mr Palmer, come to my house to speak to my parents about my plunking. The only other aspect of my life there that had any lasting effect on me was the emphasis on religion. I suppose all Catholic schools must have been the same. The school was adjacent to Saint Aloysius Chapel and there was a connecting stairway between the two buildings. On special prayer days, which seemed to come round remarkably quickly, the whole school would be marched up a steep flight of stone stairs and along a narrow passage to the side door of the chapel, where we were herded inside and shown to our pews. Once settled down we would kneel and pray and do whatever it was we had to do, then after singing a couple of hymns we would be sent home about half an hour early – whoopee!

Religion was always being rammed down our throats at school. Every Monday morning, after prayers, our teacher stood behind his desk and stared silently at his cowering pupils. It was quite nerve-racking, especially when he leaned forward a little to add emphasis to his words. Then, in a most serious voice, came the dreaded question: 'Hands up anyone who did not go to mass on Sunday?' If anyone was stupid enough or honest enough to raise their hand, a shocked gasp would rise from the rest of the class and the guilty party would visibly quake under the concentrated stare of about thirty pairs of horrified, accusing eyes. Mr Palmer always appeared to have an apoplectic fit.

'Do you not realise,' he said with a voice like thunder, jabbing his long bony finger in time to his words, his voice rising by at least an octave as he neared the end of his warning, 'that not going to mass on Sunday is a *mortal sin*? You could go to hell and your immortal soul will *burn* for all *et-ern-it-y*!' His stabbing finger emphasised every syllable as he glared accusingly at any terrified, cowering child who had been foolish enough to admit this unforgivable sin of omission. 'You will have to go to confession and tell the priest what you have done and accept his penance for your sin. And you had better not ever miss Sunday mass again,' he ended threateningly, before commencing the schoolwork for the day.

There was one incident, however, that shattered my

burgeoning belief in religion. I had made my first communion at the age of seven along with everyone else in my class and had been going to mass every Sunday and taking holy communion faithfully every first Sunday of the month. Every time I went, a miracle occurred on the altar.

I knew the priest broke bread into the silver chalice and I knew that he poured wine on top of it. Then, when he raised the chalice up on high, I actually heard heaven's bells chime out as God changed this bread and wine into his own body and blood. I didn't care that when I went forward to take communion all I received was a small round piece of white stuff. To me, it was Jesus's body, the result of the miracle that had just occurred. I almost used to quiver when I witnessed and took part in this miracle every Sunday. Like most Catholic boys, I went through the phase of wanting to be an altar boy and in order to further this ambition I volunteered, along with a couple of other lads from my class, to clean the vestry after school hours.

I suppose it was the priests' method of maintaining a regular flow of young lads ready to step into the shoes of retiring altar boys. I remember how excited I was to be permitted inside the vestry and would have scrubbed floors for the privilege. The old priest, Father O'Hara, bumbled about for a few minutes then left us to it. I dusted for a while before noticing a large cupboard that seemed to be unlocked. On pulling it open, I beamed in delight. There were boxes and boxes of biscuits stacked high inside. Without a moment's hesitation, I grabbed a box and tore the lid off. When the contents were revealed, I just stared. I can still remember the shock of realisation hitting me: they weren't biscuits. It was the little round hosts that the priest gave me at holy communion. I looked up at the ceiling, as if expecting God to give me some excuse. But there was none forthcoming. The evidence was all too clear: it wasn't a miracle every Sunday at all. It was just a bowl of these little white round things.

Then I spotted a small clutch of bells and gave them a

tentative shake. And yes, sure enough, the heavenly chimes rang out. It was as if a veil had been lifted from my eyes. The priests were kidding us. Not knowing or understanding anything of symbolism, I just thought the worst. It was all a load of lies. After that, unless I was accompanied by anyone who might have informed on me, I seldom attended Sunday mass.

The sixpence I was given for the collection plate was spent on a very different sort of plate – a plate of hot peas in the café at the foot of Balgrayhill Road. I would sit there and pass the time with my peas until chapel came out. Then I would mingle with the crowd and go home as piously as the next one. From then on, when old Palmer asked his terrifying question every Monday morning, I kept my silence.

My time at the Saint Aloysius Primary was coming to an end. However, one serious obstacle remained before I could bid farewell to the big school and move on in my passage through life: the 'qualy'. The Scottish Educational Authorities Qualifying Examination was the equivalent of the English Eleven-Plus and it was designed to sort out the wheat from the chaff. This looming event sent tremors of nervousness tingling up and down the spines of every child about to be tested.

I had a tough example to follow: my brother Tommy. He was entirely different from me. Where I was uncaring and casual, plunking school at every opportunity and generally messing about, Tommy was a swat. He won prizes for everything and every year without fail received a special award and certificate for perfect attendance. Tommy had, of course, done extremely well in his qualy: he was top of the class and even awarded a bursary. It was the talk of the steamie (public washhouse), as they used to say in Glasgow and Tommy had gone straight into the best first-year class at Saint Mungo's.

Even though I did plunk school a lot, I somehow or other managed to do quite well in my class at end-of-term exams. Arithmetic and English were always my best subjects. The qualy came and went and then we all waited for the results: I came third in the class and everything was fine. We were told what school we would be going to. There were only two possibilities. The first was Saint Mungo's Academy, the top senior secondary school, where a high percentage of students went on to university and the professions and most of the others into white-collar work. The alternative was Saint Roch's Junior Secondary where they taught you rudimentary science, basic English, a little mathematics, technical drawing, woodwork and metalwork, not forgetting the ubiquitous religious instruction. When you left the Rock, as the school was called, you were ready to slip right into the shipyards or factory production lines. If you were one of the top boys you might even get the chance to become an apprentice and actually learn a trade. The top ten in the qualy were certs for the Mungo; the dross was shunted off to the Rock.

Imagine my surprise when I was taken to Miss McGurnigan's office, an unusual event in itself and told that, even though I had been third in the qualifying examination, I would be going to Saint Roch's. I wasn't the least bit bothered by this: my father and, as far as I knew, most of my uncles had gone there. I simply accepted it as routine and off I went. It was years later, about thirty years later as a matter of fact, that my mother told me that Miss McGurnigan had sent for her and told her that, although I had pass marks for Saint Mungo's, to send me there would be wasting a place for a good student. She then asked my mother if she would agree to me going to Saint Roch's and leaving the place at Saint Mungo's for a pupil who would benefit more. My mother agreed and that was that: Saint Roch's for yours truly. I couldn't have cared less. I was 12 years old and going to secondary school. A new phase in my life was about to begin.

Chapter Two

The Rock

Sometime in 1949 I presented myself at Saint Roch's and began my secondary education. I was in class IA, the top class of the first year. I soon realised the potential for dodging classes and proceeded to take advantage of it.

One of the ruses I used to skip school was to make use of the local health clinic, which was directly opposite the school's main entrance. Very early on, I had to go across to the clinic for treatment as I had developed a bad case of chilblains. I was issued with a treatment card that I had to show to my teacher so I could get excused from class. I would wait until the teacher had marked the register, then present my card to him. 'I have to go to the clinic, sir,' I would say and with hardly a glance at my card he would wave me on my way.

There was one or two others who used the clinic cards in this way and, once in the medical centre, we would quickly get our treatment and disappear out of a side door and take off for the rest of the morning. Even though the rest of the class knew what we were up to, they thought it was all dead clever and brave of us to dodge boring classes.

JAMES CROSBIE

My particular pal at Saint Roch's was called PG Devlin: he was, of course, another truant. PG and I became good friends. During the times we dodged classes together, we went on shoplifting sprees in the city centre and collected vast quantities of useless loot. We eventually latched on to things we could actually sell and began making ourselves a little money. I am not trying to say that we made fortunes, but we always had two or three shillings in our pockets.

On the days we didn't skip classes, we would take advantage of our dinner break to travel into the city centre and launch a raid on the old fruit market, a cornucopia of apples, oranges, pears, peaches, plums and any number of strange and exotic fruits that were beginning to reappear after the long years of deprivation caused by the war – an irresistible target for any schoolchild. Once there, we would wander round the traders' tempting displays, stuffing everything we could get away with up our jumpers until we looked like rather lumpy miniature Michelin men.

It was during one of these forays that I had the memorable distinction of being the first boy in our school to steal an example of the latest exotic fruit to reach our shores: a coconut. That day, PG and I returned to school in triumph. The usual expectant crowd was hanging about the back gate and we quickly disposed of our excess plunder. There being a distinct dearth of cash among the children of the Rock, we were always happy to barter our booty for comics, marbles, dirty pictures or any gadget on offer that took our fancy.

The coconut caused a minor sensation. Most of the kids had never seen one before and it was passed reverently from hand to hand, each boy giving it a shake against his ear to listen to the magical milk sloshing about inside.

During my first year at the Rock, I had been strapped umpteen times for repeated lateness and strapped even harder for persistent truanting. At one stage I was in serious danger of being charged with causing criminal damage. I used to go to school on my bike and kept a small spanner in my pocket for loosening off my handlebars so I could twist them at right angles to prevent anyone riding away on it. One Friday afternoon, just before we finished for the weekend, I idly tried my spanner on the brass valve of a radiator in my classroom. It fitted and before I knew it, water was gushing out on to the floor.

I hurriedly closed the valve again, but not tightly. On the following Monday morning, the classroom was flooded and the ceiling of the room underneath had collapsed. I saw the janitor and the science teacher tapping at the radiator with a small hammer in an endeavour to trace the leak. 'Excuse me,' I said, leaning over, 'but isn't that valve loose?'

The janitor, who was kneeling at the radiator, felt the valve and it turned in his fingers, releasing a sudden flood.

'Here,' says I, compounding my error, 'this spanner might fit it.' I was grabbed by the scruff of the neck and frog-marched to the headmaster's office. I totally denied all knowledge. Even in the face of all the evidence I stuck to my story – the spanner was for my bike. They went off and tried it too! I insisted that the fact that my spanner fitted the valve was simply a coincidence. Very grudgingly they let me go, the headmaster warning me never to bring my bike to school again. But all that was a mere bagatelle: more serious trouble was looming.

My first brush with the law came when I was thirteen; it was at a scrap-metal-cum-rag store, a conglomeration of ramshackle, corrugated-iron sheets somehow or other jammed against one another to create a kind of tumbledown shed. What held it together I just do not know, but it made an attractive playground for us and we began to make a habit of wandering over to clamber about the place. It was easy enough to gain entry: you simply pulled a sheet of the rusting corrugated iron aside and climbed in with Ben Kerr and Jim Marshall, two of my neighbourhood pals. I made the mistake of going there once too often – three evenings in a row, if I remember correctly.

On the third visit, the owner and his two sons ambushed us. We were cornered and taken down to one of the red police boxes they used to have on street corners. A few minutes later the police arrived and we were taken to the police station. As we were too young to be locked in the cells, they held us in the station snooker room. We sat in terrified silence. Things were pretty strict in those days and by late evening we were carted off to Saint Vincent Street Remand Home near the city centre. What a carry-on! You would have thought we had robbed a bank or something. Next morning we appeared at the Sheriff Court and were remanded in custody and carted off in a Black Maria back to Saint Vincent Street.

Time there was torture. All we did was sit in a huge room all day and, to make matters worse, we could see a big clock on a building across the street ticking off every minute as time dragged slowly by. I think we did about two weeks on remand before we were given a six-month deferred sentence. It had felt like two years to me and I was never so glad to get home in my life.

That was my first court appearance and my first criminal conviction. It still annoys me that, for some strange reason, our game of jumping about on old piles of filthy rags was classified as housebreaking. That meant breaking into anything other than an actual shop (shopbreaking). So there I was, a thirteen-year-old housebreaker. It annoyed me then and it still annoys me now. I never broke into anyone's house in my life.

By this time, my parents had exchanged houses with a Mrs Buchanan and we had moved up to the top flat at 47. We now lived in a house the same size as my granny's on the ground floor. My father was always strict with me. I can still remember him taking me into the small bedroom whenever my transgressions were serious enough to warrant corporal punishment. He would march me into the wee room and present me with a choice of sticks and canes. I don't know where he got them from, but there always seemed to be a fair choice. Maybe he collected them in anticipation of my next misdemeanour. I had to pick one and he would proceed to beat me on the legs with it until it broke.

I was always smart enough to pick a wooden stick instead of

a cane. I knew the wood would break fairly quickly and I always made sure that I yelled loud enough so he would think it was hurting me a lot more than it really was. Even now I don't think my father was being cruel and I don't resent it. One thing was sure – I always deserved it. I would be kept in for a few days or a week, until things returned to normal.

I was always the only one that got into trouble. I even got caught stealing a bar of chocolate that big brother Tommy had won as a prize. He hadn't eaten it because he was saving it as a sacrifice for Lent. I just couldn't resist a whole bar of chocolate. Tommy went berserk, beating me up and screaming at me in a rage. Still, he was too late. The damage was done, the chocolate gone.

After my first conviction, I more or less kept out of real trouble for a long time. I ran away from home on several occasions, sometimes staying away for three or four days at a time, but I avoided getting into trouble with the police until I was a good bit older. I was a terrible bother to my parents, though. My mother used to say her heart was roasted over me.

Gang fights were usually settled on Paddy's Park, a large green hill behind Adamswell Street. We would arm ourselves with broom handles and home-made axes – tin cans flattened on to wooden handles – and fill our pockets with stones suitable for throwing. I honestly don't know how no one died during the hour-long pitched battles fought on Paddy's Park. I do know that I often went home with a split head or with half the clothes torn off my back.

One final incident was to mar my last few weeks at the Rock. I had obtained a Gat slug gun, the type where you had to push the barrel in, unscrew a nut at the back and insert the projectile – a slug. I took it to school and a guy called Peter Kennedy had a shot at it. He loaded it up and fired it at another boy. The shot struck this boy about half-an-inch above his right eye. I can still see it today: he was howling and we couldn't pull the slug out as the skin just kept stretching. Finally a housewife came running down from her house and the boy was taken to the Royal Infirmary. He wasn't seriously hurt, but it really was as close as you could get. I got the blame. I don't know why the police weren't called in.

Once more I found myself marched in front of the headmaster. I received six strokes of the strap and a severe talking-to. Although I still had about four weeks to go until I formally left, I was told that there would be no need for me to attend the school any longer. I suppose I was expelled and I think I deserved it. I have always regretted that incident.

So that was it. I was sent home from the Rock in disgrace. My schooldays were over.

Chapter Three

Ducking and Diving

Only 15 years of age – still more than two years away from even trying a razor – I was clumping up Palermo Street at 7.15 am on a cold, dark morning wearing a new pair of heavy-duty, tack-studded boots and a brand-new boiler suit. I had a tea and sugar tin in my pocket and I was carrying sausage sandwiches for my 'dinner piece' – just like my father.

I remember my father's anger when I told him I was starting in Connell's shipyard as an apprentice welder. After the initial shouting and bawling match was over and I continued to insist that I wanted to be a welder, I remember him telling me, 'You'll hear a lot of bad language and dirty talk in that shipyard. Don't pay any attention to it and don't listen to the things the older men will say to you.' For all the years that he had worked in the sort of environment where swearing and filthy talk was the norm, my father never used that sort of language himself. He even lost a trade union case because he refused to repeat the swearing that had caused him to bring the case in the first place. He did make an exception and said he would repeat the words if a young woman shorthand-writer left the room. The chairman denied his request and my father then point-blank refused to repeat the bad language used on him. He lost his complaint. My father also avoided alcohol. He didn't have anything against it – it was just something he personally didn't like.

So, on that winter's morning in early 1952, like thousands of Glasgow school-leavers before me, I set off for the Clydeside to begin my working life in the yards. Of course, the first days, or perhaps even the first couple of weeks, were a novelty, but I soon realised this was not for me and was on the verge of leaving. Then I was lured by some of the older lads with a couple of other new-starts away from our welding school area to roam about the shipyard searching for unattended lengths of welding cable. We would collect these cables and strip away the insulating rubber. The copper core was quickly chopped into smaller lengths for easy carrying. We would smuggle the copper out of the yard for sale to a scrap-metal dealer. There was always a few shillings in it for us junior apprentices and it was only the lure of this extra money that persuaded me to stay on at Connell's for longer than I would have had I been relying purely on the pittance of £1.25 that was my weekly pay.

There was a back way out of the yard which meant that, once we boys had checked in, shown ourselves about a bit and arranged to have our time tokens handed in at the end of the shift, we could skip away for the rest of the day. To accomplish this we virtually had to take our lives in our hands. Connell's backed on to a fitting-out dock and there was unrestricted access from this dock on to the main road. All we had to do was get into the yard and walk out the gate – but getting into the yard was the hard bit.

A high brick wall divided Connell's from the fitting-out dock. This wall projected a few feet out over the turbulent waters of the River Clyde and it had a fan of rusting spiked railings extending even further from its extreme edge. To reach our goal we had to inch out to the end of the wall then grasp the rusting spikes and swing out, under or around them, before climbing back up to *terra firma* in the other dock area. This was a dangerous manoeuvre in itself but, to add to the danger, very often one of the Clyde tugboats would come racing by just when someone was in mid-swing. The bow wave from these fast-moving tugs could easily swamp the bottom half of the spikes and caused many a terrified, panicky scramble. However, once into the next dock, you could just stroll out the gate and head for home.

All of these things made Connell's just barely acceptable. I stuck at it for about three months until one day, after a guy called Larry Downs and I had swung under the spikes and wandered off to catch the tram home, we bumped into a foreman from Connell's. He just gave us the eye and nodded. Next morning, the timekeeper, instead of giving me my brass clocking-on token, let me through the gate and told me to wait to one side. When I got inside, Larry was already standing there. We waited inside the gate for a while, then we were sent to the office to collect our national insurance cards. We were sacked and I couldn't have cared less. That was my first job and – hopefully – my last.

For several weeks, I did nothing about looking for a job. I think the relief of leaving Connell's made me appreciate my days more. All I did for that period was pedal about on my bike or pass the time of day wandering about with my pals. Of course, none of us had much cash, unemployment benefit at that time being literally only shillings, so we always had our eyes open for any opportunity to earn something. One day, as we were strolling along, I glanced into a shoe shop. Nothing registered immediately, but in the very next shop I noticed the two young female assistants from the shoe shop chatting away to a young man working behind the counter.

'Hold on a minute.' I grabbed my pal by the sleeve and pulled him back to the shoe shop doorway. I left him there and dived into the shop. There was a young girl of about 12 waiting at the counter, but I ignored her and leaped across to the till. In a second, I had it open and was stuffing all the notes I could get my hands on into my pockets. I think it came to about £15.

In another second, I was back over the counter and on the pavement. By now, my pal had begun to panic – this kind of stealing wasn't his scene. He started to run along the pavement and I followed him, pointing at a tramcar as if we were running to catch it. Of course, he ran on past the tram and I followed him. Two corners away, we stopped and split the money.

Three days later, the police called at my home and, as I wasn't in, told my mother that I was to go down to the police station to see a detective constable. I forget his name now, but I knew immediately what it was about and I must admit I felt a little apprehensive. By this time I had a half-decent bike and all the kit: shorts, racing strip, cap, white ankle socks and cycling shoes. A lot of my time was spent cycling over the country roads that were only a few miles from Springburn. I was actually becoming very keen on cycling and had been doing regular training runs. I put on the lot and pedalled off to the nick. I don't know what the DC thought when he saw me, but he didn't say anything. I was taken into the detective's room and questioned about the snatch from the shoe shop. I denied all knowledge. The detective explained that two of us (he named my friend) had been seen running away from the shop. I said I remembered us running for a tram one day in Springburn Road, but we missed it. I was never too precise with answers – being concise would have left no room for any slight alterations an awkward question might make necessary – and he finally gave up on me and left the room.

'Jimmy.' I heard a soft voice from across the room; it was the detective left to keep an eye on me. I ignored it. Besides, I have always disliked the name Jimmy. 'Hey, Jimmy.' The voice sounded again, a little more urgent this time. I looked over at another desk and saw a very sympathetic face looking over at me.

'Yes?' I replied. I have always made a point of being polite when questioned or spoken to by the authorities.

IT'S CRIMINAL

The face of the man twisted into an eager-to-help expression. 'He knows, you know.' He nodded confidentially at the door his colleague had just gone through. 'He's gone away to give you this chance to think about it. You'd be better off telling him; it could save you a lot of trouble. He can be a very nasty man, you know.' He gave me a solemn nod. 'Very nasty.'

Even at that age, I wasn't falling for rubbish. I pulled an adventure comic from one of my racing jersey pockets and started to read it. Two minutes later, the original detective returned. I watched the second guy out of the corner of my eye and he gave his mate a nod.

'Right, then...' The DC sat down and shuffled some paper. 'Tell me about it?'

'I don't know what you're talking about,' I repeated my denial.

'Right, that's it! This is your last chance to admit it, or you're going on an ID parade. Believe me, son, you're done! You'll be picked out, then you'll really be in trouble for fucking me about.'

'I don't know anything about stealing any money,' I insisted.

A few minutes later, I was standing in a line-up with several strangers they had picked up from the streets outside. Everyone was pretty roughly dressed except yours truly in my flamboyant cycling kit. The young girl came in and walked nervously down the line, not even giving me a second look. After she had left, the DC gave me a glare and told me I could go. By this time, the police were handing half-crown pieces out to the other participants in the parade, payment for their trouble. I cheekily held my own hand out and asked for my half-crown. I was roughly shown the door and told in no uncertain terms to 'Fuck off, you cheeky bastard!'

I quickly pedalled up to my friend's house and found out from his mother where he might be. His mother was very upset, having had the same message delivered by the police for her son to report to the DC. I got hold of him and told him about my experience and how I had not been picked out at the ID parade.

He then went off for his interview. When he got back about an hour later he told me that the DC had said I had confessed and

21

told that it had all been his idea. He told them I was a liar and that he knew nothing about any robbery. They kept on at him for about half an hour, then finally let him go. That was the last we heard about that incident.

On another occasion, during that spell of idleness, I spotted a Co-op dairy where only one woman worked behind the counter. This time, my accomplice was Tam Shevlin. I got him to go round the rear of the shop and fling a brick through the back window. It wouldn't happen nowadays, but the woman fled out of the shop, leaving it unattended and ran through the close to grab what she must have thought was some children. Once again, I nipped in and did the business with the till. I suppose I could have been described as an opportunist thief in those days. There was nothing great, just little bits of villainy here and there whenever the opportunity presented itself.

One day, my uncle Gerrard came into the house and made me go into town with him. Once there he took me to Peter Fisher's paint shop at Glasgow Cross and made me apply for the job they had advertised in their window. 'Boy wanted. Apply within.' Much to my disgust, I got the job and became the general gopher there. It turned out to be not as bad as I thought and it was a big improvement on the slavery at Connell's. Mind you, I had to work all day Saturday and I wasn't very keen on that. But the job had its perks.

When I wasn't sweeping floors or cleaning the bosses' shoes, I helped out on the dry-salter's counter, which sold all kinds of soap and a wide range of cleaning materials. Having unsupervised access to the basement storeroom for these goods was a blessing and it didn't take me long to get onto a fiddle, with the helpful advice of Bob McNish, the van driver. Within a few weeks of starting at Fisher's, I was humping boxes of soap and other materials Bob had taken orders for from the storeroom and putting them alongside his deliveries for that day. With his regular rounds, Bob had ready-made customers looking for bargains and he would simply load the stolen goods – soap, paint, dusters, varnish, anything that he had orders for –

into his van along with his official deliveries. Of course, I had little idea of how much he was getting for all this stuff, but I was happy enough to accept the odd few pounds that he handed me once or twice a week. Things were getting better.

By this time I was getting on for sixteen, that awkward age when you are past playing, but not old enough to get up to anything adult. In the evenings, when I wasn't out on my bike, I hung around the street corner with the rest of the gang and I suppose our ages ranged from fifteen to eighteen, when national service reared its head. Once any of the lads reached call-up age, they would disappear for about eight weeks into what must have been one of the grimmest army barracks in the country – the basic training camp of the Highland Light Infantry. The lines of the famous HLI were set in the middle of the working-class district of Maryhill. Many of the conscripted men could even look out on to their own homes, but to all intents and purposes they might as well have disappeared off the face of the earth.

Then they would suddenly reappear in all their immaculate military finery, hair cut to the bone and all. For a weekend they would swagger about in their kilts and impeccably pressed tunics, telling terrifying tales of the grim life in Maryhill Barracks. It was as if they were making their last appearance, their words a youthful valediction. And then they were gone. Once these guys finished their basic training at Maryhill and were posted off to God only knew where, they seemed to cross a divide from the rest of us.

There wasn't really a lot of villainy in my life at that time, although I do remember stripping the lead from the local library roof along with my mates. We also managed to climb on to the roof of the North British Locomotive Company (NBLC) to begin the mammoth task of trying to clear the lead off there, too. At that time the scrap-metal business seemed the only regular way to make a few quid.

The climb up to the NBLC's roof was easy enough. A pipe in Ayr Street, opposite the front doors of the library, gave us access. It was a bit dangerous because we had to scramble over a wide protruding ledge three-quarters of the way up, but we liked that. Two or three nights a week we would be up there, hacking lead off for all we were worth. Then we would manhandle the lead to the edge of the roof that was parallel with the railway line and throw it down. It was a simple matter then to climb back down and gain access to the railway line over a low wall at the end of Ayr Street and retrieve our lead. Ironically, the scrap was sold, no questions asked, to the same dealer whose ramshackle store we had been charged with breaking into as children two years before.

There was always a lot of gang rivalry in Springburn and often the Palermo Street, Ayr Street and Flemington Street boys would have running fights with youths from Cowlairs Road or Northcroft Road, or any of the four or five gangs that existed in Springburn in those days. Sometimes these fights could get quite bloody and razor slashings were not uncommon. The fights were all over nothing. There were no territorial disputes: everyone knew their area and mostly kept to their own ground. It really is quite hard to put a reason down for all the fighting and slashing that was going on all over Glasgow in the early 1950s.

Every district in Glasgow had its own public halls. The most popular activity in these halls was dancing – proper dancing like waltzes, quicksteps, foxtrots and even tangos. The ballroom-dancing scene was a big thing in Glasgow. My own father was a semi-professional ballroom dancer and a Master of Ceremonies (MC). I used to look up the dance-hall adverts in the newspapers to see if my father's initials were there. If he was MCing at a dance, the advert would have in its bottom corner 'MC – JC'. It always gave me a little tingle to see my father's initials in the paper. No one, not even the acknowledged hard cases, thought ballroom dancing was in any sense effeminate. In fact, it was considered an admirable skill and each district had its champions who were all very well respected.

IT'S CRIMINAL

Every now and again, an undeclared challenge would mysteriously materialise. No announcement would be made and nobody would make any formal arrangements, but it would be tacitly understood that anyone interested in finding out which public hall currently hosted the most talented dancers should be at whichever hall happened to be the venue for the regular Saturday-night dance that weekend. In a show of district solidarity, the local gangs would honour an unspoken truce for the duration of the event, allowing the dancers to demonstrate their skill and style on the floor. I've seen some of the most violent hard cases in the city twinkling through a quickstep and dipping into a tango with an aplomb and skill that would have earned them a guest spot on *Come Dancing*.

Only hard-eyed stares and thinned lips betrayed the barely-suppressed violence behind a veneer of sociability. At the end of the evening, no official declaration or admission would be made, but everyone present would know who had swept the floor. The last waltz was always an unarticulated admission as to who had taken the night's honours. At first the floor would be crowded, then gradually couples would glide to one side until, at the end of the waltz, the champions floated gracefully round what had become their own personal stage in a demonstration of their superiority. Actual applause would be out of the question, but quietly nodding heads, along with an air of appreciation was reward enough. A few quick bars of the national anthem, always a must in those days and the hall would start to clear.

On the pavement outside the dance hall the air would be thick with tension. There would be an unnatural silence for such a large crowd, as eyes met and faces grew stern. No one group wanted to be the first to leave the scene, as this would be seen as a sign of weakness.

It would start with a push, a quick scuffle, a voice raised in protest, a sudden flurry of fists. The night would erupt in an explosion of uncontrolled violence as the women passed blades to their men and the chibs came out. The police would be quickly on the scene, Black Marias screeching round the corner to deliver uniformed officers who pitched into the melée, clubbing everyone and anyone within striking distance of their truncheons. No one would strike back at the police – that was a taboo and they whacked with impunity.

Suddenly, as if on a silent, secret signal, the street would clear as everyone took to their heels. A few defiant voices would yell out gang slogans as they retreated into the night. 'Tongs ya Bass!' 'San Toy! San Toy!' Finally, all would be quiet and the night's entertainment would be well and truly over for another week. Only the police and a few prostrate bodies remained behind. The badly-injured were ferried to the Royal Infirmary for stitching; the walking wounded were allowed to slink away. If anyone was arrested, it would be the unfortunate injured bodies having their wounds attended to at the Royal.

Things got so bad that the judiciary appointed a very strict judge to the High Court of Glasgow: Lord Carmont. All high-court judges in Scotland are law lords. Overnight, Lord Carmont multiplied the usual high-court sentences about fourfold. People were going up to court expecting the usual two-stretch, or if they were unlucky, maybe a three-stretch. They ended up going to Barlinnie in tears, with sentences of eight and ten years still ringing in their ears.

Lord Carmont smashed the razor slashers all right and the law-abiding public hailed him as a saviour. Mind you, it has to be said that, although the old razor in the hand or stitched into a flat cap made a mess of someone's face, it was seldom, if ever, fatal. Not like now, when knives to the body are routinely causing the deaths of many young men.

I was involved in the odd gang fight just because I happened to be there at the time it erupted, but I was never really into fighting and I never carried a weapon. I suppose I had my interest in cycling to thank for that. By the age of sixteen, I had left Fisher's paint shop and started work as an apprentice electrician with the Corporation of Glasgow. I quite enjoyed my job there and I was assigned to a tradesman in the maintenance squad called Jimmy King.

During my time with the Corporation, I had taken up competitive road racing having, thanks to Bob at Fisher's, managed to buy a handbuilt Flying Scot with all the racing gear. Most of my evenings were spent training and at weekends there would be a road race. Being under eighteen, I was a junior and limited to sixty-five-mile events. I became the first and only junior rider for the then-famous Velo Club Stella. They used to say that, when they saw a VC Stella red racing strip at the start, they wondered who would be second at the finish.

I was still working quite happily with the maintenance squad, even going to Stow College of Engineering one day a week, when I was called into the foreman's office. I was being transferred to a different squad to learn installation work. I didn't mind because I thought it would be as interesting and, by this time, I was competent. For a few months I worked on different sites. I learned to install boilerhouse fittings and new pyrogenic cables. I found it interesting and was getting on very well at my work. Everything else was fine too. I had a girlfriend, Eileen McSherry and I would go out with her quite a lot. She lived in Broomton Road, quite near Springburn. I don't know how often I walked home late at night from her house.

The only criminal activity, other than the odd lead-stealing venture, which was a pretty continuous feature of my youth, was when I broke into a cycle shop late one night. That job came about because, although I was working, I was still only a second-year apprentice and earning very little money. I was still as keen as ever on bike racing, but it was expensive for me, especially the lightweight tubular tyres that were a necessity for racing. This cycle shop in New City Road had a whole swathe of 'tubs', as we called them, dangling temptingly in its window. So one night, about 11.00 pm, I pedalled down to New City Road and, after hiding my trusty bike up a close, I walked round to the cycle shop, climbed over the wooden gate and simply kicked in the glass of the front door.

I went into the window, unhooked the bundle of tubes and, while I was at it, I took a nice lightweight frame. It was as easy as that. I got back on my bike and fifteen minutes later I was in my bedroom checking out the tyres. To tell the truth, I wasn't even particularly excited. I had been more worried about getting stopped by the police for having no front light. After that I took to occasionally putting my foot through a shop doorway when I was walking home from the dancing. I would just rifle the till and grab any money that was there, then carry on walking up the road. I was always surprised at the total lack of attention I got.

I know that job transfer was all part of serving my apprenticeship, but when I was told to report to the construction site of the extension to Colston Road School, I was disappointed. Up until then, I had been on jobs of two weeks' duration. I knew Colston School – it wasn't far from my home in Springburn – and I knew that the job there was very definitely long term. I suppose I was prejudiced before I even started, but it was worse than I thought. I realise now that it was all part of serving my time and learning all aspects of an electrician's job. But squatting day after day in the cold concrete ducts of a half-built school, drilling hundreds upon hundreds of holes in hard concrete walls before fitting rawlplugs into them for the armoured cables, really sickened me. I grew to hate the job and started to take days off. I really dreaded going into Colston School every morning. I started to think about branching out.

Conduct: Exemplary

The new jet fighter aircraft were always zooming about in the skies. I could recognise the Meteors, Vampires and Canberras and felt a thrill every time I saw them flying high above me. The more I saw them, the more I thought about flying them. In those days, I used to read comics every week. There was a wide choice: the *Hotspur*, the *Rover*, the *Adventure*, the *Wizard* and the *Champion*, to name only a few. These were columns of solid print, with only one exciting picture at the beginning of each story to illustrate the key point of that week's adventure. Strang the Terrible would be left in dire straits, about to be crushed by some huge stone, or tied to a stake ready to be burned alive – you just had to read the follow-up. Each week Sergeant Matt Braddock, the modest Victoria Cross-winning bomber pilot, would overcome impossible odds. I wanted to be like him.

On the day I turned seventeen I took time off from Colston School and went into town, heading for the recruiting office of the Royal Air Force.

'Yes?' A smartly uniformed RAF officer looked up at me. Judging from his sparkling appearance I thought he must be at least a group captain. As I soon learned, he was a flight sergeant.

'I'd like to join the RAF,' I said to the flight sergeant.

He rose to his feet, hand stretched out in welcome. 'And what sort of a job would you like to do in the Royal Air Force?'

In my innocence, I thought everyone in the RAF got to fly Spitfires. 'I want to be a pilot,' I answered in all honesty.

'Just the sort of chap we're looking for!' The flight sergeant welcomed me with a confident smile and firm handshake as his free hand stretched for an application form. I signed on for a five-year regular engagement.

I knew I'd blundered the minute I jumped out of the truck at RAF Bridgnorth. It looked dreary on very first impressions. I guessed the disabled Spitfire imposingly propped up at the camp gates was the closest I was going to get to a plane.

A squad of corporals – I soon found out that they were our drill instructors, or DIs – was waiting for us, yelling and screaming at the tops of their voices as they marshalled the new arrivals into a three-deep parade. We struggled to get our backpacks and kit organised and shuffled roughly into line. Then, with four or five DIs bawling out indecipherable orders as loud as they could shout, we were marched away from the guardroom area down towards our billets.

'Halt! You bunch of useless layabouts!' One DI's voice sounded louder than the others when we came alongside a row of long wooden huts. 'You lot couldn't march to save your useless fucking lives!'

'Shut up!'

'Don't move!'

'Stand still, you bunch of fucking nancy boys!' Suddenly the shouts came from every side. There was consternation in the ranks as we bumped and pushed at one another in an effort to sort ourselves out.

'Right turn! Are you all fucking stupid? I said, *right turn*!' The voice rose to a demented scream as others bellowed and cursed around us. At last we got ourselves sorted out and facing towards the wooden huts. A nervous silence hung over us. I had heard swearing before, but never like this. Was this the way they were supposed to talk to us?

'Right!' one of the DIs shouted in a more-or-less normal voice. 'These are D squadron's billets and you miserable-looking bunch of pricks are, God help me, D squadron. You've got five minutes to sort yourselves into groups of twelve and move into a billet. I don't want to see anyone standing out here in five minutes. Right? Now *move!*' The last word was a hysterical shriek.

We had only just dumped our kit on the beds when the door to the billet burst open and in stormed a corporal drill instructor. We all turned to stare nervously at him, as he seemed about to explode from apoplexy. 'Attention!' he screamed. 'A-fucking-tention!' He put his face right up against one of the guys in our billet and screamed at him. 'Are you fucking stupid or something? Stand to attention.'

He stalked to another man and gave much the same performance. Eventually, by dint of screaming and yelling, he got us all standing by the sides of our beds. 'Now,' he breathed, looking at us in obvious disgust. 'I'll let you off this time, but the next time I walk through that door' – he pointed at the billet's entrance – 'whoever sees me first will shout, "NCO present!" And you will all jump to attention, understood?'

'Yes.' A mumbled response greeted him.

'*Understood?*' he screamed. 'Let me hear you.'

'Yes, sir!'

This set him off again. 'Corporal!' he yelled. 'You call me Corporal.' He strode round the room actually growling. I know now it was just an act to intimidate us. I wasn't scared at the time, just puzzled that a man could make such a prick of himself and think he was impressing me.

That was my introduction to RAF Bridgnorth. I've never liked loud people – I think it hides a weakness – and this corporal idiot was the loudest man I'd ever heard. I definitely knew that I wasn't going to like Bridgnorth.

Our training started right away: square bashing, weapons training and fieldcraft. It wasn't so bad when you were actually doing something and I suppose they've got to scream and shout to impose their authority and get you to jump to their attention, but I actually liked the square. I enjoyed the precision marching and the rifle drill, but I couldn't put up with all the swearing and the stupid, impossible threats to tear off my arm and beat me to death with the soggy end.

My pal there was a guy called Alan Patterson from Larkhall near Glasgow. He was a rough-and-ready type and was always getting into fights. Fortunately. he was a handy amateur boxer so could look after himself all right. I used to pal about with him and go drinking at the NAAFI when we weren't cleaning our kit or polishing the floors of the billet.

I was never a particularly good airman, as we were called, though for the life of me I don't know why we had that title. My full title was Aircraftman Second Class, the lowest form of life in the RAF, as the screaming DIs constantly reminded us. I just got on with my basic training and hoped that I would go somewhere decent when it was all over. We had as much chance of getting into the air as a one-legged man has of winning an arse-kicking competition.

One day I had to go for a haircut and, when I was sitting in the camp's barber's shop, which sold everything from cheap jewellery, watches and cigarette lighters to tobacco and sweets, I noticed that the shop took up only about one third of a billet-sized hut. The other sections of the hut held a library and an empty classroom. I looked at the construction of the internal walls. They were a soft fibreboard. I could almost press the wall in with my hand and I knew I could certainly stick a bayonet through it.

A couple of nights later I found myself entering the unlocked classroom and in five minutes I had cut a gaping hole through to the barber's shop. I needed cash, so I emptied the till and packed all the fags and tobacco I could into the old kit bag I had got hold of. The cheap costume jewellery, watches and lighters seemed valuable at the time, so they went into the kit bag too.

I knew there would be almighty hell to pay, so I hid the jam-packed kit bag in an air-raid shelter behind the firing range and was in the NAAFI before 9.30 pm. Alan was there and I told him what I had done. He didn't believe me at first, but when I showed him a small wad of notes he realised that I had to be telling the truth. Later on I showed him the kit bag of stuff and we agreed that it would be easy enough to get rid of the fags and tobacco, but too dodgy to try and sell the jewellery and other things. We also agreed that we couldn't sell the fags in the camp, as people would ask questions. In the end we split the goods into two parcels. The fags and tobacco stayed in the kit bag, the other stuff we repacked in a small case and stashed it just outside the boundary fence of the camp.

The first chance we got, we collected the kit bag and, wearing our uniforms, we took the bus to Wolverhampton. We really didn't know where we were going to sell the stuff, but picked a transport-type café that seemed to have a rough-and-ready trade and where we felt comfortable. Sure enough, the man behind the counter showed immediate interest when we told him that we had just come back from an overseas posting and had smuggled back extra fags and tobacco. The deal took about two minutes, with us accepting his offer of half his own marked-up prices. The café owner was left with the kit bag; we left with just over £50 between us.

I had been expecting to see the police in the camp, or hear it mentioned on the camp radio station. But no, nothing was said, a police technique designed to tempt the perpetrators into talking about the job or trying to sell the goods and so give themselves away.

The lift I got from the success of my job kept me going for a few weeks and everything seemed a bit brighter. It's great the difference a few quid makes and I still had the rest of the gear to sell. In order to play it safe, Alan and I had agreed to keep the other things until we went on leave at the end of our basic training. We planned to take it home with us then and try and sell it. In the end, when we inspected the gear properly, we realised that most of it was rubbish. So we tossed the 'jewellery' and split the watches and lighters between us. Then we hid it again until we would be going home.

At the end of the eight-week training course, I was posted to RAF Melksham, Wiltshire, a training camp for the electrical camp. We collected our stashed loot and took it home with us on our seven-day end-of-training leave. Alan and I had a last drink together on the train home and made all sorts of arrangements to meet up sometime. He got off the train at Motherwell carrying his little parcel of goodies and I bet he did the same as me: gave them all away. That was the last I saw of him.

I was probably the first guy that ever stood at the corner of Palermo Street in an RAF uniform instead of the usual HLI kit. The boys welcomed me back and I told them my tales of derring-do at Bridgnorth – most of them grossly exaggerated, of course, just like the HLI boys. The seven days were over in a flash and before I knew it I was getting off the train at Melksham and looking for a bus up to the RAF camp.

RAF Melksham was a lot more relaxed than Bridgnorth. No more insane screaming and shouting. No more 'Outside, D squadron!' yells every time you sat down for a minute. No more organised marching up to the dining halls. There were cleaning duties in the billet and your kit had to be up to scratch, but that was acceptable. I had brought my bike with me to Melksham and had plenty of time to train; and, surprise surprise, for the first time since I had joined the RAF, I got to touch a plane. Only thing was, it was a German plane! They had several of these aircraft in our training hangar and we practised tracing circuits and soldering joints on them. Maybe they didn't want us messing up British planes, worn out or not.

Even though things weren't too bad at Melksham, it still wasn't for me. When I signed on in Glasgow, I thought I would be flying about in the sky like Matt Braddock, not playing around with captured German aircraft. Once the novelty wore off, I fell back into my old ways of wondering how I could earn some money.

It must be true, that old proverb about birds of a feather flocking together, because out of all the guys in my billet, I found myself gravitating more and more to the company of a chap called Monty. We first got chatting because, like myself, he was Scots. It didn't take either of us long to find a kindred spirit in each other and before long we were exchanging ideas on how to earn a few quid. As it turned out, Monty was a bigger crook than me. He had discovered a lorry park behind some buildings in Melksham and he told me that it had been a habit of his to raid lorry parks in the Borders. He wanted to check the loads of the parked vehicles. 'You never know what you'll find,' he told me. 'It could be anything... tobacco, shoes, clothing, even useless rubbish. Anything.' I agreed to give it a go and off we went into the village.

We got among the lorries and checked two or three, looking for anything portable we could make money on. We were just folding back the tarpaulin of one lorry when a shout went up from the window of one of the houses overlooking the parking area. We had to run across an open area to get to the exit and whoever had spotted us would have seen our uniforms. Once on the road outside, we headed back for camp, but about halfway there we heard a lorry, obviously driving fast, coming up behind us. We ducked down in the ditch and waited until it had passed. Sure enough, it turned in at the camp gates and halted at the guardhouse. We managed to get back into the camp by crossing a couple of fields and made our way back to our billet.

We were disappointed, but felt lucky to have avoided capture. Later on, we both realised that we hadn't thought it through. What if we had stolen something? Where would we have put it? Where would we have sold it? It was one thing to raid lorries on your own stamping ground where you knew plenty of hiding places, even your own house, if necessary. Here, it was different. And now we didn't dare go back to the lorry park anyway – they'd be on their guard. We were really a bit disappointed and still short of cash.

I told Monty about my success at Bridgnorth and we decided to check out the situation at Melksham. My experience with the barber's shop had shown me what to look for and, sure enough, when I went to the camp shop the next day, I found exactly the same set-up. However, it proved to be a better target than my last effort. It was an almost identical hut, converted into three distinct sections. At one end the barber's shop flourished and looked quite an attractive prospect, every bit as easy as the one at Bridgnorth. Then there was a middle section that seemed to be some sort of reading lounge. It had tables and chairs along with three or four old armchairs in it. I think it was just used as a waiting room if the barber was busy. But the last section was an eye-opener: a post office. My heart started thudding the moment I walked inside, making a small purchase as an excuse to enter the premises. The first thing I saw was a massive safe and pound signs flashed before my eyes. The shop was also stocked with all sorts of attractive items.

It was easy, except for the safe. The waiting room windows were left open and it took seconds for us to get inside. Another couple of minutes and the beaverboard partition wall was torn open. We had the foresight to bring two large suitcases and we filled them with everything we could get our hands on. There were boxes of pens, watches, ornaments, souvenirs, lighters and other interesting stuff. It made quite a haul, definitely my biggest so far, when we counted the sheets of half-crown savings stamps we found in a drawer.

But the safe defeated us. I felt gutted to leave it untouched, but we had no option. It could have easily and quickly been ripped open along its seams, but in those innocent days this knowledge was beyond me.

We hid the suitcases in dense undergrowth on a railway embankment near the camp and spent the rest of the evening in the NAAFI congratulating ourselves on a job well done. We had found about £40 in cash; along with the savings stamps, which we intended to cash piecemeal so as to avoid suspicion, it came to about £100. It was a good haul for two skint airmen. We lived quite lavishly for a week or two on the money, going into the big NAAFI club in Chippenham and ordering fancy meals.

Once again I had got into competitive cycle racing and entered an inter-camp cyclocross event. This particular race was over a distance of about eight miles, half on roads and half across fields. I entered it on my immaculate road-racing bike – ten gears, racing wheels, lightweight tubulars and all. I only finished third in the actual event, but the two men who beat me were both top-class riders. A guy called Edney, an English amateur champion, was first and a professional road racer called Holliday finished second. I was very pleased with myself over that and won a prize of 7s. 6d.

Just before the three-month deadline for buying myself out of the RAF ran out, I put in my application for discharge by purchase. I actually thought that all I had to do was put in the form, pay the £25 and leave, all in the one day. Not so! I had to make the application, then have an interview with some wing commander. I remember him asking me if I was missing my mother. I told him that I had only joined up because the flight sergeant in Glasgow had told me I could become a pilot. He smiled at that and put my papers in for processing. He said it would take a few weeks and in the meantime I was to carry on. If I changed my mind I was to let him know immediately. He was a nice guy.

By now it was close to Christmas 1954 and we were all going home on leave. We got paid extra money, 'credits' they called it and were given travel warrants home. Monty and I had agreed that the best thing to do with our two suitcases, still hidden on the embankment, was to split up the stuff between us and sell it at home in the few days before Christmas, when we could expect higher prices. It was a good idea, only messed up by the fact that when we went to get the cases they were gone! We searched up and down that embankment in case we had missed the precise hiding place, but it was no good: they were gone and we had to write them off. It was quite a disappointment to me. On the day we left the camp to head for the railway station I walked along with Monty. There was something about him that was different. Somehow or other he wasn't as talkative as usual. Then just as we entered the station he turned very abruptly on his heel, saying something about having to go somewhere on his own and off he went. I thought it was odd behaviour because he was catching the same train as me, all the way to Carlisle. It was only later on that I thought about the disappearance of the two suitcases. Until this very day I still don't know for certain if he took them, but I can think of no other reason for his odd behaviour. As I said before, Monty was a bigger crook than me. He never returned after Christmas and was posted absent without leave.

I well overstayed my Christmas leave, but I was in the clear with the RAF because I kept getting weekly sick notes from my doctor certifying that I was unfit to travel. When I was young I used to suffer quite a lot from tonsillitis and I had discovered how to 'close' my throat by sort of clenching it tight with my muscles. I would go off to see my doctor and give my throat the clenching business and he'd sign the 'unfit to travel' certificate. I don't know how long I could have kept this up, but one day a bombshell arrived: a telegram for me! It was from RAF Melksham: 'Return to unit immediately for discharge by purchase'. Christ! I had forgotten all about it. And now I was without a penny to my name. What was I going to do?

I was spending a lot of time with my girlfriend Eileen and quite often I'd go to her house at dinner time and walk with her down to her work in the Co-op grocery shop in Auchinairn Road. A few days after I had received the telegram, I was walking Eileen along Broomton Road on our way to the Co-op, desperately racking my brains for a way to get the necessary £25 to pay for my discharge. There was and still is, a row of shops in Broomton Road. One of these shops, the biggest, a double-fronted store, was having one of its plate-glass windows replaced. I watched as two men manoeuvred a huge sheet of glass into place. The shop itself was actually closed for its dinner hour and the glaziers were just working away fitting the glass with a couple of dirty-faced kids looking on.

'Look at that,' I said to Eileen as we passed by.

'What?'

'Look at the men fixing that window,' I said.

'What about them?' She gave me a funny look.

'How do you know they're really fixing it?' I stopped to watch the workmen. 'They could be breaking into the place.'

Eileen laughed at me and said, 'Don't be so stupid.' As she gave me a dig in the ribs with her elbow she went on to say, 'It's obvious what they're doing. They're putting in a new window, so they are.'

'Hmm,' I replied, my brain clicking into gear. 'Obviously that's what anyone would think, even me.'

Two days later, during the dinner hour, I was kneeling outside a newsagent's shop in an almost identical shopping parade in another housing scheme where nobody knew me. I must admit I was a bit nervous and had walked past the closed shop several times before I finally made my move.

The pavement was clear of pedestrians when I kneeled down and, quite openly, spread out the contents of my 'tool bag'. It wasn't much of a tool kit, just a few odds and sods like a screwdriver, a wood chisel, a three-foot rule, a hammer, a duster and a huge ball of putty placed prominently in sight. I also had my workman's tea can and sandwich where they could easily be seen. With a last look round to make sure no one was actually staring at me, I held the folded duster against the glass panel of the door and smashed my hammer against it. I had to hit it about three times before the glass actually gave way. It didn't take a minute to pull out the loose shards of glass and in another few seconds I was climbing inside the shop.

Once inside, I turned and continued to work on the glass, making sure nobody was coming over to ask questions. Everyone was going about as normal – after all, I was only repairing the window – so I quickly stepped away from the door and jumped the counter. I rang up the till and grabbed its contents, silver and all. Hurrying, feeling a little nervous, I made my way back out of the hole in the door and packed my tools, not forgetting the tea can and pieces.

'OK!' I shouted into the empty shop for the benefit of anyone who might have been watching. 'That's thirty inches by twenty-four. Right! I'll be back in ten minutes.' With that I walked quickly away, turned off the pavement and on to a footpath that cut between houses, getting myself out of sight as soon as possible.

I could now buy myself out of the RAF and still have a few quid left over. My 'tonsillitis' suddenly took a turn for the better and I was soon on my way back to Melksham. On arrival at camp, I went to the administration office, produced the telegram and handed over £25.

'There you are. Can I go now?'

No. Not as easy as that. I had to complete a clearance form. I needed about ten signatures from kit stores, bedding stores, medical unit, dental unit, the flight sergeant, flight commander, officer in charge of training, the library and another two or three. It took about three days to get sorted out, but finally I had all the necessary signatures and received my discharge book. Conduct: exemplary.

Chapter Four

When I'm Breaking Windows

My parents accepted my return from the RAF with little comment. I was never questioned or censured over it, nor did they seem particularly disappointed in me. But financially, things were getting pretty desperate. I was going around with another guy from my street, Stuart Ferguson. We would wander about in our mutual poverty, wondering how to put a few pounds together and we decided that we would have to get up to something that would throw us an earner. I had sorted out this shop in Duke Street, in the east end of Glasgow and once again it was a cycle shop. There was a ready market for good racing equipment, especially the very expensive and exclusive Campagnolo stuff.

One Saturday night, we crept through the close into the backyard area and set to work on the steel bars of the rear window. In minutes we had sawn through one of the bars and bent it to one side. The interior of the shop was fairly well lit up by the outside street lights and we could see the Campagnolo boxes on the shelves through the open connecting door of the back shop.

Everything seemed to be going smoothly. Working as quietly as possible, we held the bag we had brought with us against the glass of the window and I gave it a smart punch. The breaking glass made quite a noise and we stood still for several minutes in case anyone had heard it. We didn't seem to have attracted any attention and after a minute or two I began pulling out the cracked and hanging glass until the hole was big enough to climb through.

In I went, leaving Stuart outside to keep watch. Next thing I knew he let out a yell and legged it straight across the backyard, vaulted over a set of railings like an Olympic athlete and disappeared into the darkness. A set of head and shoulders appeared at the broken window and I saw the unmistakeable silhouette of a policeman's baton held high.

I was trapped. I suppose I should have heaved something through the window at the front and made a run for it, but I didn't even think of that. It turned out that this man was a police detective and lived right above the shop. I was caught red-handed.

Tobago Street police station – the Eastern – always did have a terrible reputation. It was an old Victorian building, black from city grime on the outside, dark, murky and intimidating on the inside. Getting slapped about was part of the arrest-and-charge routine in those days and I was no exception to this. Heavy-handed constables thumped and pushed me about as I was led to the bar to be charged with breaking and entering the cycle shop. Once the CID came on the scene, I was asked who my disappearing pal had been. I gave them a tale about meeting some guy in a chip shop, café, pub or whatever and I got the usual treatment in return: heavy-handed clumps about the head and thumps to the body, as well as threats of more to come if I didn't give them a name. I held on to my story. I had met the guy in a café and we got talking. He asked me if I wanted to make some easy money and I stupidly agreed. Finally I was taken to the cells and shoved in for the night. The next day, Sunday, I was taken back down to the CID room and there was my father sitting alongside one of the detective's desks.

IT'S CRIMINAL

There was nothing I could say. My father asked me to tell the police about my pal and explained that if I did so it would go easier on me. I said I didn't know who he was and, ten minutes later, I was back in my cell.

Next morning, I was fingerprinted, photographed and taken in front of the sheriff. Four days' remand in Barlinnie Prison, the 'Bar L'. Jesus, I was terrified! The Bar L was just shocking. On arrival, I was stuck in a small box about two feet square. I'm telling the truth here – and they still use them too. At first I thought this was my cell and really didn't know what to make of it. How was I going to spend four days in here? I was too terrified to ask. It turned out that these boxes were used in reception to keep arrivals under control and easy to mind. Obviously there wasn't a toilet and kicking or banging on the wooden door only earned shouts of, 'Fucking shut up, you noisy bastards!'

You could be held in these 'dog boxes' for three or four hours, even longer if reception was busy. And if they were inundated you would be packed in, two to a box. Believe me, this still goes on in Bar L to this very day. Eventually processing would begin. We were marched across a corridor into the medical section where, on a production-line basis, we were weighed, measured, questioned on our medical history and finally marched through a doorway to stand in front of the doctor himself. The medical screw would intone his ritual speech, 'Shirt up, trousers down, name and number to the doctor and say "sir".' The doctor would inspect our hair, then bend down and shine a bright hand-held extension lamp against our pubic region. Nothing was said except your name and number: most men, including myself, just refused to say the magic word 'sir'. I suppose they must have got fed up with yelling at prisoners, because I never heard of anyone being taken to task for ignoring this instruction.

On the odd occasion the doctor would say 'disinfect' and the unfortunate subject would be hustled into a side room where his head and pubic regions would be shaved completely bald and a huge dollop of blue ointment would be slapped on them. This was all done in a most offhand, routine and disinterested manner. Medical over, unshorn and unanointed, I was marched back across the corridor and into the reception area again. It was like something out of a Dickens novel – the cowed prisoner standing in front of a high, old-fashioned desk while the screw barks questions. This ritual completed, another screw marched a group of five newly-admitted cons out of reception and over to C Hall, the grim remand wing of Barlinnie Prison.

'Five on!' the screw on the desk yelled back, his words reverberating like an echo in a dark mountain valley as he altered his chalkboard tally. With that, the reception screw marched out, slamming the steel gate and clashing his keys into the lock.

I felt quite intimidated as I stared up at the spidery steel-and-slate galleries. Halfway down the block a steel staircase gave access to the landings and on each landing cross-tie I could just make out the dark, uniformed, shadowy figure of a screw staring silently down at us. The desk screw quickly allocated cells to us, all singles in those days and the shouting began.

'One on the threes!' the desk screw shouted up.

'One on the threes!' the reply resonated like an echo as I made my way towards the steel stairway.

'Three on the twos!'

'Three on the twos!' Another echo smothered the sound of the men shuffling behind me.

'One LGF!' That one confounded me. I could understand the first two pieces of information, but this had me beat. I later found out that the screws liked to use what they fondly thought was their 'professional' language. LGF simply meant 'Locate Ground Floor'. This meant that for some reason or other – ill health, protection or someone on a capital charge – the prisoner was to be kept on the ground floor.

I was quickly marched along the landing, my loose shoes creating an awful clatter as they hit the slates. The cell door was flung wide open and I walked inside.

'You've got two minutes to get water,' the screw barked and stood to one side. I looked around the cell and saw the metal jug and basin on a shelf that was grouted into a corner. The screw pointed in the direction of the toilet arch and made an impatient jerk with his hand.

'Hurry it up, lad.'

A minute later the door slammed behind me. I stood still and looked around the bare cell. The only furnishings were a table and a green-painted metal chair. On the table lay a chipped enamel plate with a pint mug sitting between a spoon and a flat tin knife. I also spotted a set of wooden boards leaning against a wall and, when I investigated them, I found that they were hinged at the bottom and swung down to form a solid bed base. In a corner, by the window, a mattress stood on its edge, folded into a tight circle. On top of the mattress lay two regulation folded blankets. With nothing else to do I set about making my bed for the night. About an hour later I heard doors banging, the sound coming closer and closer until finally my own door was thrown wide open.

'Cocoa!' A passman stood at the door with a large can of steaming cocoa. I grabbed my mug and held it out, watching a half-pint of watery, unsweetened, dark-brown liquid pour into it. The passman gave me a nod and moved away. The door banged shut and the bolt snapped over. That was it for the night. I just sat on the bed sipping the weak cocoa, wondering what the morning would bring. Finally I slid between the stiff, chlorine-smelling sheets and fell into a fitful, uneasy sleep.

I jerked fully awake from my half-sleep by the sound of the Judas hole in the cell door sliding open as the screw made his first morning check. From my position of about four inches from the floor, the cell looked really unwelcome. 'You've got two minutes to get out of that bed and get it folded up,' a voice snapped at me before the cover fell back over the glass. A minute later, the shouts started echoing all over the hall.

'Forty-two on the threes!'

'Forty-two on the threes! Correct!' roared back from the desk.

One by one, the landing screws called out their numbers, each one getting his congratulatory 'Correct!' as if they had accomplished some difficult task. Finally, the principal officer at the desk completed his sums and yelled out his grand total.

'One hundred and fifty-four!' There was a slight pause, almost as if he was teasing his staff. Then a triumphant 'All correct!' reverberated round the hall. He kept them waiting another moment before stretching his vocal cords to the limit for his final command: 'Unlock!'

No screw ever opened a cell door quietly in Barlinnie. They would clash their huge key into the old-fashioned lock and throw the door open with such force that it swung right round on its hinges and slammed against the wall inside, accompanied by a loud exhortation to 'slop out!'

The morning parade of half-awake men queuing up in the recess with their overflowing chamber pots, the stinging stench of shit and urine almost bringing tears to the eyes: that's morning slop-out. Simply overwhelming. You just had to screw up your face and get on with it. Five minutes later, it was dub up again.

Food was always brought round the cells in the Bar L and still is to this day. About half an hour after slop-out a metal trolley would trundle its way along each landing as passmen dispensed breakfast: porridge with milk, two slices of prison-baked bread, a knob of margarine, a half-pint of grey-coloured tea and then the door was slammed shut.

At about half-past-ten I was unlocked and marched downstairs to stand outside the governor's office in the long dark passage that connected the five individual cell blocks of Barlinnie Prison. The rest of the previous day's receptions gradually filtered down to stand in the dingy tunnel, a ragged row of forlorn-looking derelicts. As we stood there waiting to see the governor, a screw handed neckties to the first two men in the queue. These 'ties' were nothing more than strips of grime-polished, once-blue cloth, already knotted so that they could be quickly slipped over your head.

As each prisoner came out of the office, the next man would be marching past him, tie correctly in place. The outgoing prisoner would have his tie whipped off and handed to the man next in line who would still be adjusting it as he was hustled through the office door. When I was marched in, filthy tie properly in place,

IT'S CRIMINAL

I stood in front of the governor who sat behind his desk, a demigod surrounded by uniformed acolytes.

'Name and number to the governor and say "sir"!' A huge highlander screw with a row of military medal ribbons stretching across his chest shouted into my ear from about two inches away. This time I said 'sir'. Not to have done so would very obviously run the risk of a severe thumping.

'Crosbie, sir! Four-day remand. Court on Thursday.'

'About turn! Quick march!'

That was it. Four days of doing absolutely nothing. Banged up except to slop out, take in meals and be ordered outside for the compulsory half-hour exercise every morning and afternoon. I was lucky enough to meet someone on exercise who promised me a couple of books the next time out. I got them too, thank God. Other than that, there was nothing.

On the Thursday morning, I was taken down to the Sheriff Court. I was lucky this time and was remanded on my parents' recognisance. What a relief! My feelings about being charged with breaking and entering never really bothered me. I knew I'd done wrong of course, but I just didn't feel particularly guilty about anything. Even then, without any conscious thought, I was just accepting that I had tried something and it had gone wrong. So what? I hadn't liked Barlinnie – who could? But already the experience had been left behind. It most certainly failed to impress me as a deterrent. The only place I'd really felt sorry – and that was for myself – was in the police cells at Tobago Street.

I saw Stuart Ferguson when I got home and he was pleased that I hadn't told on him, but he had had a scare and didn't want to know any more about thieving. I accepted that, but I knew that with his attitude he would have told on me had our positions been reversed. Still, we're all made different. About a month later I was put on probation for a year. Everyone else was far more worried about it than me.

I was still skint and I still needed money. My mind went back to the 'window-repairing' job I had done to get out of the RAF. I remembered how easy it had been and I decided to have another go. I searched for a suitable situation. What I was looking for was a small but busy shop in a location which directly faced a park, a factory, a graveyard, spare ground or anything like that, just as long as there was no chance of anyone being directly opposite. My bike came in useful for that and I found literally dozens of suitable set-ups. The thing that made it possible was that in those days every shop, except those in the city centre, closed from 1.00 pm until 2.30 pm for their dinner break.

I made my choice: it was a newsagent's opposite a graveyard wall with only a few other shops beside it. Not that that made much difference; they all closed for dinner at the same time anyway. It just meant that the street wasn't particularly busy at that time.

Everything went as easy as my first one. I pedalled up on my bike and propped it against the shop's window. Quickly, I spread out my 'tool kit' and went to work. I was very conscious of a few people passing by and alert for any sign of suspicion from them, but even the folk that did glance at me kept on going. Nobody even gave me as much as a second glance. I knew I was safe. Less than five minutes from the start, I was out and pedalling away on my bike. Good, I thought as I left the area behind, I don't need to worry about being skint again. The thought of capture on probation had never entered my head.

So things changed for me. I was able to hand my mother whatever money I got from the unemployment office and used my own money for everyday expenses. Even with the odd extra item that I bought, the money from that second glazing job lasted me three or four weeks.

In the course of the next few months I must have done about six jobs with never a sign of any bother. I even had people coming up to me while I was working to ask if the shop was open. 'Sorry,' I'd say. 'Closed for dinner. I'm only here to fix the door during the break so as not to interfere with business.' Off they would go, completely unsuspecting. Each job being individually small meant that nothing ever appeared in the papers either and that was good for me. One bit of publicity about the mystery 'glazier' would have had people diving on me the moment I spread my tools. The police are a lot smarter in that department nowadays.

I also discovered that certain types of shops held more money than others; butchers' shops, for example, were always busy and taking cash. Furthermore, it wasn't the type of shop people were expected to break into. I had hit on a good thing. That was until one day in the south side of the city when I got my tools out and put my hammer through a butcher's door and disturbed the staff at their dinner inside. Luckily my bike was handy!

My career in the glazing business was about to come to a very abrupt and unexpected end. I had been looking for a shop when I came across this chemist's. At first I was just going to pass on by, but then I had second thoughts and stopped to peer in through the door. Yes, it looked reasonable enough and chemist's were always busy. As well as the thought of the money, I could see a display cabinet full of expensive-looking cameras. Strangely enough, up until then I had never even attempted to take any goods, having limited my target to cash in the tills only. I should have stuck to that! However, I had made my choice and prepared to go to work.

Bike parked, tools out, bash, bash and through the glass of the door, all very blasé. I was inside, having a last look at the street before going for the till, when an old road sweeper appeared outside the door. He considerately cleared up all the broken glass from around the door and made a right good job of it too.

Meanwhile, I did the till and removed half-a-dozen cameras from the display cabinet. I got away from the job by telling the old man some tale about forgetting a tool or something. I asked him to stand guard for me for ten minutes or so until I got back and he was happy to oblige. I'd like to know how he explained it all to the shopkeeper.

When I got home, I inspected the half-dozen cameras I had stolen. They certainly looked very expensive, brand new and full of interesting shiny knobs. One of them even had a flash fitting on it. At that time I had no idea of where to sell the cameras; then

I remembered my 'uncle George', actually a lifelong friend of my father's whom I had grown up knowing as almost one of the family. He had actually been best man at my father's wedding. George owned a general store in Springburn Road and, among other things, he was a well-known local amateur photographer.

George had a good look at three of the cameras and told me that he didn't want them himself, but might be able to find a buyer for me. I left the cameras with him and went off to pass the rest of the day in the snooker hall until it was time to go home for my tea.

When I got home, I had the surprise of my life. Uncle George was sitting at the table beside my mother and father with the three cameras on display in front of them. I hadn't considered the fact that George was an honest man like my father. It was only because he was so close to my parents that he had not gone straight to the police. I was lucky there, all right! My explanation was that one of the older men in Alfie's snooker hall had asked me if I could get rid of the cameras for him. I had told him that my uncle George was a photographer and might know someone who would want them. So I was given the cameras to take round to show to him and that was all there was to it. If he wanted, I told George, I'd just take them back to the guy in Alfie's.

I was sent out of the living room while George and my parents had a serious discussion. I was solemnly warned that the only reason the police weren't being informed was to save my mother and father the shame. I was not getting the cameras back and George would attend to them. Further to that, I was becoming too much trouble for my parents. The new made-to-measure suit I had bought, plus the other increases to my wardrobe, had not gone as unnoticed as I had thought and suspicions about my recent affluence had already been voiced between my parents. I was to get my case packed because I was being sent off that very night to stay with my aunt Anne, my mother's elder sister, in London, until something more permanent was sorted out.

I had the other three cameras hidden in my grandmother's unused bedroom, as well as over a hundred pounds in cash inside the piano in our own room. I really wasn't very bothered about my expulsion, looking on it as a new experience to be enjoyed rather than seeing it as a punishment. And I knew too that I had been lucky with George not going to the police, which would have been a catastrophe! All in all, I thought that I had come out of a tight corner not too badly.

I didn't realise just exactly how lucky I had been, or how strong the friendship between my father and George must have been, until my father said something to me from the railway platform just before my train pulled out for London. 'You didn't know that your uncle George was a special constable, did you, James?'

I hadn't known. When my father told me that, I knew that I had indeed been very lucky. Since then, I've often thought about the strength of friendship my parents and George must have shared for him to protect them like that. Uncle George was a good man.

Chapter Six

The Great Escapes

Throughout my childhood auntie Annie visited us regularly and we also went to stay with her in London several times. The first house I remember in London was in Marcus Street, Wandsworth. We went there several times and I can still remember paddling in a big outdoor public swimming pool and losing a pair of shoes there once – that caused a bit of a panic in those days of clothing coupons.

I actually cycled to London once at the age of 16 for my annual holiday. It took me three days to get there, which was really good going. By then my aunt had married a widower, Bill Smith, a school-keeper and they lived in the schoolhouse in Capland Street near the Edgware Road. Now they were living in a schoolhouse in Shepherds Bush, just off Uxbridge Road and that was where I was sent.

My stay at my auntie Anne's was short-lived. One evening there was a television news report about a bank van loaded with cash being hijacked outside a branch of the Royal Bank of Scotland in Glasgow. I was riveted, really impressed by this audacious act, especially as it had happened in my home city. At the end of the news report I said something along the lines of, 'That was terrific! What a job those guys pulled off. They must be really clever.'

My aunt got very upset about my attitude and told me off in no uncertain terms. How dare I admire these criminals and, if that was the way I thought, then I was not welcome in her house. I went up to my room a bit dismayed at this, because I still thought the robbers had done really well.

The very next day, my father turned up at the door, probably summoned by a phone call. After a talk with my aunt, my case was packed again. This time it was to my auntie Peggy and uncle Peter in Northampton Street, Islington. They were a different kettle of fish from auntie Anne. Actually my auntie Peggy, whom I still visit, was my father's cousin on his mother's side. Her name was Peggy Kilcoyne and she was a cousin of Benny Lynch, the world flyweight boxing champion from the Gorbals who had been brought up with her family. Peggy and Peter were typical working-class Glasgow people. Both had hearts of gold and would share their last with you. Even though they had five sons and two daughters of their own living in their three-bedroom council flat, I was immediately made welcome and became one of the family. I must admit I was very happy with my auntie Peggy.

I got a job with the Phoenix Electrical Company of Marshalsea Road, Borough, as a third-year apprentice electrician. After a few weeks of jobbing around with a tradesman I was sent to work on a new building, Sun House in Fenchurch Street. The work was quite interesting too; I was left more or less on my own to install all the flat under-floor trunking for the cables.

One of the other apprentices there was Bob Shilton from Kilburn and we became good pals. He invited me home to his parents' house in Cambridge Road, Kilburn, for Sunday dinner a couple of times and we went to the local dances together. We would pick up girls at these places – nothing deep or serious, just enjoying female company and carrying on a little.

My tastes got a little more expensive and I found myself

looking for an opportunity to get more money. There was a row of shops opposite Northampton Street and I had noticed that there were no bars on one or two of the rear windows. One night I went down and managed to squeeze through the small top window of one of them. I searched around but there was nothing really worth taking. I suppose that was why there were no bars on the windows – I should have thought of that before I went in. One thing I did find, though, was a small safe in the back shop and I felt quite excited about it.

There was plenty of light coming in through the window and I had a good look at the safe. Its hinges stuck out and I could see their pivots going into metal sleeves that protruded just above and below the safe door. There were plenty of tools in the shop, including a hacksaw. That was it.

I worked for hours sawing those steel pins and when I finally got through them it made not the slightest bit of difference to the strength of the door. It still stuck in there as tight as a tungsten trapdoor. I didn't know about the lock tongues inside sliding into slots on three sides of the safe. I thought that if I just cut through the hinge pins the door would fall open.

I nearly gave myself a hernia pulling and hauling at that door. What a disappointment. Hours of work, sweating like a pig, clothes all dirty and all for nothing. I found it harder to get out of the window than it had been to get in. There was nothing on the outside I could grip to help pull myself out. I was beginning to think I'd got myself stuck when, with a last desperate thrust, I got my hips through the space and fell on to the ground outside.

My next effort was more successful – a licensed grocer's in Essex Road. I spotted this shop late one evening when I was prowling about. I noticed that it was closed and there were no lights showing, so I climbed a wall and got in through an upstairs window into a storeroom. Once inside, an internal door let me downstairs and I soon found the office. I didn't get a large amount of money – it must have been too well hidden – but there were quite a few small bundles of notes and a couple of five-pound bags of silver in a drawer. I took this, then filled an empty rubbish sack with all the fags I could find and set off for home.

Everyone was in bed when I got back to Northampton Street, so I got the sack into the bedroom unseen. John and Peter, two of my 'cousins' with whom I shared the room, were either asleep or too sleepy to care what I was doing. I stuffed the sack under the bed before getting ready for bed myself. I had the idea that I'd take the cigarettes down to Sun House a little at a time and sell them to the woman who ran the workers' canteen there. I should have known that you couldn't hide anything in a house full of people, especially with a couple of young children running about as well. About two days later, I was asked by my auntie Peggy to explain the cigarettes under my bed. One of the kids had found them and pulled them out. Needless to say my aunt wasn't very pleased about it.

There were no excuses and, although I never admitted stealing them, I think that fact was just taken for granted. My uncle Peter was told when he came home from work and I was in everyone's bad books. I was told that I had to get them out of the house that very night. I had to get rid of the fags as quick as I could.

By now I was nearly 19 and I decided it was time I rented a place on my own. My auntie Peggy and uncle Peter raised no objections, but made me promise to keep in touch with my mother and to feel free to come round to visit them any time I liked. So I left Northampton Street on good terms with everyone.

I had already discussed my plans with Bobby at work and he had introduced me to a pal of his, Don Tye from Paddington. Don was about the same age as me and lived with his parents. He wanted to move out to get some independence, so we agreed to find a place together. In those days it was easier to find a bedsit than it is today and the third or fourth place we looked at, with a Mr and Mrs Jones of Paddington, seemed very friendly. The room was really big and well furnished with a good pair of twin beds. The Joneses rented out three other rooms in their house. Our room was on the first floor and had a large bay window and another single window looking out on to the tree-lined Bravington Road.

IT'S CRIMINAL

Within a few days we more or less became part of the Jones family. Mr and Mrs Jones, Ted and Mabel, had a daughter of seventeen and adopted twin girls who were about four years old. I gave up my job with Phoenix Electrical and began to enjoy a new lifestyle. Bobby and Don were old pals and knew all the interesting places to go in the West End. It was they who introduced me to what I suppose you would call the fast life. Every day we would go up west to the Harmony Inn, a café in Archer Street, directly behind the old Windmill Theatre. This café was a meeting place for spivs – old time Del Boys. You could buy and sell anything in the Harmony Inn and we were soon involved in the buying and selling of the latest fad item – see-though wristwatches. These were wristwatches that had transparent backs to them so you could see all the works inside. They were really quite good value too, not back-street rubbish done up to con the punters. I don't know where they came from, but they were available in the Harmony for about £2 a piece in batches of ten and sold for around £5 each. Most days we could shift two or three each, quite good money at that time.

Then there were the jazz clubs. They became the places to visit. Studio 51 in Great Newport Street was our favourite haunt and we were there most nights until early the following morning. I remember some of the names: Ronnie Scott, Tubby Hayes, Phil Siemens, Allan Ganley and loads of other guest stars.

There were other clubs we went to as well, but Studio 51 was our favourite. It was all great fun, but we were spending money faster than we were making it, taking taxis everywhere, eating our meals in restaurants, paying to get into the clubs and buying other people drinks. I had even started buying clothes from shops like Cecil Gee in Tottenham Court Road. The money just seemed to drain away faster than water through a sieve.

By now there was a regular little gang of us who would meet in the Harmony and discuss all sorts of scams to earn money. One of the basic earners was the 'jump up'. This involved looking out for a delivery van or lorry and jumping up on it to grab any valuable-looking parcel, hoping to be lucky with its contents. As often as not, we got a load of unsaleable rubbish, but now and again we had a nice touch: a carton of good pullovers, a case of booze, small electrical goods and stuff like that, but it was all very hit and miss. Whenever we got something we could sell we would get rid of it in the Harmony within hours, minutes sometimes.

'Creeping' was another method of trying to make a few quid. It involved walking into office buildings and simply wandering about looking into offices and rooms for anything of value, adding machines, typewriters, desk ornaments, anything that we might be able to sell. The trouble we caused must have been out of all proportion to the value of the goods we nicked.

When we did get a good tickle, we would stop working until we were nearly skint again. Some days we would get down to the Harmony using the last coppers we had for tube fare and a cup of lemon tea to sit and sip. It was a fast and exciting lifestyle, but we weren't going anywhere. We needed something a bit more certain than casual jump ups and creeping.

Don introduced me to a cousin of his, Jack Witney, who had more progressive ideas. Furthermore, Jack could drive, something I'd not had the chance to learn. With Jack on the firm, our horizons expanded and we began to look further afield than the West End. I got on well with Jack. He was a more determined thief than Don and looked upon thieving as a full-time job – a bit like myself.

Jack had a false driving licence and some good ID he'd got hold of one way or another. In those days, driving licences were just small squares of printed paper stuck inside a little red cover that you could get from any post office by applying for a provisional licence in any name you liked. There was no tell-tale coded number on them to give your age or date of birth, so any driving licence could be used by anyone else. I'll never forget the name on the licence Jack had: Cyril Frederick Chinnery, 46 Leaver Gardens, Greenford, Middlesex. Poor Cyril, as my mother would have put it, his heart must have been roasted. Using Cyril's licence we hired cars for one day; it cost about £2 a day then, with a fiver deposit. We would keep the car out for weeks because the police didn't put late unreturned hires on their stolen list and weren't looking out for them. It was a civil matter, a debt between the hirer and the hire company. We must have had at least half-a-dozen cars out in Cyril's name and we left them if they ran out of petrol or we just decided we wanted a change.

Don and I had become very friendly with Ted, our landlord, and we began helping out with his business, which was light deliveries and private car hire. I used to go about with Ted on a contract he had to shift huge orchestral harps from one hall to another for classical concerts. It took the two of us to carry the harps and I was in and out of TV studios and concert halls all over London. I liked doing that job because I went into so many interesting places and met a lot of television actors. Ted rented or owned two large lock-up garages in Tamplin Mews, just off Cambridge Road, where he worked on his cars or garaged them if he had to. We had keys to these garages and his permission to come and go from them as we pleased. Because we had access to premises, Jack suggested that we go into the car business – stealing them, that is.

I didn't know much about cars, but Jack soon sorted that out. He got me behind the wheel of one of Ted's hire cars and in a couple of days I could drive it. Well, I could start it up, engage gear and pull away all right. I always did have plenty of confidence. Jack had lived all his life in either Hammersmith or Paddington and his father, Fred, was an old face from the racetrack gangs and now ran a coffee stall outside Hammersmith tube station. As a result, Jack knew everyone worth knowing in our new line of business. Soon we were going out at night and lifting cars from around St John's Wood and the surrounding areas.

We would take the motor to his garage where Jack and Don would strip off all the parts that we had orders for. Doors, wings, interiors, seats, wheels, mechanical parts, anything that was needed by the dozens of crooked back-street car repair shops that

Jack knew. After stripping the car we would either drive it, or tow it away if the engine had been removed, a fairish distance from Tamplin Mews and just dump it. I've driven or steered cars while sitting on a kitchen stool, cars without bonnets, boot-tops, doors or wings, sometimes even with odd wheels on. It was a good little business.

A quiet spell hit us, so I decided to show off a bit and go back home in style. Poor old Cyril's licence was used to hire a Morris Minor and after packing my bag I headed off for Glasgow. What transpired during my visit really did give my father cause to shake his head. He must have wondered what he had done, especially with him being so hard-working and good-living, to deserve a son like me.

My visit started out as a great success. Here I was, up from the Big Smoke in my new car with plenty of money in my pockets. I bragged and told lies about my success in the motor trade – I could list makes and models and values like an expert. I had an avid audience of my contemporaries who had hardly moved from Springburn in their lives.

However, the bubble was soon to burst and it really wasn't entirely my fault. I had no plans for getting into anything crooked – it just happened. I don't think I could have stopped the sequence of events even if I had wanted to.

I was minding my own business and driving innocently up Balgrayhill Road on my way to show off again to Eileen and the rest of the McSherry family, none of whom had ever owned so much as a bicycle and certainly never knew anyone who owned a car. Next thing I know, I'm being frantically waved down by the driver of an overtaking car. I drew up and the other driver stopped and hurried back to speak to me.

'Yes?' I wondered what was wrong.

'Your rear wheel is wobbling about,' this bespectacled man informed me.

I got out of the car to inspect the rear wheel and discovered that the metal hubcap was fitted crookedly, giving the appearance of a wobbly wheel. Maybe some kid had tried to steal it and got disturbed. I gave it a hard push and it clicked into place again.

'That's a nice car you've got,' my Samaritan said, having a good walk round it. 'Is it your own?'

'Oh yes,' I said importantly. 'I've had it over six months now.'

'Mine's the same model,' he said, pointing to his own car. 'A bit older right enough and a two-door, but it's a great little motor.'

I agreed with him and made suitably admiring remarks about how well he had kept it. Then this guy says to me, 'You wouldn't fancy a swap, would you?'

'Well...' I began, getting my thoughts together. 'Funnily enough, I was thinking about a two-door model. You see, I'm a commercial traveller and I'm nearly always carrying samples and stuff on my rear seat.' I was ad-libbing like anything here. 'Things are always falling out on the road when I open the doors. A two-door car would stop all that.'

'Yes, yes.' He was with me all the way. 'A two-door model is what you really need.' He looked at me again. 'Would you fancy a swap then?'

I gave it a bit of thought and decided to give him one more chance to get out of it. 'Well, actually I would like a two-door model, but I can't swap with you because I don't carry the car's logbook about with me; I've left it back home in Greenford.' There! That should kill it off, I thought. But no, he came galloping on like Red Rum winning his third Grand National.

'You could post the log book back to me, Mr ?'

'Chinnery,' I told him. 'Cyril Frederick Chinnery from Greenford.' I held out my hand to his. You would have thought that a name like that from a guy like me would have put him off. But again, no! He went for it like a big salmon leaping for a juicy fly.

'But you've got your driving licence on you, haven't you, Cyril?' He had a look of desperation on his face.

'Sure,' I assured him, struggling to hold back an urge to laugh at being called Cyril. I actually did smile. Jesus! Was he really going to do this to me?

'I could take your details from that.'

'Oh, c'mon,' I told him. 'I couldn't just swap you. My car's worth a good bit more than yours. It's practically brand new!'

'Of course, of course. But we could come to a cash arrangement, too.'

I surrendered to fate. 'How much would you go on top?'

He went over the car again, giving it a good inspection and checking on the mileage. Finally we agreed on £70 on top of the swap and shook hands on it.

I made arrangements to call at his house in Wallacewell Road later on that evening to settle the deal. 'Don't let me down,' he said as he drove off with a cheerful parp-parp of his hooter, no doubt thinking about how well he had done.

At about 7.30 pm, I duly turned up at his house and he gave me his logbook, his car and £70. I gave him Cyril's name and address and my hired car and this idiot stood at the end of his drive with a big smile on his face waving goodbye to me. 'Now don't forget to post me the logbook.' I caught his last words as I turned away from his house.

Next day I sold the car for £440 and promptly hired another one. As I have said before, poor old Cyril. I left to drive back to London that same day and going through Abington I was surprised to be waved down by two policemen. Thinking that there must have been some sort of accident or blockage, I stopped. One of the cops leaned inside my car and removed the keys. They had been waiting for me and knew the car I was driving. The police station was just a few yards away and I was hustled inside and put in a cell to wait for an escort from Glasgow. I was really puzzled and wondered what had gone wrong.

What had happened was this: the idiot who had insisted we swap cars had taken his 'new car' round to show his brother and explain how clever he had been. The brother, obviously not half as daft as him, listened to his tale and immediately phoned the police. They agreed it was suspicious and checked up on Cyril Frederick Chinnery by means of a phone call to Greenford police station. Back came the word that poor old Cyril's house had been broken into six months previously and, along with everything else, his driving licence had been stolen. The Glasgow police were also informed that Cyril Frederick Chinnery's licence had been used to hire about half-a-dozen cars in the last few months, none of which had been returned to the hire companies concerned.

The scream was up. Next day, the Glasgow CID had checked the main hire companies in Glasgow; not so many then and sure enough Mr Chinnery had indeed hired another car. An alert was put out for this vehicle and it had been spotted passing through Hamilton on the London Road. A phone call to Abington and they were ready to intercept me. That's what had happened. Simple, isn't it?

My escort from Glasgow arrived to take me back and I was handcuffed and put into the back seat of a CID car along with a huge detective. On the drive back, I gave it all I had with the chat, telling stories about London and putting myself over as a right silly bugger. My escort became quite friendly and, thinking that I was a harmless sort of guy, took the handcuffs off me.

The entrance to the Glasgow Central police station is through a short tunnel, or pen, as we call them in Scotland. We were right inside the yard when I made my move. Still laughing at some joke I had just told, the detective in front got out and opened my door. I gave it a hard shove, knocking him out of the way and ran for the exit. I made it too. What I didn't know, however, was that the very angry detective chasing me happened to be a champion runner. I might still have got away because I could run myself, but he was too close behind me when I whizzed up a short dead end. That was it. Needless to say, I got a good few thumps for that in the alley and was carried back to the police yard with my arms twisted right up my back, forcing me to point my toes like a ballet dancer in an effort to take the weight off my straining sockets. There was no laughing now at the amusing prisoner. I was sent up to the cells and flung on the floor to get a thorough going-over. I curled up, protecting my face and screaming blue murder.

I'll never forget the concerned look on the uniformed sergeant standing by the cell door. I could see he was upset, shaking his head from side to side and looking at me kneeling there. He took a couple of steps towards me and I thought to myself, Good, he's going to stop them. It just shows how wrong you can be. The sergeant came right up to me and grabbed the hair on my head to lift my face up so he could get an unobstructed swing at it with his fist. He had seen that the detectives weren't hurting me and his shaking head had only been a sign of exasperation.

A last few thumps and I was left alone for several hours. After that I gave the usual interview and told the usual lies about just being given the licence when I hired the Morris. No, I'd never hired a car before that and so on and so on. I could say that safely because it had always been Jack who had hired the cars – he was older than me and looked it. Eventually I was locked up again and in the morning was remanded for a week in the Bar L. I knew what to expect this time and accepted it as well as I could. It was easier when you knew what was coming.

One week later I was taken down to Brunswick Street Sheriff Court for a hearing. Before my case was called, I was interviewed again about all the other cars hired on Cyril Frederick's licence. I denied all knowledge. I was asked about one of the hires being spotted in Preston near the scene of a break-in. I remembered it and I also remembered the car that had followed us out to the city boundary. We had recognised it as CID at the time, but had dismissed it from our minds when we had drawn clear of the city. It just shows you how they checked out old Cyril's 'hires'. I was told that, when I was finished in Glasgow, the Lancashire Police would be waiting to see me. Christ, I thought, not more problems.

In the end I never appeared in court that day, much to everyone's surprise, including my mother who was sitting in the public benches. There was an ante-room just off the courtroom, where those appearing before the sheriff were kept waiting until their case was called and off this ante-room there was a toilet in case anyone needed to go while they were waiting.

IT'S CRIMINAL

I went to the toilet and saw that above the steel mesh covering the window was a space just big enough for me to squeeze through. I was prepared to smash my way out when much to my surprise I found that the window pulled down. I climbed through the space and landed on an outside ledge of the building one storey up. From there I hung on by my fingers and swung in to land on a broad window ledge below. I jumped to the pavement and took off up Brunswick Street like a rocket.

By now, all sorts of cars were hooting and people on the pavement were raising all sorts of noise. I just kept running. The court building was in the city centre and in less than a minute I was running along Argyll Street, the main city thoroughfare. I tried not to run too desperately – I knew that would attract unwanted attention – so I just kept a good steady pace, trying to look as if I was in a hurry, but not as if I was trying to get away from something. It must have worked because I was soon running down Oswald Street and over the Clyde via the King George V Bridge into the south side of the city. I didn't stop running until I reached Eileen McSherry's auntie Molly's house in Weir Street, off the Paisley Road West.

Needless to say, Molly was surprised to see me in such a state and even more surprised when I told her that I had escaped from the Sheriff Court. She knew that I had been captured over the car business and had been on remand, but the fact that I had been arrested and then escaped didn't bother Molly in the least. At that particular time, one of her sons, Barney, was on the run himself from approved school and Joe, another of her sons, was currently serving a sentence in Barlinnie. She looked upon my actions as a victory against the police and thought I had done really well. I was more than welcome to stay there until I could get away to London. Of course, I didn't have a brown penny, having had all my cash and property taken off me by the police and Molly, bless her, hardly had a penny to her name. I wouldn't have taken money from her anyway, even if she did have any. I was desperately in need of cash and right then I didn't know where I was going to get it.

That evening the papers came out with my escape featured on the front page: POLICE HUNT CAR CRAZY YOUTH was the headline in the *Evening Times*, along with a picture of the court building with an arrow indicating the toilet window and a trail of black-and-white marks showing my escape route. We all found it very exciting at Weir Street. Headlines! I was famous. But I was also skint.

I resorted to the same old glazing routine and it went just as smoothly as before, only this time, because I needed extra cash, as well as emptying the till I also took two full cartons of cigarettes. A friend of Molly's found me a buyer for the fags and suddenly I was solvent again.

A new set of clothes from Burton's at Govan Cross and I was ready to go. That night I took a bus through to Edinburgh and caught the train to London. I got into Bravington Road at about 10.00 am and was soon relating my story to a startled Don Tye. I was pretty amazed by it all myself, but the main thing was that I was out and ready to do some work again.

The car business had dried up a little and we had been scouting about for an earner. We had found something that looked good to us, well, to Jack and me anyway. Don wasn't too keen on it, but that didn't matter because two could handle the job all right and that suited me. I didn't like having anyone on a job who wasn't strictly necessary. The job we fancied was a quick smash-and-grab, quite a common occurrence at that time.

We had been wandering about one day and had cut through the little arcade at Victoria tube station. There was, and still is, a jeweller's on one of the corners nearest the bus terminus. The window of this shop contained some very impressive rings at well over £1,000 each.

We counted that four of the individually boxed diamond rings would come to about £5,000. We reckoned we would get about £1,500 for them, good money for us. There was a one-way service road between the two steps up to the arcade and the dividing wall of the bus terminus. Traffic on the service road was practically non-existent so there was no problem with getting the car close. It looked good to us and we decided to go ahead. Jack used a stolen licence to hire the car, a Vauxhall Velox, and a red house brick was tidily wrapped in newspaper. We were ready to go.

When I think back on it now, it was all very suicidal. Certainly the location was good and certainly the stuff was there to be snatched, but there is a time and place for everything. If I were to do the same job again I'd say that a weekday morning at about nine-thirty would give an excellent chance of success. But twelve noon on a Saturday, in an arcade which contained a busy tube station entrance next to a bus terminus and a main-line railway station, with people pouring past in both directions was, in retrospect, not exactly the most propitious time and place for a smash-and-grab.

Jack, as the more accomplished driver, stayed in the car for the getaway. I was left to throw the brick. I almost had to push people out of the way to make a bit of space. Finally I heaved the brick through the glass and made a grab for the rings. I got them too, but when I spun round to head for the car a half-circle of crouching pedestrians confronted me.

I could see Jack sitting in the car staring at me and made a rush in his direction. At least half-a-dozen men leaped on top of me and that was that. I heard the squeal of tyres as Jack took off – well, he had no option. There was nothing he could do for me. I was frogmarched into the shop and held until the police arrived on the scene. From there I was taken to a police station where I was booked and had my property taken from me and locked in a cell to await an interview with the CID. I felt in a desperate mood as I looked round the white tiled cell. Jesus! What was I going to do?

Later on, at about seven o'clock in the evening, I was taken up to the CID room and began telling the usual tales. It has always been my policy when dealing with the police to talk as much as possible, yet say nothing. This interview was no exception and I was getting to the point where they were becoming very slack with me. I reckoned in another five or ten minutes they would be leaving me on my own when other odd items of business needed their attention. Then I would be up and crashing out through a window – or something!

Things were very definitely beginning to look promising. I had just offered to sweep the floor for them and they were laughing at my innocence, when the detective handling my case picked up the phone. I heard him asking the station operator to connect him with Glasgow Central Police Headquarters. He was grinning over at me as he passed over my name and date of birth. Then the smile suddenly switched off and he straightened up in his chair. 'What?' I heard the inflexion of surprise in his voice. 'Yes, yes. I've got him here in front of me,' he said. 'No, don't you worry about that. He won't get out of here.' He put down the phone and turned to his mate.

'This little bastard's on the run from Glasgow. Jumped out of a courtroom window a couple of weeks ago.' Then he turned to me. 'Right, you! Downstairs, now!'

We were halfway down the stairs, with me in an armlock, when we met the custody sergeant hurrying towards us. When he reached me he gave me a hard clout around the ear and said, 'Who the fuck do you think you are... the Count of Monte Cristo?' I knew he had found the tiles I'd pried from my cell wall in a futile attempt to escape.

I was hauled up before the magistrate on Monday morning and remanded in custody for a week in Wormwood Scrubs Prison.

At least reception in the Scrubs was a lot more civilised than the Bar L. The stripping off and medical were much the same, as was the bath, but I got a real towel and thought things weren't too bad. One big improvement on the Bar L was that in the Scrubs remand prisoners could go to work. It helped to pass the time and if you wanted to you could get quite handy with a needle and thread and a huge sheet of canvas. Still, time passed slowly and every seven days I would be whisked through reception for an appearance in court to continue my remand. Very little broke the routine until, three weeks in, I got a visit from the police.

IT'S CRIMINAL

I wasn't bothered about seeing them and it made a break from sewing mailbags, so off I went. It turned out they were from Greenford, investigating the break-in at Mr Chinnery's house when the licence had been stolen. I told them that I knew nothing about the break-in and that the licence had been bought for ten quid months ago. They had nothing on me and because of the outstanding case in Glasgow they weren't interested in pursuing the matter. Then they started questioning me on my movements on the day I escaped from the courtroom. I told them straight out that I wasn't going to tell them where I had gone that day.

Then they asked me if I had gone straight to London or if I had stayed in Glasgow for a few days. I told them I didn't want to discuss it. Then they came out with their bombshell. Shortly after I escaped, a young woman, Anne Kneilands, had been found murdered and robbed of her purse near East Kilbride.

As I was on the run and heading south, I was a suspect. Now what did I have to say? 'Oh, well,' I stuttered. 'That's different.' I told them all about staying at Molly's, but missed out the glazing job. I realised later that I was never really a suspect. I just had to be checked out, that one-in-a-thousand possibility. It gave me quite a fright at the time, but I never heard any more about it.

I had been committed to the County of London Sessions and, as I had already made a plea of guilty, I would be appearing there for sentence. I wasn't looking forward to it, because all the feedback I was getting pointed to borstal. This was not a very attractive proposition, especially as you could be made to serve anything from nine months to four years, depending on your behaviour and the whim of the authorities.

My only hope was escape. At this time there was a high partition cutting off the bottom end of the remand wing in the Scrubs. I began to get ideas about it and gave the partition a close inspection. It rose about ten feet above the fourth-floor landing and I saw that by standing on the handrail it was possible to climb over it and drop down into the unused section of the hall. Each end of the prison wings in Wormwood Scrubs was identical in design and I had inspected the cast-iron-framed windows that rose from the first floor almost right up to the arched roof. About eight feet above the fourth landing the straight sides of the window frame began to curve over to make an arched top. I had spotted that the central pane of glass, where the curve began, was a half-round section of window that was slightly wider and deeper than the others. The more I looked at it, the more I believed it was big enough to let me through.

I had been watching the screws and had an idea that they did not pay a lot of attention when they did the count at teatime. I had seen them talking to prisoners or sorting out some argument over the food and I decided that there was no way they could keep the count in their heads through all these interruptions. As they didn't do a final check after our doors were locked, I knew that, when they shouted down 'Forty-two on the fours,' or whatever the number happened to be, they were only reading the numbers off the landing board and not giving the result of a physical count.

So one evening when we were opened up for tea, I stuffed all my blankets and things, including my door card, in the corner behind the door so that the cell looked vacant. Then I hurried along to the recess and, after a quick look to make sure no one was paying any attention, I climbed over the partition and dropped down on the other side. Once over the partition I was free to walk about, as it was impossible to see me from the occupied part of the wing.

First of all I climbed down to each landing and swivelled open the tall narrow sections that ran up to the beginning of the curved part of the window. I climbed up to the fourth landing again and stood on top of a handrail that ran across the face of the window frame. From there I could reach the half-round pane of glass; I smashed it with the heel of my shoe and cleared the broken glass away as best I could.

There is a sort of catwalk against the windows above the fourth landing in the Scrubs and I could reach this with my hands. I took a grip on it and, like a sailor swinging through a hatch, I aimed my feet out of the hole I had made and wriggled my body through. Somehow or other I managed to twist round and grip the iron frame of the window and then I simply climbed down using the windows I had spun open as a ladder. Finally I jumped down on to the small porch-like roof of the hall doorway and from there to the ground. I had the idea that I could make my way over to the reception area and try to get on or under some transport to get myself out of the prison.

The trouble was that the reception was at the exact opposite corner of the prison to where I was right then. There was nothing else for it: I had to try and get over to the reception area if I was to stand any chance of getting out. Fortunately, I was at the rear of the cell blocks and there was little coming or going of anyone there. Most of the movements were made either from the central doors leading directly on to a long corridor that connected all the halls, or from the hall doors facing the front of the prison.

I made it all the way to D Wing before I was forced to cut down towards the corridor. I managed to get across the corridor and kept going towards the front of the building. I got that far too; then, just as I stepped out to pass the front of the hall, the door swung open and I was standing there in a pool of light in my brown remand clothes.

'What the...' The screw couldn't believe his eyes. 'What are you doing here?'

'I've got to go back to reception to collect my sheets.' I tried to come out with something. But by now he had got a grip on himself. And on me!

'You're a remand. How did you get here?' Then he noticed the blood on my hand, which looked a lot worse than it really was. 'You better come with me, lad,' he said, as another mystified officer joined him.

They walked me back to the remand wing and rang the bell. The screws inside didn't even know I was missing and were amazed to see me standing there. I was taken over to the sick bay to get my hand attended to, then they marched me back to the hall to show them how I had got out. They were astonished that

I had managed to get out of the window and had climbed down the face of the building.

I was relocated to the ground floor and put on the escape list. This meant you had to wear clothes with large patches on the jacket and trousers for easy identification. At night all your clothes were taken off you and left on a chair outside your cell door. I don't know why they did that; I don't think anyone has ever got out of one of those prison cells once the door has been banged. I appeared at the County of London Sessions in Marylebone Road and got what I expected: borstal training.

Chapter Seven

The Ballad of Reading Borstal

In 1956, Wormwood Scrubs was the allocation centre for anyone sentenced to borstal training, so back I went. For the first four or five weeks of my sentence there didn't seem to be much difference in my status. I was still sewing mailbags, only this time I was dressed in the navy blue of a borstal boy. I had been taken off special watch and my clothes no longer exhibited huge light-coloured patches on strategic points; maybe it was because I was just beginning my borstal training and I was being given a fresh start.

I went through a twelve-week assessment so as to give the authorities an idea of where to send me. And the time came for allocation. '1484 Crosbie.' A rising inflexion and my hopes soared. 'Gaynes Hall.'

Yes, done it! I felt a buzz right through my body and heard a few expressions of surprise above the excited rise of whispers. 'Jammy bastard!' 'Fucking anointed!' were only two of the phrases I caught. I'd talked my way out of a hard time. Most of the lads were amazed at my result, but no one begrudged me my success. It was put down as a victory for the boys.

Gaynes Hall was in Cambridgeshire, near the small country town of St Neots and two of us had been recommended for that institution by the allocation board. Within a week we were on our way, the journey being made in style in a private car belonging to one of the escorting screws that had come from Gaynes Hall to collect us. We weren't even handcuffed and the screws wore civvies.

The dormitories weren't locked at night and there was only a night watchman on to make sure the lights went out and that there was no carry-on. I think I had been there about one week when that red flag was waved. I had arranged to meet a co-prisoner, Peter, at the rear end of the dining hall at one in the morning. I made up a bundle in my bed and simply walked out the door and over to the meeting place. Peter was already there and in a few minutes we were crossing the fields in the direction we knew would take us to a main road and then on to St Neots itself. I must admit it took us a lot longer than I thought to reach the road, but eventually we saw the glow of headlights in the distance and this spurred us on.

By the time we finally got to the main road, dawn was starting to break and instead of heading straight into the town we decided to cross the road and wait in the woods until it got dark again. I suppose it must have been about four in the morning by then and we were worried about the daylight, us still being so close to the borstal. Besides, we had been told all the stories about previous absconders hitch-hiking and being picked up by staff or police. We decided not to take any chances. It was a long day and, believe me, we were both starving by the time it got dark again.

We stayed in the woods and fields, walking parallel with the road until we reached the outskirts of St Neots. When most of the house lights had gone out, we made our way over to a golf club car park where we had spotted a couple of cars. I knew how to use silver paper in the fuse box and soon we were on the road to London.

It must have been about 1.00 pm when we arrived and I

drove straight to Bravington Road. There were no lights showing and I didn't want to disturb the Joneses by ringing the doorbell. I knew Don was out because he always pulled the curtains at night when we were in. He had to be down at Studio 51 and we decided to carry on down there. We had no sooner passed Harrow Road police station when a police car fell in behind us.

After a few moments they gave us a bell – they used bells in those days instead of the modern sirens. I had no chance of outpacing the Wolseley squad car, but tried anyway. They came alongside me and forced me on to the pavement where I had to brake. Peter and I tumbled out of the passenger door and we made a run for it.

I ran across Harrow Road and on to a bridge over the railway lines. Halfway across the bridge I saw another police car heading towards me, so I swerved and tried to cut back. The driver of this second police car must have seen this because he accelerated and crossed right over the bridge before stopping and letting his observer out to intercept me. I tried to dodge round, but I was hemmed in by the high iron sides of the bridge and ran right into the policeman. I was well whacked about by the cop who had been chasing me and got knocked to the ground; it later transpired that I had two cracked ribs. Peter had already been captured and was sitting in the first police car that had forced us off the road. My latest great escape was over.

We were taken to Harrow Road nick and our story soon came out. They took details from us but we weren't charged with stealing the car or anything. The next day we were returned to Wormwood Scrubs. I was expecting but not looking forward to the big interview and the 'you have let us all down' routine, but nothing was mentioned. This was probably because we were kept in the remand wing instead of the borstal allocation wing. I don't know why they did that. Maybe they didn't want us talking to the new borstal boys. Whatever the reason, they kept us away from there until we were transferred to another borstal.

This time there was no need for allocation boards. There was no choice. It was Reading Punishment Borstal we were going to whether we liked it or not. And believe me, we didn't like it.

The pleasant screw who had kept us supplied with fags and toffee on the way to Reading went around us and unlocked our handcuffs as the coach pulled into the prison yard. Outside, we could see one or two people gravitating towards our coach, obviously screws coming to check over the latest arrivals. We were still in quite a cheerful mood, glad to be out of the Scrubs and back into a proper borstal again, even if it was Reading. Since then I've often said that I wish they had called my name first to get off the bus. That way I wouldn't have known what to expect and therefore wouldn't have had time to get scared.

'Adams?' The screw at the door of the bus mildly called out the first name on his list. Tony Adams got up from his seat with a smile and sauntered down the aisle. When he got to the door he turned as if to make some remark to us. He didn't get the chance to speak. A surprised yelp left his lips as the mild-mannered screw clouted him roundly on the head and thrust him down on to the pavement. There were two screws standing there to catch him as he stumbled, dazed and shocked, into their arms.

One of the screws threw him against the wall screaming into his ear, 'You're in Reading now, you little bastard!' He pushed Tony against the wall as he yelled at him, 'You do everything in here at the double, d'you hear me. At the fucking double! Now.' He grabbed Tony and flung him towards the next screw. 'Get moving! And *double*!'

'Right!' The new screw took over the screaming. 'Keep doubling on the spot when I'm talking to you. *Keep doubling, I said*!' His voice roared even louder as Tony seemed to falter. 'You! You double through that gate over to that door,' he pointed. 'Downstairs, first right, right again, through the door, left turn, right turn again and mark time in front of the desk, knees up to the chest at all times.'

IT'S CRIMINAL

'Bristow!' The mild-mannered screw read the next name from his list in a calm, casual voice as if all this behaviour was a common everyday occurrence. 'C'mon, lad,' he encouraged the suddenly scared-looking Bristow. 'We haven't got all day, you know.'

We had a grandstand view of his ordeal from our vantage point on the bus and it was a nightmare! We all sat and stared at one another as the hapless Bristow high-kneed it awkwardly out of sight. Jesus Christ! Was this it? I can tell you, we were all suddenly terrified. I don't know if I was fourth or fifth off the bus, but whatever number I was, I had seen the treatment handed out to everyone before me and I was quaking in my shoes long before my name was called out. I was practically doubling on the fucking bus to try and please them!

Then, a complete bundle of nerves, I heard my name. Like those before me I was flung off the bus and bounced off the wall once or twice before being forcibly propelled towards the next sadist. Indecipherable instructions were screamed into my ear and I was thrust towards the building, completely confused by the shaking and the shouting.

Was it right, right, then left? Right, left, left? No, surely it was right first then... then...? I was totally bewildered, my mind running riot with the instructions. There was another screw waiting just inside the small doorway to reception. Another clout on the head. 'Faster, you lazy bastard! Keep those knees up! Double!' I was pushed on down a corridor. Was it right now? Please, God, don't let me fuck up! Another turn. Another screaming maniac. 'In there! There, you stupid bastard!' Pushed through another door to come up against a desk. Three screws now, all shouting at once. 'Strip! Clothes off! Don't stop doubling, you bastard!' Another clout.

Knees pounding up to my stomach, I tried to undress. I honestly don't know how I, or anyone else, managed but somehow or other, between staggering and stopping for bare seconds of time, I got my clothes off and my borstal gear on. Then I had to stretch my arms out in front of me while blankets, sheets, clothes, boots, overalls and all the other kit I needed was loaded on to them. There was no slackening in the doubling and no slackening in the shouting. It was a thousand times worse than the RAF had ever been.

Once loaded with kit, my arms feeling as if they were being drawn out of their sockets, I was doubled out of the room and up an almost impossible steel spiral staircase to end up out on the prison centre.

'Double!' The first word I heard again as the screw behind the desk yelled when I threatened to come to a faltering halt. 'Double while you answer my questions.'

I gave him my name, puffing and panting as if I'd just run a marathon and answered his questions about medical treatment, religion and diet between wild gasps of breath. Eventually he slapped a door card on top of my kit. 'Now double!'

Jesus! What did he think I'd been doing for the last half-hour? I was beginning to think it was the only word they knew.

'One-twenty-two!' He shouted my cell location and pointed to his right. 'Now double away and bang your door. And *double*!'

I turned into 122 at the trot and fell to the floor across my blankets. 'Bang that fucking door!' the voice screamed from the desk. I shoved the door with my foot and collapsed across my kit again, almost sobbing with relief. What had I let myself in for? This was Reading Borstal.

On my very first morning I made the mistake of trying to make two trips to the toilet recess. An Arran-sweatered screw was on to me in a flash. 'What do you think you're doing? One slop-out, that's all.'

I put on my 'reasonable' voice. 'Sir,' I began. 'It's imposs ...'

That was as far as I got. Whack! A full open-handed slap across the side of my head. 'Don't talk back to me!' he raged. 'One slop-out, that's all!'

In those days there were no such thing as watches or radios

in prison, even for borstal boys, so we had no way of knowing the time. And the work was murder too... Sewing mailbags! A bundle of them were thrown into your cell, along with a huge needle and a hank of waxed thread. Instructions were screamed – 'Get bloody sewing!' You had to get bloody sewing just as hard as you could, hoping you were doing enough in the time. On my first day I could hear the opening and slamming of doors as the screw came round the landing checking our work. I was feeling quite pleased with myself as I had almost completed a whole bag. Gradually, the sound of doors opening and closing came nearer and I began to hear voices, but nothing clear as yet. Finally the cell next door to me opened and I could hear what the screw was saying.

'How many?' His voice was sharp, very businesslike.

'Two, sir. I've done two.' I could even hear the tremble in his voice.

Two! My mind shrieked. *Two!* Oh my God! And I was happy with one. I bent over my bag in a futile attempt to produce a bit more work.

'Two!' The screw's voice echoed my thoughts. 'Two! You better get three done in future or you'll find yourself in serious trouble, m'lad.'

'Yes, sir.' I heard the submissive reply.

I was shaking with nerves as I plunged my needle in and out of the heavy grey canvas. I should have put the bloody stitches further apart! Oh, Jesus, he was coming.

My door burst open. 'How many bags?' I looked at him and held out my meagre offering.

'*What*?' He tore the bag out of my hands and threw it on the floor as if in a temper. 'Three! It's three bags I want, not half a bloody bag.' He ranted and raved at me for several minutes, uttering dire threats if I failed to meet this target. Believe me, the sound of that 8.00 pm bell from the centre was the only welcome sound of the day in Reading Borstal.

After the first month of this sort of torture we were upgraded from the basic grade and given a job in the wire shop, where they made diamond-mesh fencing wire and safety nets for the Prison Service. This was a vast improvement on the mailbag sewing and you were even allowed a few words with your work partner as long as they were about the job. It was a great relief to get away from that quick-change routine and settle down to a proper job.

I made a blunder on my very first day in the wire shop. The works screw in charge of the shop came up to me with his location board. Anywhere else if a screw wanted to know your cell number he would ask, 'What is your location?' Obviously you would give the appropriate reply. However, this screw held the board in front of him and asked me, 'Where do you live?' Then he added, 'And don't say Glasgow.'

I was happy to please him and said in all innocence, 'Oh no. I live in London.' *Whack*! The location board bounced off my head. 'Don't try and get funny with me, Crosbie.' I was warned. 'You'll find yourself starting another month of basic if you're not careful.' It was only then I realised it was my cell location in the borstal he wanted to know, not my outside address.

Normally a borstal boy under punishment at Reading served between three and four months before being returned to normal conditions. When you are serving time in Reading, three months seems very long indeed and all sorts of schemes and excuses are used to try and get this term shortened. I was no exception in trying to get away from there early, but I had a really good excuse to put forward. The charge of fraud – selling Mr Chinnery's hired car – was still outstanding against me in Glasgow and this meant that when I completed my period of borstal training in England, I would have to appear in court in Glasgow to stand trial for that offence.

I wrote a petition to the Secretary of State requesting that I be transferred to Scotland so that the outstanding charge could be dealt with and my sheet would be clean when I finished my borstal training. Nine out of ten petitions are dismissed with the phrase 'No grounds for complaint'. However, I wasn't complaining and my petition did make some sense: what was the point of me completing my borstal training and becoming a rehabilitated person, only to be arrested and taken to Scotland to answer to an old offence? If I was transferred to Scotland and had the case dealt with now, I would leave borstal with no outstanding charges.

About four weeks after I had sent out the petition, I was marched into the governor's office and told that my request had been granted and that I would be going back to Wormwood Scrubs to wait for transport to Glasgow. This decision cut about four weeks off my time in Reading and I was quite happy about the idea of being transferred to Scotland. Within a week I was heading back to the Scrubs and two weeks after that my journey to Scotland began. It was almost with relief that I got off the prison transport outside reception at Polmont Borstal, six weeks after my journey had begun.

Because I had completed nearly six months of my sentence, I skipped quickly through the classification hall and was allocated to Wallace House which was the block where they kept the troublemakers and inmates they thought might give them problems. With my record it was the only house I was getting into.

I had been at Polmont for about four weeks when I was escorted through to the Sheriff Court in Glasgow for my fraud charge. It was all an anti-climax. The sheriff noted that I was serving a sentence of borstal training and simply admonished me on the car charge, ordering that I be returned to carry on with my current sentence and that was that. If I hadn't already been serving the borstal sentence, I would probably have been dealt with very differently.

Wallace House was more or less a cell block. Everyone had a single cell and the routine was identical to that in an adult prison, slop-out and all. Whatever the 'training' was supposed to be, it escaped me completely. My time there passed pretty uneventfully, although I did get one surprise about a month before I was due to be released. The housemaster sent for me and informed me that I was to be taken to Edinburgh for a medical to see if I was fit for military service. 'That can't be right,' I told him. 'I was in the Royal Air Force and bought myself out in 1955.'

'Yes, Crosbie. The military authorities are aware of that. But as you only served six months before leaving, you have to serve a further eighteen months in the army to complete the full two-year period of national service.'

I had no answer to that and the following day I was taken, along with two or three other lads, to the medical centre in Edinburgh to be examined. I did my best to fail the medical, hoping for a grade-three rating which would disqualify me from service. When I was doing the rising on the toes exercise I made out that it hurt my tendons and barely made it halfway up. Then I thought I would display colour-blindness by failing to pick out the numbers on the dotted colour charts they showed me. Needless to say, I messed that up. I actually felt quite self-conscious when I looked at the bright, colourful cards and saw the numbers leaping out at me clear as crystal. How could anyone not see them, I thought. But I persisted in my plan to prove my colour-blindness and denied being able to distinguish any numbers among the coloured clutter.

I thought my act was going well but, when they showed me a grey dotted card with a bold red number sticking out like a sore thumb, I really felt that it was so obvious I would have to admit to being able to see it. What I didn't know was that the red against the grey of this card was the least visible to a colour-blind person. The tester gave me a resigned look and marked me with a pass. In the end, I passed the whole medical and was really fed up about it.

Around October 1957, I finished my borstal training and went home to my parents in Palermo Street. They had been visiting me during my time in Polmont and were happy to have me at home again. I suppose knowing that I would soon be getting called up made them worry less about me. I had been at home for just over a week when the brown envelope dropped through the letterbox with my call-up papers and a travel warrant to Aldershot, Hampshire. I had been selected for service in the Royal Army Service Corps (RASC) and was to report to Blenheim Barracks, Farnborough. At least my 'bad tendons' had kept me out of the HLI.

Less than a week later I was on my way to serve Her Majesty again.

Chapter Eight

Sharpshooter Crosbie

I was prejudiced against the army even before I arrived at Farnborough. I knew it would be all the same mad shouting again, just like the RAF. Still, after nearly two years of borstal, I wasn't very concerned about that and at least I wouldn't be getting locked up at night. It turned out that Blenheim Barracks was basically a kitting-out camp, but they also spent some time there doing the usual aptitude and IQ tests and I found myself filling in the same forms yet again. They did make us do a little bit of square bashing there as well, probably because we were national-service conscripts and they didn't want to let us think it was too easy.

I shot off to London at the first opportunity and called on Ted. Don had left the flat by this time, but was still around and Jack Witney was living nearby in Kensal Rise. Shilton had got himself married and was the manager of a fruit shop in Queensway. Ted made me welcome and told me that I was free to use his home for my 48-hour leaves whenever I got any. He had also kept all of my clothes and, a pleasant surprise, my bike.

Naturally I wanted to know what had happened during my

two-year absence and it was Jack who told me all about the trials and tribulations they had gone through during my incarceration. As I had never contacted anyone at Bravington Road, I had no idea that the car ring had been, in modern terms, 'bust' and that Jack had served an 18-month sentence for car theft. Jack told me how it happened.

After I had been captured at Victoria and disappeared into the prison system, Jack and Don had resumed business with the stolen cars. Jack had found a customer who required mainly engines and other mechanical parts like the clutch and exhaust systems. This meant that the stolen cars, or shells by now, had to be towed away from Ted's garage to be dumped and this was the most dangerous part of the operation. Jack and Don always dumped them as quickly as they could. This meant that all the stolen cars were being abandoned fairly close to the garage.

The police soon realised that cars stolen from places as far away as Neasden, Wembley, Acton and more or less any outlying district to the north-west were all being found in the Paddington and Kilburn areas. As every abandoned car had obviously been towed to its dumping spot, they reasoned that the crook's garage couldn't be far away.

Police surveillance in the area was intensified and early one morning the crew of a police patrol car spotted Jack unhitching a car in Sutherland Avenue. The police pulled up, checked the towed car and discovered that it had no engine. Jack and Don immediately came under suspicion and were taken into Harrow Road police station.

Knowing the dangers of this happening, Jack and Don had a prearranged story. They had always taken turns when they had a car to tow away for dumping and it was Jack's bad luck to be the 'driver' that night. Don's story was simple, as all the best stories are. He had received a phone call from Jack asking him if he could come along to Saltram Crescent and give him a tow in a car he had just bought. Don had obliged and towed Jack to Sutherland Avenue and had just untied the tow rope in preparation to return home when the police arrived. It was as simple as that. He knew absolutely nothing about a stolen car or missing engine.

Don gave his home address and as his driving licence and other odds and ends bore his name and Chippenham Road home address, it all checked out. The police didn't connect him to Bravington Road or Ted and therefore missed the connection to the garage, which would have been fatal for everyone, Ted included. Jack's story was that he had bought the car very cheaply from a guy he had met in a pub – the usual tale. With no engine? The police knew full well he was lying. That was the reason it was so cheap, Jack boldly told them. Logbook? Oh, that was to be handed over the following evening in the same pub.

The police knew that they had undoubtedly caught the car thieves who had been plaguing them, but they couldn't break Jack down. He stuck to his improbable tale and confirmed that he had phoned the unsuspecting Don for a tow. There was no evidence to charge Don, so he walked; but Jack was charged.

The jury, like the police, didn't believe his tale either and Jack got a guilty verdict at the same court as me – the County of London Sessions. As he was only done for the one car he was sentenced to 18 months – a heavy sentence under the circumstances, but still lucky for Jack. If the police had managed to trace Ted's garage they would have found evidence of over 20 car thefts there, because magpie Ted had taken and kept the tool kit and spare wheel from every car that had passed through his premises.

Jack had served a year in prison, but with his three-month remand he had actually been away just over 15 months. Time spent on remand was not counted as serving your sentence then, as it is today. He had only been out about six months and was fiddling about here and there trying to scratch a living. Whatever had happened, I was glad to see him and it felt good to be around my old haunts again. But I had the army to contend with, as well as the fact that I was on borstal licence for the next year as well.

My company had a second lieutenant who didn't like me. A friend of mine called Robert Loughry and I were out one evening and we spotted this officer driving into the car park of a pub in Farnborough. When he went into the pub we wandered over and looked inside his car. There was a large trunk in the back seat and he had left the keys in the car's ignition. I looked at Robert and we grinned at one another. A minute or two later we were driving along the road towards Guildford. We just drove around in it for a while then headed back to our barracks. There was a parking area under the buildings that held the classrooms and I decided to leave it there. Just as we were leaving the car, I looked at the trunk in the rear seat and became curious.

I really think if I hadn't developed a dislike for the pompous pig I would have walked away, but that dislike, caused by his attitude to me, just tipped the scales. I opened the trunk to find that it was full of uniforms and other clothes. On a sudden impulse we got back into the car and drove it round to the incinerator, stuffed all his gear into the still glowing interior and gleefully watched it burst into flames. I realise that it was all very juvenile, but it seemed hilarious at the time.

The following weekend, I went off to London on an official 48-hour-pass and, as usual, I spent it at Ted's house. I had such a good weekend going round my old haunts with Jack that I decided to stay longer than my pass permitted. I went to Ted's doctor and he gave me an 'unfit to travel' certificate for three days. Everything was fine and I was sitting in the living room of Ted's house when there was a knock at the front door. When I opened the door, two CID men from Harrow Road were standing there.

'Are you James Crosbie?'

'Yes,' I answered, a little bit wary but not feeling I had anything to worry about. The upshot of it all was that Robert Loughry, my so-called pal, had become torn with remorse, or something and had gone and told the duty officer about stealing the car and burning the clothes.

As stealing the car was a civilian matter, the officer had informed the police and they had got a warrant for my arrest. I was taken to Harrow Road nick and held there until police arrived from Farnborough to take me back.

Both Robert and I were charged with stealing the car and its contents. We were taken up before the magistrate's court; Robert got three months and I got nine. As I had just turned twenty-one, I was taken to Wandsworth Prison in London to serve my sentence. Robert went to some young offenders' institution. I never saw him again after that.

Wandsworth was a frightening place for me. First of all they weren't going to accept me as a prisoner because they thought I was too young. Of course, when they inspected my committal papers and found out that I really was over twenty-one, I started to get a lot of stick from the reception officers who were, to a man, all ex-military with their campaign ribbons plastered all over their chests. I was in uniform and they made a right monkey out of me, making me stand to attention and calling me a disgrace to the armed forces.

Nothing untoward happened during my sentence and my date of release gradually came round. I was released on a Good Friday morning and was given an envelope with a travel warrant and instructions to report at 6.00 am on Saturday to 10 Company, RASC Bulford Barracks, Salisbury Plain District.

By this time, I was looked upon as a very suspect soldier and I remember once when I was working in some lieutenant's office I found a half-dozen old lemonade bottles in a cupboard I was cleaning out. I took the bottles out to the NAAFI van that came round every day and cashed them in for an orange drink or something. This little lieutenant practically accused me of stealing them and I felt really embarrassed. If I'd known he was so skint I would have loaned him a few quid. Finally I just got fed up with the whole childish carry-on and took off for London. Goodbye army and good riddance too! Why didn't they just chuck me out? That would have been the easiest solution for everyone. My main problem was that I just could not generate any respect for them because I knew they were treating me unfairly. So fuck them: I went AWOL.

Chapter Nine

Tea Shops for Two

It was 1958. I was 21 and back living in London again. I was lucky to be able to move in with Jack at his cousin's house in Kensal Rise, but I knew that this could only be temporary. I could have gone to stay in Ted's house in Bravington Road, but because I had been arrested there before, I thought it possible that the army authorities might come looking for me. So I moved into Liddell Gardens until I was in a position to get a place of my own.

Most days Jack and I just mooched about, getting up to the odd fiddle or quick piece of work here and there. Opportunist thieving was probably the best description of the way we were grafting then. I remember one stroke we pulled in the Dudley Arms pub, used by the cops who worked out of Paddington Green police station, which was just across the road. The Dudley was always full of loud-mouthed coppers and we were in the habit of going in there two or three times a week just to pick up the local police gossip about what was going on.

As happens in many pubs, the bar staff in the Dudley used to put all the banknotes, other than ten shilling and pound notes, in a tumbler standing on the shelf alongside the till. One night, we were in the Dudley and the tumbler was particularly full of fivers, with even the brown colour of £10 notes showing between the blue (the cops always had plenty of money for booze).

I had toyed with the idea of pulling this stroke before, but things had never been really desperate and the money in the tumbler was seldom that much of a lure. I knew it could be taken, but I had always shrugged the idea off. This night, however, money was a bit tight with us and the tumbler full of notes was really very tempting. It was a busy night and I saw yet another fiver stuffed away. I nudged Jack and indicated the tumbler.

'I'm going to nick that, Jack,' I told him. He raised his eyebrows at me over the rim of his pint then glanced round expressively at the noisy, clustered cops. 'C'mon with me,' I said and headed towards the toilet.

Up on the wall between the first door off the bar and the second door that opened into the toilet itself was the main electrical switch box. I pointed it out to Jack and told him to go into the toilet, have a slash and pull down the switch box handle on his way out. He gave me a long sideways look then broke into a grin, nodding his head in understanding. I made my way back to the bar and began psyching myself up.

I was beginning to think that Jack had got lost when suddenly the pub plunged into darkness. I was ready, with one foot on the brass foot rail and the second the lights went out I launched my body over the surface of the bar and stretched my arm across the space and grabbed the prize. There was a lot of good-natured shouting about putting the lights back on as I slipped away to meet Jack outside. There was over £140 in the tumbler when we counted it out and I've often wondered what the bar staff thought about it being stolen while the pub was full of cops.

That's how it was then: something always turned up and we scraped along, one day good, another day poor, but always ready and on the lookout for that quick, sometimes split-second, opportunity.

Jack had been left an old Wolseley car by a friend of his who had got nicked and was in jail; we would pass the days driving around in it, keeping our eyes open and our hands ready. It was in the course of this prowling that we latched on to a series of jobs that threw us a few modest earners.

We normally went into a Lyon's tea shop – there was a huge chain of them in London in those days – for our breaks and it didn't take us long to notice that none of them was particularly secure. I suppose it was because they were only cafés and didn't appear worth breaking into. A more critical eye, however, would have noticed that every Lyon's tea shop sold cigarettes and as cigarettes were always a good seller for us we decided we would have a go at one of them.

When we made an inspection of several shops, we discovered another feature that made them even more attractive. Every tea shop had at least one emergency door and right in the centre of this door hung the key to unlock it. This meant that even if it was an awkward entry, we could get out nice and sweet through the emergency exit, usually on to a back alley or into a corridor that led to the street.

We decided to have a go at one near Kensal Rise and picked a branch on a main road. We got on to the flat roof at the rear of the building where we could work comfortably on the first-floor window bars. Once in position, we opened the jaws of our bolt cutters to their maximum and placed them over the bars. They cut through like strings of liquorice and once inside we soon found the storeroom that held the tobacco.

In those days, the tea shops carried a stock of about 25,000 to 30,000 cigarettes and getting rid of them was no problem at all. Sure enough, the emergency key opened the door out on to the same alley we had used to access the roof. It took only a minute to throw everything into the car boot and five minutes later we were stacking the cigarettes in Jack's bedroom. We had hit on a good thing and began sorting out a Lyon's tea shop to break into on about a weekly basis. I suppose we must have done about ten of them before their insurance company came to its senses and made them install burglar alarms.

We always sold our cigarettes to a café owner in Acton. We were getting paid six pounds ten shillings per thousand for upmarket fags – Players, Senior Service and Capstan – and five pounds ten shillings per thousand for 'cheap' fags – Woodbine, Player's Weights and Park Drive. It seems very cheap compared to prices nowadays, but in 1958 that was good money. With things going so well, I decided to find myself a flat, or at least a room to live in. It so happened that a friend of mine, Les Beavis, who owned a licensed drinking club in Oxford Gardens, off Ladbroke Grove, knew a café owner who had a vacant one-room flat above his place in Portobello Road. The café owner got a tenant and I got a flat with special attention in the café for my meals. It suited me fine and I was happy to find a place of my own with an understanding landlord.

With plenty of free time on our hands and money in our pockets, our daily prowling tapered off to almost nothing and Jack started taking me over to Fulham where he knew a lot of people. Everyone knew everyone else's business over there and Jack and I got a bit of respect from them because they knew we were grafters and doing quite well. In the criminal world this sort of socialising is important. It is through becoming known and earning a reputation as a good grafter and solid if it 'comes on top' that you become accepted by your peers and allowed into their circles. In this way you increase your knowledge of what work is available and who's doing what, when and where.

Funnily enough, we spent more time socialising in the cafés over cups of tea than we did drinking in the Lion. I met a lot of up-and-coming villains in Fulham in those days, the most famous being, I suppose, the little 'snouter' firm of Mickey Ball, Joey Docherty, Charlie Wilson and Roy James – the last two went on to play major roles in the Great Train Robbery. Mickey Ball would have been on the train robbery too if he hadn't got five years for his part in a pay snatch in Heathrow Airport. And Joey Docherty was doing a five for a snout warehouse in Weymouth, or he would have been there as well. It was about that time I met Bert Mathers, a pal of Charlie Wilson's, who had just signed off from the merchant navy and was thinking about doing a bit of 'work'. He asked about grafting with Jack and me, but we weren't doing enough to require another hand.

Doing the tea shops had tapered off due to the new security precautions and because I had moved away from Kensal Rise I began to see less and less of Jack. I would meet up with him in Fulham and sometimes he'd visit Les's club for a late drink. As well as this I had a steady girlfriend now, Jo Taylor from Ruislip, whom I'd met through a relation of Jack's. Gradually Jack drifted away and soon a few weeks passed without my seeing him. I really didn't notice it all that much as I was going out with Jo two or three times a week and travelling backwards and forwards to Ruislip took up a lot of my time. I was also spending a lot of time over in Fulham with my new mates.

It was at about this time something happened that reminded me of my army days. I used to visit Ted and his family at Bravington Road; one Saturday Mabel asked me if I would give her a lift up to Finsbury Park where she wanted to visit a friend. I was happy to oblige and soon I was motoring along Finsbury Park Road. I couldn't help seeing the bright shop front of Ted Gerrard's Cycles. I remembered that I had got things from him and never paid for them.

After I dropped Mrs Jones off at her friend's, I made my way back to Ted Gerrard's and went inside. It was a proper racing man's shop with all the latest bikes and equipment on display. The owner was behind the counter. I introduced myself and told him I owed him for some equipment I had got from him months before.

'Crosbie ... Crosbie ...' he mused, his face wrinkled in thought after I told him my name. 'You were in the army or something, if I remember correctly?'

'Hey,' I said. 'That's nothing to do with you. I only want to square up my bill.' I looked up at the bikes dangling from their hooks in the ceiling. 'And I want to buy a track bike.' I had tried to train on the Paddington track with my road bike, but it wasn't allowed.

'Oh, I'm not concerned about your army business,' Ted said,

grinning. 'But I sent you a letter and someone replied to it. Here, I've got it on file. I'll let you read it yourself.' With that, he went to his filing cabinet and in a moment or two he handed me a letter.

Dear James

I have been going through my accounts and find that you are four weeks in arrears. Would you therefore please leap upon your bicycle and pedal to the nearest post office and send me £2. This will serve (a) to keep you in my good books for any future orders and (b) to keep you fit.

Yours sincerely

Ted Gerrard

I smiled at the friendly tone of the demand and went to hand it back. 'No, no,' he said. 'Someone typed an answer on the back.' I turned the letter over and read:

Dear Mr Gerrard

I regret to inform you that Private Crosbie took your advice somewhat prematurely, leaped on his bicycle and has not been seen since. If he is still pedalling, he is either (a) very fit, or (b) nearly dead.

Yours sincerely

Sgt Laffy

IT'S CRIMINAL

It was about then that Bert put a proposition to me and we began working together. Eddie Matcham, a Co-op driver who occasionally passed on information to Charlie Wilson's firm, wasn't too happy with them. Apparently he had told them about a big delivery he had made and they had underpaid him for his information. He wasn't very happy and wanted to know if Bert would speak to Charlie about it. Bert told Eddie that he didn't think he could do that, but if he wasn't happy about getting properly paid he should pass on his information to us and we would guarantee him his correct money. Bert and I became the recipients of Eddie's valuable information.

Our first requirement, if we were to exploit our source of information, was good transport and this presented us with a slight problem. It had been easy enough with Jack and the old Wolseley – the registered owner of that car was in jail doing two years and couldn't care less about the motor. Bert didn't drive and I didn't have a licence, yet a car was essential to us. It also had to be a car that I could explain away to the police if I ever got a pull or was involved in an accident. I couldn't afford to be on offer – at serious risk of arrest – every time I drove the car and most of my day was going to be spent behind the wheel.

What I had to do was find someone who, for a small financial consideration, was prepared to 'lose' his wallet along with his driving licence and other identification papers. The loss would be reported to the police and this would cover the person against any problems which might arise later on due to the criminal use of the lost licence. The licence and another piece of ID material was then used to hire a car and that was us mobile. This meant that we could drive around without worrying about being stopped for any reason by the police. If we were stopped, I only had to produce the hire contract and driving licence to get waved on. It meant that the only time we would really be on offer would be when we were driving back from a job with the car loaded with snout. If the police spotted us in that situation I would just have to try to lose them, or at the very least get out of their sight long enough to abandon the car and escape on foot. Whatever happened, the police wouldn't be able to trace us through the car and the chances were that the person whose licence I had used would not even be questioned. It wasn't a bad deal all round and once we had a car our next priority was to find a safe lock-up garage.

A safe lock-up was, as they still are today, hard to come by. Certainly there were plenty of private house owners who didn't have cars and sub-let their garages for the sake of the few pounds' rent they could ask. But for people like us who needed a garage to store stolen goods and burglar's tools, this sort of set-up was too dangerous. Private house owners tended to be inquisitive about who rented their garages and the odd hours we would be coming and going would make them even more curious.

We finally managed to track down and rent a lock-up in a small square of garages just behind Clapton railway station in East London. Now we could start taking advantage of Eddie's information.

I worked with Bert on several of Eddie's jobs and we never had any bother. On every occasion, entry was gained through the skylight on the roof. We would fold back the lead flushing and lift out the pane of glass in one piece, then step inside the skylight structure on to the framework 'floor' of steel bars. Bert would position the bolt cutters on a bar, letting one handle lie flat on the barred surface. He would then sit on one handle of the cutter and stretch up to grasp the other one with both hands. This was an ideal position to get his full weight and strength behind the pull and he could easily cut through the bar on his own.

Once the bar had been removed, I would lower myself down into the shop to locate the cigarette store, then pass the stuff up to Bert through the gap in the bars. We always tried to finish our work before midnight so we could drive to our lock-up and get the cigarettes put away while there was still plenty of traffic about. We did quite well working on Eddie's information and always paid him as agreed.

As well as the work Eddie was feeding us, we also found jobs of our own. It was the same routine as when I worked with Jack, just driving about, keeping our eyes open and doing our police work in reverse: the police patrolled to make sure everything was secure; we patrolled to try and find anything insecure.

It is really quite strange the way you come across a possible job. All you do is drive about looking here and there, more often than not finding nothing of interest, then out of the blue you spot something and bells ring in your head. One time, it was a British Road Service lorry in the process of delivering cartons of cigarettes into a shop up Highbury Road, a sight that more than warranted a closer look. Once the premises came under inspection, we would check the outside for alarm bells and security precautions and whether the shop was a liver (persons living on the premises) or a lock-up – this could make or break a job for us.

If everything looks encouraging from the outside, the next step is to go inside and check the interior of the premises. A look at the inside of the shop can often expose a weakness that is invisible from the pavement and you might be able to look into the rear section of the shop and see what sort of stock they carry, or how secure the back door might be. Depending on the shop's layout, you might even be able to go right up to the rear door to check it for an easy exit – a great asset for carrying out the cartons of cigarettes and if the door can be easily opened from the inside it means that the actual entry point only needs to be big enough to admit one person, involving a minimum of work and noise.

If everything from the front and the inside looks good, the next thing to check is access to the rear of the premises. Usually we would find a lane running behind the shop premises and the shop itself would normally have a small yard at the rear. A backyard was attractive because there would normally be a fence or a wall to protect the area and this would hide us from anyone who might use the lane – someone walking a dog, or maybe courting couples looking for a dark corner to canoodle in. A lane was always handy too for getting the car close up for speedy loading.

If everything looked good, we would make a similar check after dark to see how much activity we could expect and whether or not there were lights on in premises above or to either side of the target. If everything still looked good, we would go ahead as soon as possible.

Everything was going smoothly for us and we thought we were doing very well for a couple of snouters. I had made enough money in the last three or four months to rent a large unfurnished basement flat in Devonshire Gardens and I had bought furniture through a friend in Hammersmith.

I remember feeling a twist of envy when the newspapers headlined a job that had been pulled on a branch of Barclays Bank in Stamford Hill. Now that was a job I could admire. The villains had rented empty premises next door and broken into the bank through the dividing wall in the basement. Once inside the bank, they had cut open the vault using a thermic lance and had stolen a *lot* of money. Once they had cleaned out the vault, the crooks took off with the cash and the thermic lance, no doubt thinking of future uses for this magnificent burglar's tool. They left the rest of their easily replaceable equipment behind —oxygen bottles, carbon rods, heat shields and the heavy protective clothing necessary when using the lance. As far as I remember, this was the first time a thermic lance had been used in a robbery and no one was ever done for the Stamford Hill job. I looked at the bank as I drove past it on my way to pick up my own more mundane burglary equipment and was conscious of what small fry Bert and I were compared to the men who had pulled off the bank job. Maybe one day I would be in on something like that.

We had two jobs to do within a couple of nights of one another. The cigarettes and some cases of spirits we had taken from a licensed grocer in Golders Green were still in the lock-up as we had decided to wait until the second job was done so we could deliver the goods in one go. I had gone on my own to collect the tools, having made arrangements to collect Bert later in the evening. As I turned the car into the square of garages, my headlights shone across the door of our lock-up and I spotted immediately that the padlock had been removed and hasp was open.

In retrospect, I should have simply turned the car round and driven off, but the place seemed dead quiet and I decided to have a look. I drove the car right up to the garage doors and stopped, leaving just enough room to pull the doors open a few inches.

When I looked inside I saw two men sitting on ordinary kitchen chairs. They must have dozed off because I can still see them lurching into life as the door rattled a little. They threw themselves off the chairs and lunged towards me, but the car jammed them in. I didn't stop to stare. I just turned and ran, hearing shouts of 'Police! Stop there, you!' Their voices faded as I sprinted out of the yard and disappeared towards the main road, where I jumped in a taxi and headed for Liverpool Street Station.

Later on, I realised there had been no need to panic. The detectives couldn't have got out of the garage unless the car was moved. I should have stayed and had a laugh at them before running away. If they had any brains they would have sat in the garage next door and waited until I was inside my own lock-up before pouncing – or is that me just being smart in retrospect?

Later on, we figured out what had gone wrong with our lock-up. It was all down to the thermic-lance bank robbers! Because they had left so much heavy equipment behind, the police reasoned that they must have stored it fairly close to the bank in the first place, so they wouldn't have to transport it very far when it was required. As a matter of routine they had checked out all the people who had recently rented lock-ups in the immediate area and when they couldn't trace the person at the address I had given, they forced the lock and found our stuff.

The same thing had happened to one or two other crooks in the area who were not as lucky as me. This sort of fall-out always happens when the cops are galvanised into action by a particularly spectacular robbery. I suppose all the small fish they net during their massive investigation and crackdown serve as a consolation prize for them.

A few days after losing our garage and equipment, not to mention the stolen goods, I was sitting in my room above the café when there was a thumping on my door. It turned out to be a couple of Notting Hill detectives who were searching the premises for a load of stolen booze that Les, the club's owner, was supposed to have something to do with. The search warrant, if one existed, was for the Kimberly Club premises. The cops hadn't found any of the stolen booze there and decided to search the whole building, including the café and the rooms above it. In the course of our cigarette-stealing activities, Bert and I always ended up with some strange brands. As these fags only came in relatively small amounts, hundreds rather than thousands and no one wanted to buy them anyway, I had been in the habit of taking them home and tossing them into a cardboard box on top of my wardrobe. I used to give them away down the club or to friends of mine.

I had accumulated several thousands of these odd cigarettes and now, like an idiot, I was caught with them sitting on top of my wardrobe. Needless to say they found my cigarette stash and to make matters worse the cops also found a complete set of twenty-six double-ended skeleton keys in my chest of drawers – a proper professional set of 'twirls'. These articles attracted a lot of attention and I was bundled off to Notting Hill police station to explain myself. I was nicked for the fags as a holding charge; then they found the 'lost' driving licence on me and this started another line of inquiry. This then led to the car I had left outside the lock-up, to the embarrassment of the policemen trapped inside. Of course I admitted nothing. I had found the licence and never been to Clapton in my life. After several appearances at the magistrate's court, I was remanded until 3 December 1958 to the County of London Sessions for sentence.

This time my good behaviour on remand backfired on me. When I finally went up for sentence I got glowing reports from my interviewers and they all said, more or less, that I wasn't really a bad fellow. Another guy on remand who was about my age, but a right rebel, told them all to stick their interviews up their arses and got a terrible report. My remand reports, on the other hand, were all very good and it was the governor's opinion that I would benefit from a period of rehabilitation. The judge agreed with this opinion and, after warning me that this was my last chance, proceeded to sentence me to three years' corrective training. The rebel, however, was considered 'untrainable' and sentenced to nine months in prison.

Chapter Ten

Working for the Kray Twins

Corrective training – CT – was simply another name for imprisonment and the induction prison for anyone sentenced to CT in the London area was Wandsworth. When I first arrived there from the court, I was put into a cell on C Wing and even with my previous experience I found it all very dingy and intimidating.

During my remand in Brixton, I had known about the possibility of a CT sentence, but I had been convinced that it was more or less an adult borstal. Instead, here I was doing time like any other con in the jail sentenced to ordinary imprisonment. At just under twenty-two, three years seemed a helluva long time and I immediately lodged an appeal on the grounds of the severity of the sentence. Ninety-nine times out of a hundred this is a hopeless cause but, when you are twenty-two and have just been lumbered with what seems a massive sentence for 'receiving' a few thousand cigarettes, you tend to clutch at straws.

The problem with appealing, however, was that in the late 1950s you automatically lost forty-two days of your sentence if the appeal failed. After waiting about three months for the result I found myself deducted forty-two days and passed on assessment and allocation to a prison deemed suitable for corrective training.

I was just about at the end of my assessment period when I was sent for and escorted over to F Wing, the administration block. When I got there, I was taken to a small office and introduced to a little fat man in a greasy-looking trench coat. It turned out he was a sergeant in the Special Investigation Branch of the army. He didn't like me at all, scowling at even having to talk to me. I was a bit concerned at first, until I discovered that he was only there to serve me with my army discharge papers.

'We don't want your sort in the army,' he sneered at me in disgust and pushed a pen into my hands. I couldn't sign fast enough. I had been wondering when the military would catch up with me and worrying if they intended waiting until I finished my CT to grab me back. Getting discharged was good news to me. Then, just when I thought everything was over, he pulled out an envelope and handed it to the screw who was in the office with us.

'Here's his money,' he said and at the same time pushed another form at me. 'Sign here for it.' I was amazed. Chucked out of the army and they even gave me money! I think my smile annoyed him and he pushed past me out of the office without even shaking my hand. I was escorted back to C Wing with a smile on my face.

Eventually I was allocated and sent to Verne Prison. I really do think the Verne would have bored me to death and it was only through an incident completely foreign to my character that I was thrown out of there.

One evening when we were all sitting round the stove in the dormitory, this Scottish guy who was always telling improbable tales was going on about his time in the RAF. He was a big boy and the Verne's top football player. He used to swagger around a bit and he looked quite a hard ticket. He said he was in charge of the gym and ran the football team at Bridgnorth. Then he said that he used to nip into Birmingham for a drink in the evenings. I asked him how far Bridgnorth was from Birmingham and he told me it was about five miles down the road. Then I asked him what sort of RAF camp Bridgnorth was. By now he was giving me funny looks. But I persisted and asked him if he knew the address of Bridgnorth.

'Just RAF Bridgnorth,' he snapped back at me.

'No it isn't,' I told him. 'I was in the RAF at Bridgnorth and if you had been there you would know it is Number Seven School of Recruit Training. And what's more,' I went on, everyone staring at us now, 'Wolverhampton is the nearest city to Bridgnorth and that's twelve miles away. Birmingham's nowhere near Bridgnorth – it must be fifty miles away at least!'

By now the guy was getting red in the face, but I carried on with my logical demolition of his story. 'So that means you've never been to Bridgnorth and you're telling a tale.'

Suddenly he lunged at me, obviously prepared to do me serious injury. I got a fright, because, although I knew I was showing him up a bit, it really wasn't that serious. I jumped up to protect myself and we grappled together, the usual jail fight. We staggered around a bit then he fell against a bed and, as he was underneath me, I swung a punch at his head. I was amazed when he started squealing as if he had been really hurt and he rolled into a ball, not even attempting to fight back. I gave him a couple more swings and a couple of kicks as well. Then it was all over and he crept away to his bed. I was amazed, but I knew that it wasn't my abilities that had defeated him – it was just that he was utterly useless.

Next day, I was dragged out from the blacksmith's shop and marched in front of the governor. The guy had gone and reported that I had attacked him and beat him up. It turned out that he had ripped his leg open on a spring at the edge of the bed and had required stitches. The governor remanded me for the visiting court and I was immediately taken to Dorchester Prison to wait for adjudication. Three weeks later I was taken back to the Verne and appeared before the Visiting Committee (the VC).

I argued that all I had done was defend myself and that the damage to his leg, which was the thing that was bothering them, was an accident. Luckily, two guys from the dormitory came forward and agreed with my version of the story. Nevertheless I was found guilty of fighting and assault, but because of the circumstances I was only sentenced to twenty-eight days' loss of remission.

The Scottish guy who had already given his version to the VC was called back in and sentenced to twenty-eight days' remission too. He would have been better off keeping quiet about Bridgnorth. Or maybe I should have kept my mouth shut and let him rattle on. Two days later, no doubt as a direct result of the incident, I was transferred to Maidstone Prison in Kent. I can't say I was sorry to leave the Verne.

Because it was so close to London, there were live concerts and plays almost every week in Maidstone and lots of top stars came down to entertain us. I also bumped into one or two people I knew there. Charlie Wilson and Mickey Ball were two of them. Charlie, Mickey and Roy James had all been jailed for conspiracy and possession of explosives for blowing safes. Roy got a three and Charlie and Mickey both got thirty months.

A City and Guilds printing course was about to begin not long after I arrived at Maidstone; I put in for it and was accepted. Now I only had to get myself something to do in the evenings and my time would be fully occupied.

As it turned out, the printing shop was quite a boring place to work. The letterpress machines were all ancient, hand-fed types; once a job was locked into their bed all you had to do was stand at the roller and feed sheets of paper into it. Some of the print runs were huge and every single one of them fed into the machine by hand. I honestly fail to see how anyone of average intelligence could not fail to master machine minding in a couple of months.

One day, I was working away on the small Heidelberg platen when someone approached me. He gave me the eye and pulled me to one side.

'Would you do a job for the twins?' he asked me.

'Who're the twins?' I asked, not having the faintest idea who he was talking about.

'The twins,' he hissed. 'Ronnie and Reggie, the Kray twins.'

I had never heard of them up to then. 'I don't know them,' I said. 'But what is it they want?'

He held up a small, red driving-licence holder. 'Driving licences. Can you run some off?'

I looked at the licence that was gummed inside the small book's covers. In those days a driving licence was simply a tiny sheet of white-gummed paper with the issuing authority and the words 'Driving Licence' plainly headlined on it. There was a space for the licence number to be typed in, then half-a-dozen dotted lines for the name and address of the holder. The bottom line showed the classes of vehicle that could be driven and the final printed item was 'Fee 5/-' in the bottom corner of the paper. The licence was printed on gummed paper so that it could be securely stuck inside the little red booklet, which was issued along with it. This booklet contained half a dozen blank pages to be used by the courts if any endorsements were required. New licence holders were easily obtained by applying for a provisional licence in any name you could think of at the local county council offices and once issued with the provisional licence all you had to do was tear it out and you had a brand new booklet to stick any licence you liked into.

The issuing authority of the licence he had handed me was the West Kent County Council and it really was the plainest-looking licence I had ever seen. I estimated that it would take about five minutes for a compositor to have it set and locked into a forme.

'I could print that easy enough,' I said. 'How many are you looking for?'

'Five hundred,' he told me. 'Print up five hundred and they'll pay you a fiver a piece for them.'

I looked at him in surprise. 'A fiver each? That'll come to two-and-a-half grand!'

'Yeah,' he nodded. 'That's what they'll pay. Everyone's looking for a bent brief these days.'

I thought for a moment. I knew that the current price of a stolen licence was £10 and villains were always trying to get their hands on them. A new blank licence would be even more desirable as they could fill it in to suit themselves. They could easily be sold for £15 or £20 a piece.

I had a pal in the compositing shop and I knew he could set it, two up, in a matter of minutes. Running them off on the speedy little Heidelberg would take five minutes at the outside. I decided to be more realistic. 'Look,' I said. 'I can run them off no bother, but pay me a pound a piece and I'll be happy.'

I was thinking to myself that the chances of getting the two-and-a-half grand would be slim, but £500 might well materialise and that wasn't bad money for fifteen minutes' work. I know that it would have been sensible to ask for some of the money up front, but the job was nothing and I decided to give it a whirl. It wasn't costing me anything and I might just get the money. The licences were duly produced and handed over and I never saw a brown penny for them. So much for my business with the twins.

With four months of my sentence to go, I heard that Bert had got himself done. He had been working now and again with another guy from Fulham and had been spotted unloading snout from a car into his basement flat in Eustace Road. He was in remand in Brixton and expecting to go to jail. Three months before my date of release I was granted, as part of the CT deal, five days' home leave and spent it with friends of Bert's in Hanworth, near Hounslow. I went with his friends, Betty and Dave Pegler, to visit Bert on remand and he was very down in the dumps. I was surprised because he was only looking at months rather than years. He couldn't get lumbered with corrective training, because as well as being a bit old for it, he only had one minor previous conviction and you had to have at least two previous indictable offences on your record to qualify for CT.

He just couldn't handle it inside at all and swore he was packing up the thieving game. I was disappointed to hear this, but it really didn't make a lot of difference to my position. He would, after all, be doing time when I got out. I would need to find someone to work with. The snouting game had run its course and the up-and-coming game was good, hard cash blags. I saw Jack during my leave and we decided to team up again when I got out. This suited me because I knew Jack would be prepared to have a real go. At the end of my five days' leave he drove me back to Maidstone where, despite the influence of several large vodkas, I reluctantly banged on the prison gates to be let back inside.

At half-past-seven on a Thursday morning in February 1961, I stepped to freedom through the huge gates of Maidstone Prison and into a waiting car. On the drive into London, Jack passed me a bag containing overalls, a woollen hat and a heavy lead-filled cosh. Less than three hours later, along with Johnny Thomson and Chick Harris of Paddington, I was on the pavement outside a bank in East Acton carrying out my first payroll blag. It all went off well and we raced away from the scene richer by almost £4,000. It was a good start to my freedom.

The three years of CT had no beneficial or reformatory effect on me at all.

Chapter Eleven

Pavement Artists

Jack drove the car that took us away from the robbery scene as Johnny, Chick and myself struggled in the confined space to get out of our overalls. We only had a couple of minutes to do this, as it was essential to dump the car as quickly and unobtrusively as possible. There would have been at least half-a-dozen 999 calls already made about the incident and police cars would be closing in on the area. Any car carrying four men would certainly get a pull.

Jack dropped Johnny and Chick as soon as they got out of their overalls. With their outward appearance changed beyond anything that might have been phoned in, they split again to make their separate ways to our meeting at Jack's house.

Jack and I continued in the car while I hurriedly stuffed the overalls and tools into a holdall. We'd changed from being pavement artists into respectable members of the public. When I was ready, Jack dropped me near a bus stop. Any bus that came along would do me – the important thing was to get on one, any one, and keep moving away. Public transport is by far the most innocuous and safest way of getting away from a crime scene. In the meantime, Jack drove on a little further to park the stolen getaway car in a side street before walking round a couple of corners to where he had parked his own motor.

I was the last to arrive back at Fernhead Road, where Jack lived with his girlfriend Yvonne and the rest of her family. He had a nice set-up there with Yvonne's divorced mother, Lily, looking after the house and another daughter, Evlyne, who was a year or so younger than Yvonne. There was only the four of us in the house when we settled down in the front room to count the cash – always the most exciting part of the job for me. The count-up came to £4,215, the payroll of a small engineering firm in Park Royal and we ended up with just under £1,000 a piece after ten per cent was taken off to pay the worker who had put Jack on to the job. London's streets were certainly paved with gold.

Not having any immediate cash worries was a great relief and I just loafed about for a couple of weeks. Nobody seemed very eager to look for work now that they had a few quid; this was a fault I found with a lot of London firms. Whenever they had a good tickle they would lie back and enjoy it, only seriously looking for work when their cash became dangerously low. Me, I always wanted to sort something out while we had plenty of money so we would be able to set it up properly instead of trying to operate on a tight budget at the last minute. Still, this time I was content enough to let things slide.

Not once since I had left the army had I contacted my family. The last thing they would have heard about me was that I had gone AWOL. I couldn't write to my mother with any sort of reasonable explanation, so I took the coward's way out and said nothing. Then, with me getting the three years' CT, I thought it would be better if I just didn't tell anyone. To be honest, I was a little embarrassed. When I look back, I realise I should have at least let my mother know. I don't think I realised how much worry I was causing her.

Now, with nearly four years gone and the army business settled, for the first time I found myself thinking about going home. The more I thought about it, the keener I became. Suddenly the urge became irresistible. Within a day I was packed and with my two bikes dismantled for easy carrying, I was off to Heathrow Airport. I couldn't go home without my bikes: they would be almost a status symbol up there, especially the track-racing machine, a rarity in Glasgow cycling circles.

I arrived by taxi in Palermo Street and carried my bikes one by one up the three stairs of the tenement, waiting until I had all my things on the landing before I turned the key in the door. The idea of knocking never entered my head. I simply turned the same key that had been in the door when I left almost four years before and stepped into the hall, shouting out the time-honoured Glasgow salutation, 'It's only me.'

When I think about it now, I realise my mother must have got the shock of her life. Scottish people really are very undemonstrative with their emotions. In Glasgow working-class families there's none of the hugging and crying business, but the moment was quite emotional as we looked at one another.

'Are you home for good then?' my mother finally asked in a normal tone of voice.

I held my hands out and shrugged, not knowing what to say. Finally I got out a few words. 'I don't know. I'll see how it goes.'

'I'll put on the teapot,' my mother said, turning to put the words into action. 'Are you hungry? Do you want something to eat?' She busied herself about the cupboard.

'I'll just have a cup of tea.' I sat down at the table and that was me home.

At half-past five my father came in from his work and you would have thought I had never been away.

'Oh, it's yourself, is it?' he said, placing his working bunnet on the sideboard and emptying his pockets into it as I'd seen him do literally thousands of times throughout my childhood. It was as if time had stood still. I wouldn't have minded betting that it was the same bunnet too.

Later on I went up to the corner to see all my old pals. Most of them were happily working away at their jobs and were, as much as possible, enjoying life in Springburn. What struck me most was the realisation that my boyhood pals were still standing at the same corner doing exactly the same things they had been doing when I had left for the army four years before. Other than growing older and getting married and having children, nothing had changed in their lives. They hadn't been anywhere, or seen anything of life other than Glasgow and most of their time had been spent in Springburn.

They all knew about me, of course. I don't mean about being in prison – no one in Springburn knew anything about that but myself. But they all took it for granted that I was a crook and that I had been living the same high life-style as all the other crooks in London. My sudden reappearance, well dressed and with plenty of money, did nothing to dispel this idea. It wasn't long before we were all in the Snug Bar at the top of Palermo Street. Although it was at the top of my street, it was my first time in the place, but for the others it was their main social centre. It didn't take them long to bring me up to date with what had happened during my long absence: very little. There was no doubt though that it was a close-knit and friendly life and I felt quite at ease in the company of my old pals.

Needless to say I was the man of the moment that night. Everyone wanted to hear what I'd been up to in 'the Smoke', as they called London, and I was questioned and cross-examined on every detail of my life there. It wasn't nosiness, just a natural curiosity about the kind of life they could never imagine themselves living. From their point of view, I was a success, getting away from the rat race in Glasgow and into the Promised Land to return with plenty of money in my pockets. I had a pleasant feeling of belonging as I walked down Palermo Street that night after the pub closed.

Gradually the weeks slipped past. I was spending my time much the same as my brother, Tommy. Nearly every day we would pedal out into the Campsie Hills, or head for places like

Loch Lomond. At the weekends there would usually be a road race to watch, then the Sunday run home again. If the weather was wet or dull, I would end up in the snooker hall and most evenings would see me passing my time at the corner along with my pals. It was a quiet, peaceful existence, far more relaxing than London could ever be.

I had been there for almost four weeks when my brother William gave me an idea for starting up a business. He was always telling me about his job with the blacksmithing company he worked for. On more than one occasion, he mentioned that he got extra money by doing 'homers' – jobs of his own done in his bosses' time – for his own private customers. He turned out loads of things for himself, like door grilles, plant-pot holders and fancy pieces of ironwork. When I asked him if there was a lot of that sort of work available he told me he was always turning down jobs because they were too big to work on and smuggle out of the workshop.

At that time, there was a vacant single shop in Ayr Street, not a hundred yards from our house. As I could weld and cut metal to size myself, I suggested to William that I rent the shop and set it up for doing wrought iron so that I could start turning out the extra work he was knocking back. He jumped at the suggestion and within days I had rented the shop and bought a new electric welding machine and a small hand guillotine. William obtained some tools and anything else we needed I just went out and purchased. Then I bought a small van cheaply and that was us ready for business.

The shop gave me something constructive to do and for the next three or four weeks I was happily doing most of the rough work on jobs William had found. He would come in and tidy them up after he finished his own work and the following day I would paint them and deliver them in my wee green van. It was quite enjoyable, but we really weren't making a lot of money and my own cash was now running dangerously low. I suppose it is the optimist criminal in me, because I wasn't really worried about the worsening money situation. I always felt that, one way or another, I could get my hands on some more.

The habits I had picked up in London had never left me and, as I drove about in the van or rode my bicycle, I always kept my eyes peeled for any decent-looking opportunities for an earner. I spotted plenty of good bits of work. One of my pals, Jim Marshall (with whom I shared my first conviction), was a bit like myself but had never really gone beyond the lead-stripping stage. He used to go about with me in the van now and again and on one of these occasions I showed him a newsagent's shop I had spotted in Milngavie, a fairly well-off district just outside Glasgow heading westwards.

One day when I had been out that way I had gone into this shop for directions and noted the large stock of cigarettes stacked just inside an interior door. The sight had made my pulse quicken. I noticed an open fanlight above the door and spotted that only a thin metal arm on each side prevented it from falling right down inside.

Even in its closed position, it would only be secured by one of those old-fashioned sprung snibs where you hooked your index finger through a ring and pulled to release the catch. That type of catch was never very strong or secure. I had gone back after closing time to check if it was left open – they sometimes were, but not this time. It was obviously their habit to snib the fanlight when closing the shop at night. With Jim and me almost skint, the time seemed right and we were ready to go.

I got some tools together and one night we went off to screw the newsagent's. I parked the van a couple of streets away and walked towards the row of single-storey shops. The newsagent's was the first in a line of about six lock-up premises that faced on to the main Milngavie–Glasgow Road.

The plan was crude, to say the least, but I had successfully used similar methods of entry before. I intended to vault the wooden gate at the shop front, then climb up and jemmy open the fanlight above the shop's door. Once that had been done, I only had to bend both the retaining arms aside and the fanlight would swing inside to lie flat against the door, leaving the gap completely open. I would climb inside and locate the cigarette stock, then stack the cartons by the door. I was confident of finding a pair of stepladders in the back shop – there had to be a set to pile the stock on the high shelves. With the ladder in position, Jim would come over the gate to catch the cartons as I dropped them down to him. He would stack them behind the wooden gate and when they were all outside I would climb out myself and follow him back over the gate on to the pavement.

Jim would by now be crossing the road to take up a position where he could keep his eye on the shop front and check that no one came along and noticed anything. In the meantime, I would be walking smartly towards my parked van so I could bring it round to the shop for loading. It would all be over in a matter of minutes and we would be on our way home, back into a few quid again. It all sounded so easy the way I explained it to Jim and he, believing me to be an expert, felt confident too.

It was getting late when we arrived in Milngavie and it must have been well after eleven o'clock. However, there were still some late-night pedestrians wending their way home so we decided to hang about until the streets were clear. Although we would have preferred rain instead of the mild weather that night, we weren't bothered about waiting. There was a close about fifty yards up from the shop on the opposite side of the road where we had a good view of people coming and going as we waited patiently for the pavements to clear.

We saw a police jeep drive past, heading towards Glasgow. It never slowed and disappeared into the distance. Another fifteen minutes passed, but there was always some straggler heading in our direction; we needed the road completely clear for my initial entry.

Then we spotted a police jeep again, this time coming from the opposite direction. We were very aware of it, but continued to stand as if waiting for someone. They all look the same, but this must have been the jeep that had passed us earlier because as it drew level the driver stared over at us; twenty-five yards on, his brake lights flared and the jeep swung into a U-turn.

I was going to say Jim panicked, but in truth we both did and bolted from the close. I ran directly across the road and through some bushes, heading towards the bungalows and the shelter of their gardens. I didn't hear anyone at my heels so I presumed that the cops had chased Jim. I leaped over a fence and disappeared round a corner. Two minutes later, I was in my van and heading for home.

The next morning, I discovered Jim had not returned home and I knew then that he had been done. I made a few phone calls and found out that he had appeared in front of the sheriff on a charge of loitering with intent and been remanded in custody with bail set at £10. It was just as well that I had been carrying the jemmy bar, or the charge could have been far more serious. I went round to the dry-cleaning shop where his girlfriend worked and told her what had happened. She got into a bit of a state, but I told her not to worry as I would get his bail money and he would be home again that day. The problem was that I didn't have the money and I didn't know anyone who would lend me it either.

I felt responsible for what had happened to Jim because it was me that had talked him into going on the job in the first place. I thought hard about it and came to the conclusion that there was really only one chance I had of getting the money. As far as I was concerned it was a case of trying my last resort, so I got out some tools and set off in my van to do a bit of the old faithful – glazing!

It was after midday when I made my decision and I would have to be quick if I was going to pull this off and get the bail money for him. My geography of the city was good, but I honestly didn't know where to start so I just drove around. I knew what I was looking for and I was hoping to run across something that fitted my criteria of being in quite a busy spot but with nothing on the opposite side of the road to overlook me. It must have been all of five years since I had last done it and my panache of those early days had gone. I passed a few likely places, but my nerves made me see dangers or problems that didn't exist and I made excuses not to do them. Time was running out.

The 'dinner hour' was still the same – 1.00 pm to 2.30 pm – and it was just before two when I forced myself to make a choice. It was a grocer's shop on a busy road with the house windows on the opposite side shielded behind a high hedge. The shop next door was open for business, but the pavement was quiet. I drove my van round to the back of the block, parked it in the street parallel to the main road and walked back round to the front.

My tools were slung over my shoulder and I looked pretty well the part of a working man, but my nerves were keyed up and jangling like a man in the electric chair. I walked past the shop on the opposite side of the road, crossed over and turned back towards the doorway again. I stopped to look in the shop window and saw the till positioned in a small cash desk near the door. I could see a metal Oxo box sitting on a shelf below the till and knew from experience that it would contain cash. I walked on again, sweating from every pore. It was after two and I knew that the shop would open at half past. The staff could easily start arriving ten minutes before that. I tried to psyche myself up. I felt very conspicuous as I walked back yet again, passing the shop and looking about to see if anyone was staring; I certainly felt as if a thousand eyes were focused on me.

Ten past two! I was getting desperate. I told myself it was nothing. My entire body was as tense as a steel cable. I couldn't wait any longer. If I didn't do it now, it was off. The clock was touching a quarter past two when I finally turned into the shop doorway. I didn't even take my jacket off, just exhibited my tools on the ground in front of the door.

When I put my hammer through the glass it sounded like a chandelier crashing in a cathedral to me. I waited for a shout. Nothing. Quickly I bashed in a few large shards of glass and pulled at some of the shorter pieces to take away the jagged peaks.

As soon as I thought the gap was big enough, I grabbed my tool bag, put my head and shoulders through the hole and stepped inside. Still no one bothered me. I was right next to the till and, hands shaking, I pushed at buttons until the drawer slid out, hoping to God there was no one looking in the window.

Next I picked up the Oxo tin, its weight telling me it was full, then my eyes caught sight of some £1 bags of coppers. They went into the tool bag too and seeing nothing else I turned to leave. I could only have been inside the place thirty seconds, but when I turned, two girls in white shop-workers' coats were staring wide eyed at me through the broken glass of the door. They were only feet away from me and looked quite scared – so was I. Quickly, I bent my head and shoulders and began stepping out through the gap.

'What are you doing?' one of the girls asked me, her hand held nervously to her mouth.

'I'm repairing the door,' I replied. 'It got broken half an hour ago and I was sent to fix it.' I kept climbing out as I spoke.

'You took the money out of the till!' the other one accused. 'We saw you!'

By now, I was outside the shop and felt a wave of confidence as I smiled at the girls. 'Well,' I said with a grin. 'The truth is, I'm not really fixing the window. I'm a burglar. But don't worry, I'm not doing anything to you.'

By this time, I was past them and walking away. The girls just stared at me, then looked at one another. Then one of them said, 'Quick! Run and tell Mr Graham.'

One of them turned and began running towards the shop next door. I broke into a trot and disappeared round the corner before breaking into a sprint towards the next turning where my van was parked. I got into the van and was reversing towards the far corner when the girls, led by a man in a white coat, came running into sight. I actually read her lips as one of the girls mouthed the van's registration number.

I turned the corner out of their sight and pounded the steering wheel in anger. Fuck it! What was I going to do now? The van would be traced to me and I would get done. Fuck it! I was really angry and could hardly think straight. I drove in the direction of Springburn wondering what the hell to do. Both girls had seen me, spoken to me! My mind was in turmoil. Everything was going wrong. I would have been well away if I had used my bike.

I began to think a little more clearly. It was imperative to dump the van – it was bright green and the police were probably looking out for it right now. What was I to do? I didn't want to dump it just anywhere. It might sit for days and even get vandalised. And I didn't want to lose such a valuable asset. I had to find a place to park it where it would be safe. Luckily my bike was in the back of the van – I had intended using it to ride up to whatever job I picked out, but because I had been so late and the place was so close I hadn't bothered. There was only one place I could think of that was close and safe: Maryhill police station. It was even on my route home. So that's what I did. I parked my van in Maryhill Road, just outside the nick and pedalled away on my bike.

Twenty minutes later I turned into Palermo Street and the first thing I saw was a police jeep parked at the top end facing downwards towards my close. Jesus Christ, I thought, that was quick. I kept pedalling and turned into Ayr Street then back up Flemington Street to Springburn Road again.

I was in a state and didn't know what to do. Finally I went into the dry cleaner's where Jim's girlfriend worked. She knew straight away that something was wrong and I explained what had happened. One of my pals, Ronnie, was passing by and spotted me through the window and came inside just in time to hear the story too.

'You better come round to my house,' he said. 'Have a cup of tea and straighten yourself out a bit.'

I was able to relax over a cup of tea and began to think a bit straighter. I got Ronnie to walk round to Palermo Street and check on what was happening with the jeep. He was back in about ten minutes and much to my surprise he had my brother

Tommy with him. The jeep was still sitting there, apparently waiting for the green van to turn up.

'What's going on?' my brother wanted to know.

I explained about Jim and the bail money and what I had done up till then. I ended up by telling him that I would have to get away back to London. It was lucky for me that Ronnie had bumped into him because Tommy went up to the house, packed all my things and brought them back to me. I divided up the money – I forget how much it was, but it was enough to pay Jim's bail and get me back to London with a good few quid left over.

The only thing bothering me now was the van. I wanted that returned to Tommy and William as soon as possible and there was only one way I could think round it. William would have to become involved. At that particular time he was working in a department store fitting new railings on the stairways and I knew he would be in there until eight o'clock that night. I got hold of him at work and explained what had happened. He was a bit upset at first, but when he realised he was being left with the van (a prized possession), the shop and all the tools, he soon cheered up again. I told him that when he finished his work at eight o'clock that evening he was to go straight to police headquarters in St Andrew's Square and report that the van had been stolen from where he had parked it that morning. He was to explain that he had been at work all day in the department store and hadn't returned to the van until he was ready to go home at eight o'clock. It must have been stolen while he was at work. If they asked him anything about me, he was to say I was in my bed when he left for work, but I had said goodbye to him last night because I was catching the ten o'clock train to London in the morning.

That was the story. Nothing fancy. No big tale. Tommy had already been briefed to say that I had left the house in the morning with my bags to catch the train to London and that was the last time he had seen me. Satisfied that I had done my best, I went round to the station and finally bought myself a ticket for London.

IT'S CRIMINAL

Things had been recovered from what had seemed a disastrous situation. Jim would be out on bail, Tommy had a few quid and two good bikes (temporarily, I hoped) and William had a van and a fitted-out workshop. I was back where I started and not really sorry to be heading back to London.

Chapter Twelve

Pay Days

I had telephoned Ted before leaving Glasgow, so my appearance the following morning wasn't totally unexpected. Later that day, I telephoned Tommy at the snooker hall and he told me that the police jeep had been in Palermo Street until half past five before being driven away.

Half an hour after it had gone, the CID arrived at my parents' house wanting to know where I was. Tommy told me he had explained my absence as we had agreed and the CID had left the house in a very dissatisfied state. Then William had turned up at Central Police HQ to report the van stolen and had gone through everything again with them. Tommy and William stuck by their stories and everything just fitted right, or so the cops appeared to think. They didn't like it at all, but without me to put on an ID parade there wasn't a lot they could do, especially as no one could furnish them with my address in London. Apparently the cops weren't happy about it all and their final words had been, 'Tell that fucking brother of yours that he better stay well clear of Glasgow.'

I had also, Tommy told me, made the front page of the *Evening*

Times: CHEEKY BURGLAR STRIKES. I thought that I would take heed of the detective's advice and decided that it would not be wise of me to return to Glasgow in the near future. So now it was back to work in London and Jack soon filled me in on what was going on in our circles.

He had been knocking about with Chick and Johnny Thompson from Paddington and a chap called Eddie Hearn, one of my old mate Bert's friends from Fulham. Three of them, Jack, Eddie and Chick, had recently had an earner on an easy little blag in Church Street, just off the Edgware Road, when the guy carrying a wages box on to a building site showed good sense and dropped the box as Chick and Eddie, both hard faced and holding coshes, confronted him.

In the early sixties you couldn't pick up a newspaper on a Thursday or Friday evening without reading about at least two or three big wage snatches that had gone off in London and these were only the blags big enough to make the national press. Every local paper regularly reported its own crop of smaller robberies in the district it covered. It didn't seem to matter how often it happened or how many times the police warned companies about their wage-collecting methods; no one seemed to learn.

In the course of the next four months, we did three different jobs stuck up by employees of the firms we robbed. It would surprise you how many 'loyal' workers were only too happy to pass on information about how their company handled the weekly wage collection from the bank. We usually found that this information came to us second hand. A worker with a slightly crooked bent would pass on the word to some close pal whom he knew consorted with more serious villains. The close pal would make an initial approach, usually in a bar over a friendly drink and vaguely touch upon the job. If the work sounded interesting, a more serious discussion would develop and the close pal would be instructed to obtain more precise details. This suited us because it kept us away from the inside man and we didn't have to worry about being identified by him. If everything still sounded sweet, the job would be properly cased, just to check out the veracity and accuracy of the information. Once we were satisfied that the job was a 'good 'un', we would swing into action.

The routine was always the same: steal a car a couple of days before and change its number plates, then tuck it away somewhere safe. The rest of the gear we would need – overalls, masks and coshes – were always at hand and presented no problem. On the morning of the job (funnily enough, now I think about it, I've never been on a blag in the afternoon), we would park our straight car fairly close to the robbery site, then make our way over to where Jack would be waiting with the 'ringer'. All the gear would be with Jack and we would change into our overalls and prepare ourselves as we drove back towards the bank or the place selected for our ambush. The only time I worried about anything was when I was in the ringer driving to the job, all geared up and ready to go. At that time, we were definitely on offer for a charge of conspiracy and possessing offensive weapons at the very least. And there was always the possibility that if the robbery squad spotted us, they would follow on and let us commit ourselves to the job. This was so they could call up reinforcements and get us bang to rights for the more serious offence of assault and robbery. That way they would make themselves look good and we would get the maximum jail sentence. We couldn't afford to hang around for very long, so our timing had to be cut rather fine.

The job itself would only take ten to fifteen seconds on the pavement, then we would be into the car and away. Two or three turnings later we would start to drop off and once out of the ringer we would be safe to go our separate ways. It was Jack's responsibility to dump the ringer and fetch the money back and if everything was sweet he would even bring the bagged-up kit for future use.

Most of the time, everything went very smoothly for us and we were successful blaggers. We never got into any of the big blags, like the Roote's Group payroll robbery near Ladbroke Grove, nor were we as active as the Robin Hood gang, so called because they wore green-felt hats with little feathers in their hatbands when they were performing. We seemed to be stuck around the smallish two- or three-grand jobs. This wasn't a reflection on our ability or bottle, it was just that unless you were lucky, or a well-known face, you never received information on any of the big jobs. Every week we would scan the newspapers and read enviously about the latest big payroll robbery. We were just itching to get put on to a big one.

One of the problems in our business was getting bad information and the two things I used to ask myself when someone was explaining the details of some proposed snatch were: (a) is this guy in a position to know this information and (b) does the story make sense? If the answer to both these questions was yes, then the job was worth looking at.

Even then, when everything sounded sensible and looked good, mistakes were made and serious risks taken for nothing. One of the three jobs we had been put on to was a contract-cleaning company in Fulham. We were told by an employee that the company worked out of premises in a side street off Fulham Road and employed about 130 cleaners and other staff in various schools and office buildings throughout West London. The total payroll was about two-and-a-half to three grand and pay day was Thursday morning when the staff could call into the offices to pick up their wages any time after eleven. The story was that the manager took the ledgers and pay envelopes home with him on the Wednesday night and made up the wages in his house.

The guy who gave us the information worked in the place and swore blind he'd seen the boss putting the books and the pay packets into his briefcase plenty of times. Well, he was in a position to know this and at the time we thought it made sense for the manager to make up the wages at home so they would be ready for handing out in the morning. I suppose a lot of these sorts of tales sound genuine because you want them to.

We decided to go ahead with it and, as only one man carried the cash, there would be just three of us on the job. This suited everybody: Eddie didn't fancy working on his own doorstep and

IT'S CRIMINAL

Johnny was busy at the time with his small plumbing business. It was arranged that Jack would be driving, with Chick and myself on the pavement to take the bag. The manager always parked in a private bay to one side of the office building, leaving him a walk of about twenty-five yards to the entrance. We would have plenty of time to move in and take the briefcase.

Everything went smoothly. The car appeared on time and Chick and I were on the pavement walking towards the manager as he locked up and turned towards his office. Just as he passed us, Chick spun round and gripped him around the chest, pinning his arms helplessly against his sides. I grabbed the briefcase, striking it really hard to break the ends of the handle because he refused to let it go. Two hard hammer thumps with the edge of my clenched fist snapped both ends of the handle.

While I was doing this, I could hear the manager shouting, 'Fools! Stupid fools!' When I heard that and the way he shouted it, I just knew there wasn't any money in the briefcase. By now, I had the bag and Chick shoved the man away from him just as Jack pulled up alongside us in the car. We were away in seconds, going round the block and crossing over Fulham Road to dump the car.

'There's no money in this bag,' I said as I unbuckled the flap of the old-fashioned briefcase. 'There's no fucking money in it! He was too calm, that guy.' Sure enough, I didn't find a penny. What I did find was the ledgers and the details of each employee's wage neatly written in longhand on the front of the pay envelopes, ready to have the appropriate money put inside. Our informant had been nearly right. Because he had seen the office manager putting the envelopes and books into his briefcase, he had assumed that he was making the pay packets up at home. All that risk for nothing!

Something happened one day that sent a charge of excitement surging through me like a bolt of lightning. When I heard the news I said to myself, Yes! That's the way! No information required and definite knowledge that the cash was there for the taking. I confronted Jack and the others and slapped the paper down. 'That's what we should be doing,' I said. 'Robbing banks like these guys!'

What had happened was that three men had run into a bank in Cricklewood, just up the road from our manor, fired two shots from a handgun and snatched about four grand in a lightning raid. Five minutes later, they ran into a bank in Salisbury Road, Queen's Park, right on our own doorstep, fired a shot and grabbed several thousand quid. Ten minutes later, the same three men repeated the performance at a bank in Bayswater, escaping with even more cash; then they had simply disappeared. I was stunned. So fast. So easy. So smooth. And a bank meant money guaranteed.

But none of my mates wanted to know. They just weren't interested. Guns? No way. The cops would go crazy, they said.

'C'mon,' I told them. 'If nobody knows you did it, how can you get caught?'

My logic didn't make any difference: guns and banks were out. Besides, Jack told me, he had been put on to a factory payroll job in Ruislip with more than six grand in it. In those days, six grand was a good job; equal to around £40,000 in today's terms. It was a good turn, but we all ended up being lifted, thanks to an inside tip-off to the police from a new gang member. We were all taken straight to Harrow Road nick and charged with conspiracy to rob person or persons unknown. Three months later we were up for trial at the Old Bailey. It was three-and-a-half years for me. Eddie got a three, Jack a two-and-a-half and Johnny, being a first offender, got away with eighteen months. The meat wagon came to take us off to begin our sentences in Wandsworth.

Chapter Thirteen

Zombie Nation

In December 1961, for the third time in three years, I found myself being processed through reception in Wandsworth Prison. It was like taking part in a recurring nightmare as I sat on the same well-worn, pew-like bench, waiting for my name to be called out by the reception screw. I wouldn't mind betting it was still the same fat-arsed, red-faced screw who scowled at me from behind his sloping, school teacher's desk as he inspected my committal papers and began the ritual of reducing me to a number. Then it was the four-inch-deep lukewarm bath, the ill-fitting prison greys and the loose, clattering shoes that seemed to be standard issue in Wandsworth.

After we were processed, I found myself allocated to a cell in B Wing. Eddie went to C Wing and Jack, playing up on his ulcers, was sent straight to the sick bay. Johnny Thompson, as a first offender, had been taken on to Wormwood Scrubs and I wouldn't see him again.

Wandsworth was different this time. I was no longer considered a trainable prisoner, so it was straight into the mainstream for me. Next morning, after seeing the doctor and being interviewed by the assistant governor in charge of receptions, I was allocated to work in the pouch shop, which in actual fact meant sewing mailbags. Things in the workshops had improved a little since my last visit. The silence rule had been relaxed so that you could talk to the men on either side of you, but not to the men in front or behind. But it was still the hand in the air for a 'sit down' or a 'stand up', then waiting for the screw on his high throne to nod you off to the toilet. From now on I would make few, if any, decisions for myself. My every movement, bowel or otherwise, would be controlled by the rules of the prison or the order of the screws. I wouldn't have to think, simply obey.

When I first walked through the centre of the main cell block in Wandsworth Prison, I saw right away why its radiating wings were always likened to the spokes of a wheel. At first I had thought the description apt, but after a few weeks I began to see the spokes more as the tentacles of an octopus gradually sucking and squeezing at the lives within its grip, remorselessly reducing them to an obedient, grey, common sludge with no will of its own. The prisoners' lives were so controlled and dominated by the strict, unchanging daily routine that they were little more than zombies. And I was becoming one of them.

Obviously, because of the monotony, nothing much went on in Wandsworth worth writing about. I did run into one well-known figure in the pouch shop who has been mentioned in every London crime book that I have ever read – Big Frank Mitchell, otherwise known as the Mad Axeman, whom the Krays, for some reason known only to themselves, spirited away from Dartmoor.

All I can say about Big Frank is that when I worked beside him in the pouch shop, he was a very decent sort of guy. I never saw him taking a liberty with anyone and he always had a broad smile on his face. I don't know why the villains got him away from Dartmoor just to end up killing him.

I must have sat and sewn in the pouch shop for over a year when I was offered a job as a cleaner in the library. They say that everyone remembers where they were when they heard the news of President Kennedy's assassination. All criminals remember where they were when they first heard the news of the Great Train Robbery. I was in the library of Wandsworth Prison and a screw called Leeson told us about it when he came in on duty. The morning papers hadn't arrived and in those days we didn't have radios in prison. I remember feeling a surge of excitement and thinking to myself what a brilliant a job it was and wondering who had carried it out. Later on, of course, when the word got out and it all started to go wrong, I felt even closer to it when I heard that Charlie Wilson and Roy James were two of the main parties involved. It gave everyone inside a frisson of excitement and something to talk about for the months up until the trial at Aylesbury Crown Court.

I remember wincing at the sentences when they were handed down: a diabolical thirty years for the main men and massive sentences for everyone else involved. In the jail we had all reckoned about fifteen to eighteen years, certainly no one ventured as high as a twenty. The train robbers were victims of establishment outrage. It was and still is, in the eyes of villains and the general public alike, a prime example of political and judicial revenge. I've always wondered if I had been out and around at the time if I would have been declared in and whether or not it would have been a good thing or a bad thing. Not everyone who was on the Great Train Robbery was captured.

My sentence at the Old Bailey had been three-and-a-half years, but with one third off for good behaviour I only owed Her Majesty two years four months. I had thought about my release. I had thought about it every day since I came in, as a matter of fact. But I still hadn't made my mind up about what I was going to do. This sentence had been a lot harder than my previous three-stretch in Maidstone, even with the luxury of the library job. Working in the library had been an enlightening experience, too. Every week I had seen the same faces pass through and watched the spirit in their eyes gradually dim. Men who would once stand and chat brightly for a moment or two now responded in dull monosyllabic mumbles. Where they used to stride in with a bit of a spring in their step, they now mooched about like tired old men, before fitfully choosing their books and slouching upstairs to merge back into the greyness. Sometimes it made me shiver and I didn't want it happening to me. But now I had other things to think about: I would soon be getting out and I had to be making some plans for my future.

When I first got nicked on the conspiracy charges, I had written to my brother Tommy to let him know what had happened to me. He had replied and asked if he could take over the little metalwork shop I had started because William wasn't bothering with it. I knew Tommy was unemployed, so I wrote back and told him he could. I even sent him some money so he could advertise for work in the newspaper. I had very little contact with anyone except the occasional letter to Ted and now and again a short note to some of my mates. Jo, my girlfriend from Ruislip, had been very good at first, writing regularly and visiting me almost every month for nearly a year, but eventually she had found someone else. She had been nice about it, writing to explain herself and asking me not to feel badly towards her.

There is a strange thing about doing time: the closer you get to your date of discharge, the slower each day seems to pass. It is almost as if the devil is enjoying your impatience. Every moment of every day is measured and weighed against time to go. Your last weekend. Your last Monday. Your last Tuesday... Every long, dragging, last day counted off with the monotony of a slow metronome. On the penultimate day, even the meals are counted down, right to your last breakfast on your last morning. During the final hours, your body feels as tense as an astronaut waiting for blast-off.

I have always been fairly casual about goodbyes and I made no great fuss about leaving. I was ready and waiting when the screw unlocked me at a quarter to seven in the morning to take me over to reception. Everything seemed all right. Suddenly, the door of the cubicle rattled open and an orderly stood there with a tray of food.

'Breakfast?'

I looked at a bowl of porridge alongside the mug of tea and a sausage sandwich and thought about it for a moment.

IT'S CRIMINAL

Throughout my sentence, I had never supped the porridge at breakfast time. I liked the stuff all right, but not with sugar, the way they served it in Wandsworth; I took my porridge with salt. However, there is an old superstition about your last breakfast in jail: 'If you don't sup your last bowl of porridge, you will be back for it another time.' I must admit, I did hesitate, but I've never been superstitious and I settled for the mug of tea and sausage sandwich.

I heard my name called out and walked round to the reception desk, my feet feeling strangely light in unfamiliar thin socks and soft, leather shoes. Once again I had to give my name and number before my 'valuable property' bag was unsealed and I was given back my watch.

As I leaped in the taxi I had just flagged down, I shouted to the driver, 'Paddington.' I had made up my mind and knew where I wanted to go, what I wanted to do. 'Bravington Road, Paddington. Do you know it?'

'No problem, guv.' The driver spoke over his shoulder. 'Off the Harrow Road, isn't it?'

'That's right,' I said. 'Past the Prince of Wales boozer, then third on the right.'

'Got it, guv.' The driver turned out into the traffic.

I leaned back in the seat and nodded to myself. The decision had been made and I knew I wouldn't change my mind. I looked at my wristwatch and saw that it was still not quite half-past seven. I could easily make it to Ted's and collect my things in time to catch an early train out of London.

Chapter Fourteen

Anything, Anywhere, Anytime

hen I arrived at my friend Ralph Benson's door in Kent, he made me welcome and I moved into the spare room of his three-bedroom council house. Ralph had been released from Wandsworth about six weeks before me and was still mooching around doing very little. He hadn't actually turned back to what I would have described as 'real' thieving, but he was hanging about with the local guys, working fiddles with them and doing a little dealing in stolen metal from the factories in the Medway Towns district. On other occasions, he would make a few quid by acting as an intermediary in the odd sale of stolen property. It wasn't the sort of life that I would describe as really criminal. It was more like a survival existence. I arrived there with the vague idea of perhaps finding a job and maybe going straight. At the time I really did think it was a good idea and I even made a fair start at it.

There was plenty of work available in the area and I took a job at a brick-finishing works. The change was all right for a few days, but then it became boring. My hand got used to the stinging and I could cleave the stones quite well, sometimes even getting an extra slice now and again and feeling proud of my achievement! But in all honesty, I couldn't really say there was any job satisfaction in sitting like a dummy, whacking stones with a hammer all day. I think I lasted until about halfway through my second week. The boss wasn't the least bit bothered about my leaving. I mean, it wasn't as if I was a vital part of the brick-production operation and no doubt there were plenty of other young men waiting to take my place.

Ralph told me I could get a job in an engineering factory in Strood. I still remember its name: Hobourne Aero Precision Ltd. 'What as?' I asked. Two or three days later, I was well into the swing of being an internal grinder and tossing out cogs like an expert. I have always had the habit of racing myself whatever I am doing, and this job was ideal for trying to go faster. But I left Hobourne Aero Precision the day before I was due to begin working on the night shift. I just couldn't face it. The staggering monotony of my future terrified me!

Now what? I looked up jobs in the newspapers and wrote away for several attractive-sounding positions. I answered one ad that said: 'Ambitious young men urgently needed for dynamic company. Earnings of up £1,500 per annum. Apply immediately.' It was the only reply I got and I went to the office for an interview. I don't know what I was expecting, but it certainly wasn't door-to-door selling for 'Betterwear Products'! What a farce. And a con – in order to obtain employment for this 'dynamic' company I had to pay them for my sample case before I could even hope to earn my 'up to £1,500 per annum'.

Good intentions were getting me nowhere. What next? Well, the Co-op store on the main road suddenly began looking like a good job to me. It was a busy shop selling cigarettes and spirits as well as the usual Co-op groceries. There was no alarm and the rear windows were only protected by thin steel bars which could be seen from inside the shop. Ralph was delighted with the idea and a few nights later I walked across a field and jumped over the fence of the brickyard where I had once slaved. In the workshop, where my stone-breaking career had come to an end,

IT'S CRIMINAL

I found a set of four-foot-long bolt cutters still hanging in their position on the wall.

Ralph borrowed an old banger of a van from someone and a couple of nights later we were round the back of the Co-op. It took us about two minutes to chop out one of the window bars at the back and we were inside. The snout and booze went into the van first, then we went back and ripped the safe open. There wasn't a large sum of money in it, but along with the sale of the snout and booze it came to a nice few quid.

Suddenly Ralph and I went from being skint, and I mean skint, to having a few quid to spend and plenty of time to lounge about the pubs with the rest of the local 'chaps'. I must admit that, despite all my good intentions, I felt a far greater sense of accomplishment in successfully screwing the Co-op and ripping open the safe than getting a bonus for turning out a thousand cogs at Hobourne Aero.

Still, I really did want to do something other than simply revert to snouting. I actually wanted to do something constructive, something different with my life. But what was it to be? I was looking through the adverts in the papers for the umpteenth time and moaning about the lack of interesting-looking opportunities on offer, when Ralph made a suggestion.

'Why don't you advertise yourself?' he said one day.

'What?'

'You advertise,' he said again. 'You put an advert in the paper asking for a job.'

Yes... I turned the idea over in my mind. That's not a bad idea. Not a bad idea at all. I had always been in the habit of reading a half-decent daily paper, the *Daily Telegraph* at that time and I always looked at the Jobs Available columns, but I had never thought about reading or using the Jobs Wanted bit:

Young man, 26. Seeks employment, prepared to do
anything, anywhere, anytime. Reply to Box No 1234

Within three days, I had five replies. Four out of the five offered me some kind of job but only if I sent money for further information. The fifth offer was from a company at an address just off London's Oxford Street. It was interesting enough for me to get on the train and take a trip to London. Selling air humidifiers on a commission-only basis around offices in London: that was the adventurous life I was offered when I arrived for my interview. I know my ad did say 'do anything', but I was actually looking for something more exciting than this.

It was the forces of law and order that finally made me make up my mind to leave Gillingham. One day Ralph and I were walking up from town when two CID officers in an unmarked car stopped us. They were quite friendly, just asking us what we did with ourselves and if we knew of anything they should know about.

Then they asked us about the Co-op shop and quizzed us about where we were the night it had been broken into. I was sweating. If they had a report about the bolt cutters being stolen and found out that I had worked in the brickworks, I could be in a bit of trouble. However, they weren't too busy with us and after a few more questions they let us out of the car with the warning that they might want to speak to us again. As I said, they weren't very heavy with us. We were probably only two in a long list of probables they chatted to, but I decided that Gillingham was too small for me. I decided to do what I should have done in the first place when I got out of Wandsworth: to go home and see my family.

I will always remember my mother leaning over the wide well of the close as I ascended the stairs. I saw her shape leaning over the banister and realised she had spotted me.

'Is that you, James?' I heard her voice.

'Aye,' I called up to her. 'It's only me.'

Then she said something that I have thought about a thousand times, trying to analyse what she actually meant. It was nothing drastic, just a simple question. 'You're not home for good, are you?'

I was actually stuck for words for a few seconds. In fact, I don't really remember how I replied to her question. Still, I was home for the moment and that was all that mattered. My young brother William had got married and had a place of his own by this time, so there was plenty of room for me in the house and I took my place without any upheaval.

Of course, I was a seven-day wonder again. All sorts of tales had been heard about me and most of the lads I grew up with knew that I had been in jail down in the Big Smoke. Naturally I told a few tales, adding bits and pieces now and again to make my story more interesting, but when I think about it now, I realise that even the bare facts of my story were infinitely more exciting than the lifestyle my old mates had experienced.

Within a few days, it was as if I had never been away. My elder brother Tommy had kept the metal workshop on and, although not exactly busy, he was turning out a fair amount of work. I still had some money left from the Co-op job, but I knew that if I wanted to stay in Glasgow, and I wasn't sure yet whether I wanted to do that or not, I would either have to work along with my brother, or find some way of making some money. One thing I did know was that I was not going to work on some daily grind for meagre pay.

I had been at home for just over a week when a large envelope arrived for me from Ralph. I didn't think much about it as I opened the envelope until several smaller envelopes fell from the packet when I tipped it up. There was a short note from Ralph explaining that these letters had arrived from the *Telegraph* a couple of days after I had left for Glasgow.

I think there was about four letters in the envelope. Three of them were the same as the last lot, all offering 'exciting opportunities' as long as I bought this or that from them to get started. The letter that I kept until last was in an airmail envelope with a very bright, floral stamp on it. Ghana, that's what it said on the stamp. Ghana? I wasn't very sure where the country was.

I read the letter. It was an offer of work in a place called Takoradi. The writer, George McFall was his name, told me that he was the manager of a cocoa mill in Ghana and that he had read my advertisement in the *Telegraph*. He wondered if I might be interested in working as a general assistant to him in the cocoa mill. Some driving and office work was all that would be involved. If I was interested, I was to reply as soon as possible before he put an advert about the job in the paper himself.

I felt quite excited about this offer and wrote back immediately, telling him I would take the job. It was exactly the sort of break away I was looking for. Africa! I could hardly believe the possibility had arisen and waited anxiously to hear from George McFall again.

He replied about two weeks later enclosing a letter to take to the BOAC ticket office in Victoria, London and a cheque for £50 expenses. I arranged myself a passport and even took a last-minute driving test which I passed. My mother accepted my latest departure with her usual equanimity, simply asking me if I had everything I needed and asking me not to forget to write this time. I don't think big brother Tommy even bothered to get out of his bed to say goodbye.

The errant son just picked up his bag, said 'cheerio' and walked out of the door on his way to his latest adventure. I know my mother watched me halfway down the stairs before I heard the door quietly close behind her. I wonder what she really thought about all my carry-on as I set off once again from Palermo Street, this time headed for darkest Africa.

Chapter Fifteen

Gracious Living

I could still hardly believe what was happening to me. Here I was, just a couple of months out of jail, flying over Africa in a 707 jet. As the plane thundered its way southwards, every passing second brought me closer and closer to Accra and the adventure of Africa.

I had always had a picture of Africa in my mind: thundering herds of wildebeest, galloping zebras and bounding antelope raising dust clouds across the plains; lions roaring in the jungle; the screeching of monkeys swinging in the trees; clutches of thatch-roofed villages inhabited by noble, half-naked savages bearing primitive knives and spears, stoically facing life against a constantly cruel jungle while the constant throb, throb, throb of jungle drums made the very air vibrate with a deep, dark, African passion. Of course, I knew this was a false image, but all I knew about Africa had come to me via the Hollywood film industry. Tarzan had a lot to answer for!

The final moments of my flight were breathtaking. As the jet dropped lower and lower in the air, I was able to see the forest in greater detail. Then the jungle started to thin out and I began to catch glimpses of the red, roasted earth that was the soil of Africa. Gradually the jungle petered out altogether until we were flying over baked earth and scrub instead of the thick greenery of the forest canopy.

I had no idea what the West African city of Accra would look like, but I certainly wasn't expecting the modern, skyscraper buildings that suddenly leaped into view when the pilot banked into a turn and lined the aircraft up for the final approach. I got my first real impression of Africa when I stepped from the air-conditioned plane on to the top step of the passenger ramp. It was like stepping into the boilerhouse of some steamy Chinese laundry – hot and humid and not a breath of wind to cool things down! Halfway down the passenger stairs I was already sweating and shrugging my jacket off as perspiration trickled down my face. I walked the short distance to the terminal building, removing my tie and fumbling to loosen the buttons of my shirt. The vest I had put on that morning was already clinging to me like a wet rag.

I had been a little concerned that I might miss George McFall at the airport, as neither of us knew what the other looked like. My fears turned out to be groundless. Most of the passengers aboard my plane were flying on to Lagos, Nigeria and there were only about a dozen of us disembarking at Accra. As we straggled across the tarmac towards the small, whitewashed terminal building, I noticed a man in the outside waiting enclosure studying the arrivals, as if he wasn't quite sure who he was looking for. As everyone else seemed to be waving and smiling at someone, I guessed the inquisitive-looking guy must be looking out for me. We smiled tentatively at one another and he stretched his hand towards me as I approached.

'James Crosbie?'

'That's me.' I smiled and extended my arm, looking him over as we exchanged handshakes. George McFall was slightly taller than me, but his shoulders slumped a little, making him look shorter. Wearing off-white trousers and a white, sweat-wilted shirt, he looked to be in his early forties. Thinning fair hair emphasised his sun-reddened face and his eyes looked tired, as if the heat was wearing him out. When he smiled, the dried lines of his face gave him a distinctly gnomish look. I got the impression that he was a decent enough sort of bloke.

'I'll pick you up when you come through to the concourse,' he said, as I carried on to immigration control and customs.

I passed customs and entry controls without delay and when I went through to the concourse I saw George waiting for me with a friend. We shook hands once again and he introduced me to his friend and colleague Brian Smith, the cocoa buyer for the same company he worked for. Brian was based in Accra and worked out of a large villa in a prosperous suburb not far from the airport. This villa was company property and as well as being Brian's living accommodation it served as the main Ghanaian office and communications centre for the mother company in London – Gill and Duffus. Other company employees also used it when they passed through Accra on their way to and from Takoradi, or for weekend breaks in the city. George told me that we would be staying at Brian's place overnight before catching a flight on to Takoradi in the morning.

Later on, after a welcome cold shower and changing into fresh, lightweight clothes, I went downstairs to the lounge where Brian's houseboy served the three of us with ice-cold bottles of Heineken. It felt a little strange to be waited on by a servant; I sat back in a huge, squashy armchair, held the lager glass in my hand and looked around.

The room we were sitting in was palatial by any standard I was used to. Heavy drapes had been pulled across the window, the maroon, gold-trimmed velvet curtains contrasting luxuriously against the pastel-coloured walls which carried huge, obviously native, oil paintings on any area large enough to warrant a frame. The furniture was all very plush: fat settees and armchairs formed a huge square in the centre of the room around a rectangular, dark-wood coffee table of which the main feature was three carved elephants, their broad backs supporting a polished glass surface that seemed acres wide to me. There were display cabinets and sideboards against every wall and a huge hardwood dining table was placed near the entrance to the kitchen. Where there was space, native ceremonial masks, crossed spears and wood carvings decorated the walls and every flat surface boasted its own explosion of colour as huge displays of flowers contrasted against the pastel shades of the room. I looked around and decided that it was definitely the largest and most luxurious living room I had ever been in.

No mention had been made yet of what work I was expected to do, but I supposed George was waiting until we arrived at Takoradi before bringing the subject up. So I just sat and sipped contentedly at my ice-cold beer, listening as Brian chatted away about collecting soil samples from a cocoa plantation the next day. Part of his job was to extract soil samples from freshly planted fields and send the earth to London so that Gill and Duffus could have it analysed. This chemical analysis enabled the company to estimate the quality and quantity of cocoa beans a particular plantation would yield and armed with this knowledge Gill and Duffus would make a confident advance bid for the crop. It seemed the sort of job I would like, skulking about in fields stealing soil and I suspected it was a form of industrial espionage.

I was politely brought into the conversation with questions about my journey and the weather back home and soon had George and Brian laughing when I told them that I had almost decided to wear my heavy Crombie overcoat for my trip to Ghana because of the cold weather in Scotland. 'Winter at home is the hottest time of the year here,' George explained. 'I don't think anyone out here as much as owns an overcoat.'

I was feeling very relaxed and asked George about Takoradi. Was it a very big place? Was there much to do there? 'You'll find plenty to do with yourself once you're settled in,' he told me. 'There's the Takoradi Sports Club, which has an excellent nine-hole golf course and a first-class swimming pool to lounge around. There's even horse riding if you like that sort of thing. It will be one of your jobs to drive me down there every day,' he said, smiling at his first acknowledgement of my job. Then he looked at me inquisitively. 'Do you play golf yourself?'

When I told him I had never played the game, he simply nodded and told me he would round up a set of clubs for me and I would soon learn. This all sounded great to me, playing golf, swimming, horse riding, all in the wonderful sunshine of Africa. 'And then there are some very interesting places to visit,' George went on. 'The Volta dam scheme at Akosombo, the diamond fields at Tarkwa and the gold mines at Obuasi. You'll find plenty to keep you occupied. Don't worry about that.'

My ears had pricked up at the words I was hearing. 'I thought all Ghana had was cocoa beans,' I said.

'There's a lot more to Ghana than just cocoa beans,' Brian broke in. 'There is a huge timber industry and vast bauxite mineral deposits, as well as the diamond fields and gold mines.'

Diamond fields and gold mines: so far all I'd ever done was read about things like that. Now here I was, actually within striking distance of them. Again I felt that quiver. We sat and chatted away until Brain's houseboy, Koffi, announced that dinner was ready and we sat down to a lovely meal. Not long after the meal was over and Koffi had cleared up and gone home, Brian excused himself for bed, pleading a pre-dawn start to collect his soil samples.

I felt a little awkward with George as we sat there in the living room, but we just chatted away, George asking me questions about my past education, work experience and that sort of thing. I gave him a highly sanitised and edited version of my life and he seemed quite happy with my answers. I supposed he was more or less constructing an oral CV and I thought that was fair enough. After all, I was going to be working for him. At about ten o'clock I was feeling quite tired and said so to George, who showed me to a bedroom in the upper part of the house.

I had a huge bedroom to myself with en-suite facilities – another first for me (excluding, of course, the in-cell piss pot) – and after a shower I lay back on the bed and considered my situation. I couldn't help comparing my present conditions to my old cell in Wandsworth and realised I was smiling. Things were looking good to me. I lay in bed listening to the hum of the air conditioner as it blew cool air into the room and I dropped off to sleep with my mind still turning over the tantalising prospects of diamond fields and gold mines.

I was awakened in the morning by the sound of Koffi placing a cup of tea and some biscuits on the bedside cabinet and sat up feeling great, ready for anything in this new life. When I got downstairs, George was already up and about. Brian was long gone on his soil-sampling expedition and by ten o'clock George and I were at the airport boarding an ancient Dakota of Ghana Airways for the domestic flight to Takoradi.

It was a memorable experience, travelling in the venerable old DC3 as it rattled and smoked its way the 120 miles westwards along the coast to our destination. At one stage I was almost on the point of calling the stewardess to point out some rivets on the wing that seemed to be revolving in time with the engine vibration. I felt sure that rivets shouldn't turn like that, but I didn't want to make a fool of myself and appear a nervous flyer. Other than my concern for the mysterious revolving rivets, it was a flight I enjoyed immensely. The slow old plane droned westwards at no more than 150 miles per hour and just a couple of thousand feet above the coastline, the speed and low altitude allowed for views that were simply sensational.

On the seaward side, I could see line upon line of boiling surf endlessly tumbling, frothy white, into the bluest water I had ever set eyes on. The inland view was even more impressive. From the right-hand windows of the plane, I could see a low range of tree-covered coastal hills that tapered right down to the shoreline, the brilliant green leaves of ancient hardwoods etching a ragged, natural line against the sparkling silver sands of the long beach; every now and again a picturesque fishing village would float into view and appear to drift lazily by underneath our wings.

We began flying over some stone buildings and George pointed out the university township of Cape Coast and then its

Top: James Crosbie, *far right*, pictured with his two brothers and parents.

Bottom: James Crosbie, *middle left*, with his parents and, *right*, brother Thomas Anthony and, *bottom left*, younger brother William Ireland.

In the army, 1957, James (*left*) with a pal.

Top: In his living room in 1969, James relaxes.

Bottom: The house in Takoradi, Ghana, where James Crosbie stayed.

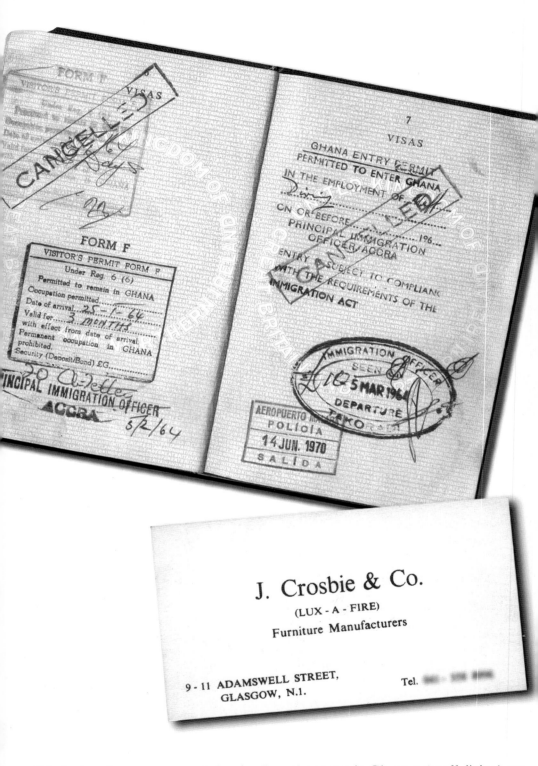

Criminal on the go: a passport showing James' purpose in Ghana as 'muff diving', *top left*; a business card for a legitimate furniture-making business, *bottom left* and flying licences (including member number 008 – licenced to rob! *Top right*).

Glasgow Flying Club

Saint Andrews Drive, *Crmlsie dr.*,
Glasgow Airport,
Abbotsinch,
Renfrewshire.
Tel. 041-889 4565 (direct) 041-887 1111 (Ext.208)

Name.... JAMES CROSBIE

Address.... 100 PARK ROAD.
BISHOPBRIGGS · GLASGOW
(Please notify the Club of any change of Address)

Signature.... *James Crosbie*

Membership number 008

Available to 31st December, 197**3**

The holder of this card is a.... PILOT
member of the Glasgow Flying Club and is
entitled to all the rights and privileges
prescribed in the Club Constitution and Rules
for the said Class of Membership until the
date stated opposite.

.... *January* .... HON Secretary

Club membership includes membership of
The Glasgow Air Centre, affiliated to The
British Light Aviation Centre, London.

Club Shop

Members may purchase navigation
instruments, manuals, maps, training
publications, ties, badges etc., in the
Club Shop.

THIS CARD IS ONLY VALID UNTIL 31st. March, 1973

E.F.C.

THE EDINBURGH FLYING CLUB LTD.
Incorporating
WEST OF SCOTLAND FLYING CLUB (see overleaf)

This card signifies that the holder:

Mr/~~Mrs~~/~~Miss~~.... J. Crosbie

Address.... 100 Park Rd
Bishopbriggs, Glasgow

No. and Membership
Classification .... 421 A

Is entitled to all privileges relevant to
the above classification of membership
as laid down in the club's rules. .... A. McQ
Secretary's Initials

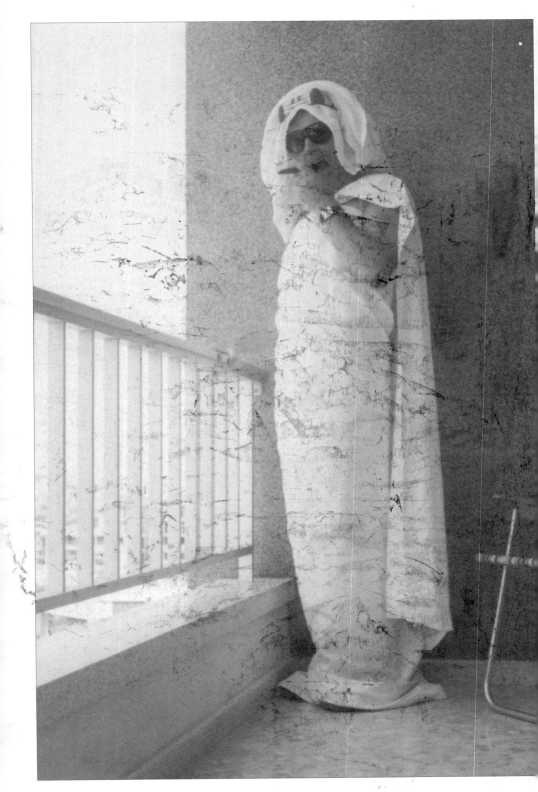

In Cyprus in 1972: 'I was acting the goat!' laughs James.

Part of the winning sports team at Saughton Prison in Edinburgh, *far right*, James Crosbie. They were victorious in the marathon between 1984 and 1986.

Later life: in Madeira with Marlene, *top*, and also on a cruise.

neighbouring Cape Coast Castle, an old Portuguese-built fortress that had, in the past, held captured slaves before they were shipped off to the West Indies in the diabolical conditions of the 'triangular trade'. Ironically this ancient fortress, once witness to so much of man's inhumanity to man, now served as a bastion of law and order as the training college for the Ghanaian Police Force.

Twenty minutes later, the buildings of another large town began to appear beneath us. Sekondi, George told me, straightening up to fasten his seatbelt. 'This used to be where they loaded and unloaded boats before they built the harbour at Takoradi. We should be landing in about ten minutes' time.'

A chauffeur-driven company Mercedes met us at the airport. The African driver took my case and put it into the boot of the car, then held the rear door open for me to step in. On the way to the cocoa mill I saw monkeys capering about high in some trees and turned my head to watch them. It was then that it really hit me that I had actually moved continents.

George McFall was the manager of a British-owned company called West African Mills that bought and processed cocoa beans, exporting the produce — fresh cocoa beans, cocoa butter and cocoa cake — all over the world by ship from Takoradi harbour. The cocoa mill was about three miles east of Takoradi on the road to Sekondi and was a fairly big affair. The actual mill was a large, strangely shaped building made mainly from black corrugated iron on a high steel frame, its walls rising about forty feet into the air.

There were other smaller, single-storey buildings huddled around the main structure that contained the offices and workers' medical centre. A railway spur allowed direct delivery of raw materials and was also the means of getting the finished product down to the Takoradi docks, where it was loaded on to boats and shipped to ports all around the world. I was quite impressed by the size of the place and realised that the cocoa mill was a much bigger operation than I had imagined.

Once through the factory gate the car turned left along a narrow tarmacked road, taking us past the side of the factory and up a steep hill that spilled us out on to a large, landscaped area containing the living quarters for the European employees of West African Mills. I could see several bungalows nestling among the neatly trimmed trees and bushes and was wondering which one was George's when the chauffeur turned the Mercedes into the second driveway on the left and parked outside a large, white-painted bungalow.

I had expected that George would have good accommodation, but the beautiful stone bungalow we had pulled up outside went beyond my expectations. The front door of the house was reached by twin flights of stairs at opposite ends of a spacious balcony area. The balcony itself was big enough to contain a selection of wrought-iron garden furniture set around a large, circular, glass-topped table and there was still room for a huge cage on a stand that contained, or should have contained, a parrot. When I arrived, Marmaduke the parrot, an African grey as I later found out, was perched on the roof of its home, treading anxiously and cocking its head from side to side, no doubt considering the new arrival. The front door opened before we reached it and a young African man came out to greet us, his face beaming in a wide, welcoming smile. This was Sam, George's houseboy. I was introduced and we shook hands before he went to the boot of the car where the chauffeur was unloading our luggage.

The bungalow was spacious, its large living room running into an equally large dining area, where open arches led off to two enormous bedrooms, giving the place an expansive, open-plan look. There were only two doors inside the house: one led to the modern kitchen and the other to the bathroom. A house like this was a new experience for me and I was suitably impressed. As for actually having a servant running about after me – well, that was very definitely a first.

There were about seven or eight bungalows in the small estate and only three of them were being used. George Merriman from Hull, the resident engineer for the factory and his rather quiet and retiring wife Frances lived in the bungalow furthest away from the road and deep in the shade of the trees. The only other occupied bungalow was an even grander affair than the rest and was lived in by a Mr Theodore Sloot, his wife, their twelve-year-old son, also named Theodore, and the son's long-time nanny or nurse, a woman of about thirty-five called Rosemary.

Mr Theodore Sloot was in overall charge of the entire complex and a director of the parent company, Gill and Duffus. He was actually the architect who had designed and built the mill in Takoradi, as well as a 'twin' factory in Hull, England. I never did find out what actual work Mr Sloot did in Takoradi. He just seemed to pass his time there without noticeably doing anything. Maybe that's how it is when you're the boss!

The other bungalows of the small estate lay empty and unused, only opened up when the odd visitor arrived, such as the annual relief manager, or very occasionally some company representative from Britain. George told me I could stay with him until such time as a bungalow could be prepared for me and when I asked him when I would be starting work he told me to forget it for a week or so until I settled in. The arrangement suited me fine and I happily moved into his place.

Looking back at it, I suppose that time of my life was the nearest I came to what I would call 'gracious living'. Sam would serve me my breakfast from hot serving plates and wait on me throughout the meal, topping up my tea and tidying up as soon as I finished with anything. It took a bit of getting used to and I don't think Sam knew quite what to make of me. I'm a very loquacious person by nature and I was treating him just like a pal, chatting away, asking him questions about Takoradi and about himself, his family and so on. Then I gave him all the clothes I had brought with me that I knew I wouldn't need – heavy pullovers and some long-sleeved shirts. On my third or fourth morning there, I heard a knock at the front door and Sam admitted the local town tailor whom George had sent for to measure me for cotton trousers and shorts. I was amazed. Here was the tailor coming all the way from Takoradi just to measure me up for a few pairs of trousers. I felt really important. This was the sort of thing the gentry did, wasn't it? With every passing minute, I was getting to like the place better and better.

I was actually quite keen to get started on my work, but it turned out that George didn't actually have a proper job for me; what he was really after was company. I could understand this too, because although George had the use of a company car, he couldn't drive. Therefore, with walking about at night being out of the question, he was virtually a social hermit, marooned in his bungalow on the factory estate every night. His neighbours were of no help to him. George Merriman, no doubt under the influence of his introvert wife, kept to himself and seldom went out at night unless in her company. The wealthy Mr Sloot had his own social circle among the higher echelon of ex-pat businessmen in Takoradi and had little or nothing to do with the social activities of his underlings.

So it turned out that I was more or less there to keep George company and to drive his car so he could get out and about a bit. It was all very casual and I didn't get a pay packet or anything, but it suited me very well. If I needed any money, I had George's permission to help myself from cash he kept in a drawer in the house.

Funnily enough, I hardly ever needed cash. I was allowed to use the mill's credit number and could obtain everything I needed simply by signing my name. That credit account number, 3M33, is one of the things I will always remember about my stay in Ghana. I could buy almost anything with it. I could even hire cars, which I did when we wanted a decent model to drive through to Accra for the weekend. If I left the house with a pound cash in my pocket, I was loaded!

One evening, we were sitting on the veranda, quietly enjoying our regular evening beer and watching a freighter as it approached Takoradi harbour. 'You mentioned something about diamond mines, George.' I finally broke a long silence, keeping my voice casual as I broached a subject that had never been far from my mind. 'Remember... when I first arrived? You said I would be able to see them.'

'That's right,' George said and nodded absently. 'Well, nearly right,' he added with a quiet laugh. 'There is a gold mine, right enough. But there's no diamond mines in Ghana. It's diamond fields they have out here. Surface diamonds. Alluvial diamonds, to give them their proper name. The natives dig them out of the ground.'

'What!' I exclaimed. 'You mean they just dig about and find diamonds?'

'Well, it's a bit more complicated than that,' George admitted. 'But basically that's it. They just go out and dig.'

'Can anyone dig for them? Could I have a go?'

He laughed at my keenness, but shook his head. 'No,' he said. 'The diamond business is government controlled, part of the national resources. Anyway, they're not the sort of diamonds you would recognise. It's industrial diamonds they have out here, not the polished gemstones you see in a jeweller's window.'

I felt a little deflated at this news, but was still intent on investigating the possibilities I had dreamed about. Industrial diamonds might not be as interesting or glamorous as gemstones, but they still had a high market value and I wanted to see the set-up for myself.

'But I can go and see the place, can't I?'

'Of course you can,' George agreed. 'Not that there's a lot to see. Bit like looking over an oversized shale pit.'

'Are they very far away?' I asked.

'The nearest fields are in the Tarkwa district, about forty miles north of here. Mind you,' he added, 'the road is a bit rough once you leave the coast. Not much more than a track, as it happens.'

'I'd really like to see them,' I persisted, not allowing George's pessimism to put me off. 'Do you think I could find them on my own?'

'You couldn't miss them,' he told me. 'Once you reach Tarkwa there's nothing else. Why don't you take a trip up there tomorrow? I would go along with you myself, but quite honestly I really don't fancy making that particular trip again. I'll get Sam to prepare a packed lunch and a few bottles of beer for you.'

'Good!' I said. Terrific, I thought. Diamonds, industrial or otherwise, suddenly held a great attraction for me. Surely there would be an earner somewhere in this. I happily began making plans for the next day, my mind overflowing with tantalising possibilities.

Chapter Sixteen

All That Glitters

By nine o'clock the following morning, I was in the car heading for Takoradi and the road that would take me to the diamond fields. As George had promised, Sam had prepared me a packed lunch with a few bottles of beer to wash it down. I was feeling quite content as I drove along, dreaming about diamond fields and the possibilities that lay just forty miles ahead. I drove through town, turning right on to the Tarkwa Road just before the airport, then settled down to enjoy a drive in the brilliant morning sunshine. I was barely one mile out of town when the badly maintained metalled surface disappeared altogether and I found myself wrestling with the steering wheel as I bounced and skittered from pothole to pothole like a ping pong ball in a cloud of dust. Even with my speed reduced to less than fifteen miles per hour, it didn't take me long to realise why George had not been keen to join me on the trip.

After more than three hours of rocking and rolling, surrounded by a constant cloud of red dust, I was almost on the point of turning back when I spotted a lopsided road sign telling me that I had arrived at my destination. It should have been a relief, but when I saw the single-storey, run-down buildings that made up the town of Tarkwa, my spirits sagged. Surely, I thought, nothing of value could possibly come out of this place? However, if nothing else I desperately needed a drink and I kept my eyes open for a bar or café.

At last I spotted the familiar Coca Cola sign and pulled up in front of a small roadside bar, parking my car behind a dust-covered jeep that was already sitting there. It was a relief to get inside into some shade and I was surprised to see a white man sitting at a table. When he looked up and gave me a friendly, welcoming nod, I ordered two beers and went and sat beside him, sliding one of the beers across the table in his direction. The guy accepted the drink, smiling his thanks and seemed pleased to have some company.

After we had introduced ourselves and started chatting, it transpired that the guy, Walter Ellis, originated from Leeds and was working in Tarkwa as a maintenance engineer on the diamond fields. Over another couple of beers, I told him about my 'job' in Takoradi and how I had driven up for the day to see the diamond fields. It seemed to amuse Walter that anyone would actually want to see round the place, but he offered to take me back with him and do the honours. 'Not that there's a lot to see,' he warned, as we walked out of the bar together.

I trailed behind him in my own car; avoiding the thickest of the dust cloud the heavy tyres of his jeep threw up. After about five minutes, Walter turned through a gateway into an area of barren-looking earth that was almost black in comparison to the red surface I had been driving on all morning. We rattled along an uneven dirt track for another few miles through a moonscape of desolate, ravaged land, its surface gouged and scraped into long shallow troughs and deep valleys where the diamond-bearing gravel had been stripped clean by man's continuous quest for the precious stones hidden inside.

Eventually, after a bone-shaking ride along the deeply rutted track, we pulled up outside some dingy-looking buildings. Walter waited until I had parked alongside him then, after picking up a fat-tyred rough-terrain vehicle, he gave me a guided tour of the diamond-extraction operation at Tarkwa. It would be an understatement to say that I was disappointed. In my innocence, I had expected to see diamonds glinting and sparkling on the ground and in my mind's eye my pockets were already bulging with precious stones. In reality, all I could see for miles around was barren, dark, gravelly earth, every stone and pebble looking just that – like stones and pebbles. As for diamonds, well, Walter *had* told me in the bar that they had to process tons of earth to garner a few of the things. I had heard his words, but being an eternal optimist I had interpreted 'diamond fields' in my own way.

There was no doubt that Walter knew his stuff as he showed me squads of sweat-streaked Africans digging into the surface soil. He explained that as each area became worked out, the security fence was extended and the necessary equipment moved into place on the fresh ground. Workers would then dig deep into the ground, shovelling the earth into scurrying dump trucks that tipped it on to the nearest rumbling spur of a long, snake-like, conveyer belt. From there the raw ore trundled slowly across the landscape to disappear inside the diamond-extraction plant, close to where we had parked our cars.

We climbed out of our vehicle and stood on one of the conveyer belt's inspection platforms to watch the excavated earth trundle slowly past. It just looked like crushed slate to me. I was definitely unimpressed. I had set out on my tour full of interest and optimism, but that had faded as Walter led me around.

Uninterested now, I watched the dross drift by, listening politely enough as he explained things. But as far as I was concerned, I might as well have been touring a gravel pit in Essex. Even when we made our way back to the processing building, there was nothing worthwhile to see. The loaded conveyer belt simply disappeared behind a screen into a secure area where the diamonds were extracted and taken to the sorting room for grading and weighing. The conveyer belt moved on through the security area to dump the looted soil back on to the earth's pockmarked surface, where men driving bulldozers scooped it back into place like make-up artists repairing a ravaged face.

I finally got to see some of the elusive diamonds when, on Walter's request, a security guard unlocked a door and allowed us to pass through into the secure area. 'I expect you'll be wanting to see the finished product,' Walter said as we stepped into the brightly lit sorting room.

At first sight it looked a bit like a laboratory to me. Everything was white – the walls, the tiled floor, the Formica table, even the overalls of the four men intently going about their work, grading and weighing the pickings from the field. Walter walked over to the table and spoke a few words to one of the men who smiled and handed him a small metal tray. 'There you are,' he said, holding the tray out for my inspection. 'This is what it's all about.'

'These are diamonds?' I was more than surprised. Even after seeing the workings and realising that my ideas had been radically wrong, I still expected the finished product to look more impressive than the spoonful of coarse grey grit being held out for my inspection.

'You're looking at some of the highest-quality industrial diamonds in the world there,' Walter informed me, shaking the tray a little so that the largest grains 'floated' to the surface of the small heap. 'Hardest substance known to man,' he went on. 'Machine-tool makers, oil-drill manufacturers, even gemstone cutters themselves take all we can produce – and come back for more. It takes a diamond to cut a diamond, you know.'

I nodded my head, listening, but not really paying attention. My bubble had finally, irretrievably burst. Half an hour later, after a final cold beer from the fridge in Walter's office, I was on my way back to Takoradi, still shaking my head at my naivety. But even though my visit to Takoradi had been disappointing, I was still glad I had made the trip. Otherwise I would be wondering to this day whether or not I had missed out on a great opportunity: if there is one truism in the world of villainy, it is that you never know when the Big One will turn up.

The drive back to Takoradi was hot, dry and dusty, with nothing to occupy my mind other than dodging potholes. Then, ever the optimist, I remembered the gold mine at Obuasi and the fact that George had promised to arrange a weekend there for us. The mine manager was a friend and they exchanged visits three or four times a year for a change of golf course if nothing else. Diamonds forgotten and dreaming of gold, I pressed on in a happier frame of mind.

I had settled into a routine at Takoradi by now. George was always up early and away down to his office by seven in the morning; I would stay in my bed until about half past eight when Sam would bring me in a cup of tea and a few biscuits on a tray. After a shower I would be served breakfast and by ten o'clock I was ready to wander down to the cocoa mill and do my daily 'tour'.

It was an experience for me to be treated by the workers as if I were someone important, but I am sure that most of them found my behaviour rather strange for a white man. I have always been a gregarious, outgoing person and I chatted away to the labourers just exactly as I would with my workmates in the old shipyard days. Every now and again I would give a hand to someone struggling with a loaded trolley, or help to shift a heavy sack of cocoa beans about. I even surprised the blacksmith in the repair shop by picking up a set of tongs and demonstrating my welding skills. I don't think they knew quite what to make of me. I'd end up in George's office in time for a cup of tea, pass half an hour or so chatting with him, then wander about the outer office annoying the giggling female staff.

My only real job each morning was to drive into town and pick up the mail from the company's PO box at the central post office. This took me about an hour and after I had handed the mail into the office I was free to return to town for a few beers and pass my time exploring Takoradi, or lounging about the pool at the sports club.

Sometimes I would perch myself at a bar where I could watch the incredible hustle, bustle and colour of the huge circular marketplace in the town centre. On these occasions a group of small, solemn-faced children would inevitably gather to stare with innocent wonder at this strange white man. I felt like a king when beautiful, doe-eyed little girls, index fingers to chin, executed perfect curtsies, while serious-faced small boys puffed out their chests and saluted like soldiers in front of me. All this in return for the copper penny pieces I handed them. Small price for the pleasure I got from seeing their chubby black faces break into huge banana smiles, before they scampered back to their waiting mothers. When I had finished my couple of beers, I would take a stroll round the market stalls, always finding it a lively experience. The Ghanaians loved their loud 'hi-life' music, constantly swaying to its infectious, pulsating rhythm. I'm sure that if I really searched my mother's house today I would come across a couple of the 'hi-life' records I bought then.

Between my factory walk, collecting the mail and visiting the town, my day was pretty well filled. Now and again I would take a ride on a half-decent road bike I had found in Mr Sloot's garage, amazing the passengers on the trundling 'mammy wagons' I often kept pace with. No Tour de France leader got more cheers than I got from them. When I suddenly thumped into a spoke-bending pothole, their good-natured laughter rose even louder than the cheers.

Around three o'clock I would collect George and we would head to the sports club for a round of golf. I was never a good golfer, not treating the game seriously enough according to George. But I quite enjoyed myself, strolling round the nine-hole course as if I were a champion.

Passing the time in the evenings was another matter. Except for a once-weekly projector-style film show at the club, I found myself spending most of my evenings sitting in the bungalow with George drinking beer. I had rapidly discovered that drinking was an inescapable feature of life in Ghana. At first I wondered why a small table stood at the side of every armchair.

IT'S CRIMINAL

I soon learned that they were there solely to hold drinks. The moment we came through the door in the evening, Sam would appear with two large bottles of Heineken and two tumblers and would place them on the tables. We would each take our chair and automatically pour the beer. It was as routine as kicking off our shoes and, except for the film show or a special night at the club, that would be us for the night.

I asked George several times about going out, but he told me that, other than the sports club, there was nowhere else for Europeans to go.

'What about the bars in town?' I asked.

He told me that it wasn't the done thing for Europeans to frequent the local bars. It was considered too dangerous. We could be mugged just for the shoes on our feet, never mind anything else, according to him.

Well, I never had been one for paying attention to what was or was not 'the done thing' and one night I told George I was going into town. He didn't seem too happy about it and refused to come with me, once again telling me it was dangerous. Well, I didn't mind keeping him company, but I certainly wasn't going to sit in the house every night because he was scared to go out and I told him so. In the end, I went off into town on my own.

At first I was a little wary, but then I thought about the men in the cocoa mill and all the different, friendly people I'd met during the day at the marketplace. I had never once felt the least bit threatened and everybody had always made me feel welcome. I realised that this talk of danger was all in George's narrow, clerical mind. And besides, I thought, I'm a villain myself!

As it turned out, all George's fears were groundless. I had a great time and ended up spending the night with a beautiful black girl. I admit I did hesitate at first when Comfort (a lovely name) invited me home with her. But she was so lovely and such friendly, easygoing company that it was difficult not to give in. Especially since it had been nearly two months since I had enjoyed the intimate company of a female. I had been getting a little desperate in that department, to be honest. Much to my surprise, Comfort's small apartment was as modern as any I had ever been in, with plenty of flowers and family photographs decorating her smartly furnished living room. And I certainly didn't expect the modern double bed that met my eyes when she led me into her very comfortable bedroom.

She told me later that her last boyfriend had been a white man who had recently gone home and it had been he who had helped her with the apartment. I was really impressed. When Comfort first invited me home I had visualised a more 'native' set-up in her house. I couldn't have been further from the truth and it taught me a lesson about jumping to conclusions.

As for danger, well – if sexual exhaustion was dangerous, I was in serious trouble …

Needless to say, once ensconced in Comfort's huge bed I was reluctant to leave and it was next morning before I arrived back at the bungalow. What a carry-on! You'd have thought I had been murdered or something. When I blithely turned into the drive, I was met by a deputation of George, Mr Sloot and George Merriman (the engineer). I felt like a naughty lad, as George demanded to know where I had been all night and what I had been up to.

There I was, a man of twenty-six, making up a story about getting too drunk to drive and falling asleep in the car. I felt really stupid and don't know why I didn't just tell them all to fuck off and mind their own business. Actually, Mr Sloot didn't seem to care at all; I think he was really more concerned about calming George down. The other George just gave me a knowing leer and went off, as he said, 'down t'mill'.

Of course, George had only been worried about my welfare and I should have been grateful for his concern. I apologised and agreed that my behaviour had been very inconsiderate. I still didn't admit I had stayed the night with a black girl, so I made up a story, partly true, about meeting a crowd of Dutch seamen and ending up too drunk to drive home. With the drink and the humid heat of the night, I had climbed into the car and fallen asleep

IT'S CRIMINAL

It was shortly after that first night out that George finally organised a trip to the Ashanti gold mine at Obuasi. I was quite excited about it and couldn't wait for the weekend to come.

Obuasi was only about a hundred miles north on the Takoradi–Kumasi railway line and I was surprised when George told me he had booked a sleeping cabin on the Friday night 'express'. But when we boarded the train and it set off on its journey, I soon found out why he had booked the sleeper. It was still daylight when the little puffer engine steamed slowly out of Takoradi station. I kept waiting for it to speed up, but no, our train just kept chugging away at no more than fifteen miles per hour. I remember looking out of the carriage window, watching palm trees drifting gradually by as we slowly chugged along. Several times I saw dark figures leap from the rattling carriages and disappear into the dense undergrowth at the side of the track. Every now and again, as if to compensate for the deserting passengers, I would spot ghostly figures darting from the greenery to clamber aboard the dawdling train. With three or four routine halts at isolated, unlit stations and a two-hour layover in a siding to allow southbound trains through on the single-track line, the hundred-mile trip took a total of eleven hours.

At half past six in the morning it was still dark when our train wheezed to a halt and deposited us, complete with luggage and golf clubs, at the small wooden platform that was Obuasi station. A driver and car from the gold mine had been sent to meet us and we were driven straight to one of the mine's guest bungalows. Neither of us had slept well on the train and we were glad to get into a real bed for a few hours' proper sleep.

At ten in the morning, a loud banging on the door of our temporary abode awakened us. John Ogilvie, George's friend who was also the mine manager, had arrived to greet us and treat us to breakfast in the mine cafeteria. After introductions over breakfast, John arranged for one of his foremen, a Welshman called Gareth Williams, to show me around the mine. John and George had their golf routine already set up and they both headed straight for the course. In the meantime I got kitted out in the full mining kit: big boots, white overalls, hard hat, battery-operated light and I was ready for the big drop into one of the deepest gold mines in Africa.

Before I went to Obuasi, I had visions of pulling nuggets of gold out of the walls of the mine, like you see in some of the old cowboy pictures. But long before I actually got there, I had learned that the Ashanti Goldfield at Obuasi, the richest gold mine in West Africa, only produced something like ten to twelve grams of gold for every ton of ore that they processed. There were no nuggets of gold there. It was the diamond mines all over again. But I had known this all along. I knew I was kidding myself about getting my hands on any gold, even if there had been nuggets. It was just another imaginative, idle dream.

Being so deep underground was an almost eerie experience. It grew cooler as we dropped and by the time we hit level fourteen, the working level at that time, it was almost cold. I don't know how far we walked along the long, dimly lit tunnels, but I felt as if I was walking inside the body of some gigantic monster. And in the distance, growing louder as we approached, I could hear the steady throb of machinery, like the heartbeat of a living thing.

Once we reached the workface, Gareth got the culling-machine operator to demonstrate his skills, but the flying dust and debris was so thick I could hardly breathe. After an increasingly red-eyed look around, I was glad to head back to the surface. Above ground I was shown round the smelting sheds, ending up in the vault where the finished gold bars were kept before being transported to the treasury in Accra. This was an experience in itself and my last chance to earn. They have an old custom at Obuasi which says that, if you can pick up one of their gold ingots with one hand, you can keep it. Every visitor gets a try at becoming rich, but they only say that because it is impossible to lift the ingot. In the first place, they weigh twenty-eight pounds apiece and, in the second place, with their tapered sides, they are the wrong shape to grip properly. As well as that, pure raw gold has a greasy feel to it, which means that the harder you grip, the quicker you squeeze it out of your grasp. It is impossible. It is just a game for visitors. It adds a bit of spice to their visit and they can always say, like me, that a fortune literally slipped through their fingers.

Later on I met up with George and John and the rest of the weekend was passed either in talking about golf or playing golf. And of course drinking. I tried a round of golf myself on the Sunday, but John Ogilvie couldn't put up with my slow play and I was politely left behind. I enjoyed my weekend at Obuasi, even if I didn't manage to pick up the ingot of gold. It is another experience I will never forget.

A few days after we arrived back at Takoradi, a job turned up for me. Not long after we visited the gold mine, the London office of Gill and Duffus telexed the Accra office to report that they had received several complaints from customers about the condition of the cocoa butter being delivered to them. The problem had been traced to ships' loading officers stacking the packages of butter too high in the holds of their ships. The cardboard cartons were sturdy enough to allow stacking up to seven cases high. But the loading officers were filling the cargo holds to their limit, sometimes as high as twelve cartons in each stack. This over-stacking meant that the lower cartons were buckling under the weight, crushing the hard butter into crumbling lumps, which severely reduced the quality of the product.

Gill and Duffus were well aware of their packages' limitations and actually paid for the empty cargo space above the agreed height. This was to avoid the crushing and to maintain the high quality of the butter. However, the loading officers, being on a tonnage bonus, were ignoring the instructions and stacking the cartons as high as they could, gaining space for extra cargo. What George wanted me to do was go down to Takoradi harbour when they were loading the boats and check that they were stacking the cartons to the correct height.

I was pleased to be of some use and after being issued with my harbour pass, I became a regular visitor to the docks when a ship was being loaded with our cocoa butter. As a result of this, I became friendly with ships' officers and on two or three occasions I was invited to stay on board their craft for a free cruise down to Nigeria, usually returning on the same ship a few days later.

On one occasion, owing to berthing problems at Port Harcourt and again at a place called Burutu, I was away for three weeks. It was a great experience, steaming at full speed upriver to the inland ports, some as far as a hundred miles from the coast. On one of these trips, I experienced a couple of incidents I will never forget. Waiting mid-river for a berth at Port Harcourt, the ship's captain, a German called Meyer, lowered the painter's cradle into the water so I could swim off the side of the ship.

I quite enjoyed this break in the monotony until, one day on the bridge, I picked up a pair of powerful binoculars and saw that what I had taken to be canoes pulled up on the beach were actually a row of basking crocodiles! I was assured that these monsters never ventured mid-river, but I thought, Fuck that! Crocodiles! And that was the end of my swimming.

A few days later, in a river port called Sapele, I was being 'taxied' ashore from our mid-river anchorage in a native canoe. I suddenly became aware of a terrible, rotten stench. It was really bad and I made a pinched nose sign to my 'driver'. Immediately he veered off to the right and approached an odd-looking lump sticking up out of the water. He bumped alongside it and although the stink was making me screw up my face, I was curious to know what it was. As we drifted past the floating object, I realised it was a pair of water-swollen human buttocks. As I stared in amazement, I saw that they belonged to a headless corpse. I was a little stunned to say the least, but the boatman was unperturbed. 'He be t'iefman,' he told me, pushing at the buttocks with his paddle. 'He be catched. They chop him for head, then he go for river.'

Well, thiefman or not, I felt that I should report this discovery to Captain Meyer and instructed the canoe owner to take me back to the ship. I really felt quite excited about it – my first dead body! 'Captain Meyer, Captain Meyer,' I gabbled as soon as I had rousted him out on to the bridge. 'Look!' I said, pointing dramatically at the floating buttocks.

'Ja, ja,' Captain Meyer looked over the side for a few seconds. 'What about it?' He looked at me with a faintly puzzled expression on his face.

'It's a dead body,' I repeated. 'Look! Floating in the water. It's got no head.'

'Ja, ja, ja,' he said, making an irritated gesture with his hand. 'So?'

'Well.' I was nonplussed by his offhand attitude to the most dramatic moment of my life to date. 'Shouldn't we report it to someone?'

'This is not my business,' he told me, shaking his head as he turned away to return to his comfortable cabin.

'I'm going to report it to the harbourmaster,' I said, thinking this was pretty important.

'You do what you want,' the captain told me. Then he raised his eyebrows and gave me a little smile. 'But if you do report this body, it will cost you £75.'

'What?' I turned back to him. 'Why's that?'

'In this country, James,' he said, his smile widening, 'it is what the English call finders keepers. If you report finding the body, it becomes your responsibility. You will have to pay for its recovery and burial.' And with that he left the bridge.

It was two days before the bloated body finally disappeared, either sunk or eaten by crocodiles. Apparently it was not an unusual thing to find a body in the water at Sapele and certainly no one was going to pay £75 to have the corpse of a t'iefman buried. Mind you, I made a mental note not to be tempted by anything during my stay.

Back in Takoradi, my social life had picked up considerably. George had got used to the idea of me going out on my own once or twice a week and I spent many a pleasant night dancing in the Zenith and Jamboree clubs in Takoradi. Of course, I met local girls in these places who were quick to show that a romance would be welcome and it would have been easy to chalk up trophy after trophy, but I had to restrain myself in that area. Takoradi was a small town and whereas my visits to the nightclubs would be tolerated, fraternising with the local girls would soon cause gossip within the European community. I soon found out I wasn't alone in my nocturnal activities. Most nights I was out I would spot familiar white faces tucked away in smoky corners, enjoying the company of some local beauty. Sometimes we would exchange a nod or a smile but, largely by tacit agreement, we mostly pretended not to see one another.

Although I was enjoying my stay in Ghana and lacked for nothing, socially or materially, I was quite conscious of the fact that I wasn't actually making any money. What I was 'paid' by George was really only pocket money and to be honest it was all I was due. After all, the work I did was no more or less than I would have done even if I had been out there as a *bona fide* guest. At the back of my mind I knew I was really just marking time and I didn't want to go back home at the end of things and find myself in exactly the same position I had been in when I left. I wasn't interested in asking for official recognition and payment for my cargo inspections. Besides, I had entered Ghana on a visitor's visa and was not supposed to do any paid work at all. So I had to try and figure out some way of making and saving a few pounds for when I went home.

One of the first things I had noticed in the cocoa mill was a huge stack of fifty-gallon oil drums. They took up most of the large forecourt in front of the processing plant and seemed to be serving no purpose at all that I could see. One of the times when I was gossiping in George's office, I asked him why they were there.

A couple of years earlier there had been a scare within the company when the Ghanaian government announced its intention to suspend imports on certain small manufactured items. The government stated that in order to provide more jobs for the people, they intended to produce certain goods themselves. The list of embargoed goods included manufactured cardboard cartons and this caused concern in the offices of Gill and Duffus.

IT'S CRIMINAL

As a result of these new proposals, the Ghanaian customs authorities had held a shipment of cartons back. This caused a panic at West African Mills and Mr Sloot had to make hurried decisions regarding alternative means of packaging the cocoa butter. In Ghana there were not a lot of choices. One idea he came up with was to buy up a huge stock of fifty-gallon oil drums that were no longer needed by the military. However, once they were purchased, it was soon discovered that although the liquid cocoa butter could be poured into the drums easily enough, once hardened inside it became, short of hacking the heavy steel containers to pieces, impossible to get it out again. The oil drums were unusable and Mr Sloot's apparently brilliant idea came to nothing.

So the huge oil drums basked in the sunshine of the factory forecourt, leaving the workers to enjoy their shade during meal breaks. I dare say they even thought that they had been placed there for that very purpose. In the meantime, no one dared mention the embarrassing oil-drum stockpile to Mr Sloot. No one, that is, but me.

I suppose it was because I was not connected in any way to the company, but old Theodore seemed quite amused when I asked him about the oil drums. He told me the story, adding that just shortly afterwards the government had given exemption to West African Mills regarding the importation of cardboard cartons.

'What's going to happen to them, then?' I asked.

Mr Sloot, a phlegmatic Dutchman, pulled a face and held up both hands. 'Nothing,' he replied. 'There's nothing I can do. No one wants them.'

'What about scrap value?'

'I thought of that,' he admitted. 'But it's not worth the dealer's time coming to pick them up. Too bulky for the weight, they say. I'd have to pay the dealers to take them away and I don't think G & D would like that. Anyway, it doesn't cost anything to leave them in the yard.'

I already had the glimmerings of an idea for the oil drums, but I wasn't really sure if it would work.

'What if I could sell them?' I asked. 'Would you let me have them on the cheap?'

'But they are worth nothing to the company now, James. The accountant wrote them off a long time ago. If you can get rid of that damn mountain, you can have them for nothing. I'll be only too happy to see them gone.'

'OK then,' I told him. 'I've got an idea, but I'll have to see if it will work out.'

'You go ahead and do what you like, James,' he assured me. 'You've got a free hand as far as I am concerned.'

So I became the proud owner of about two thousand fifty-gallon oil drums. Now, what was I going to do with them?

I had noticed that most of the water supply in Takoradi was drawn from outside stand pumps. This meant that the women were constantly going to and from the pumps, drawing water into plastic buckets or similar containers and, with limited storage facilities, this was often a timely inconvenience. I had the idea that the women of Takoradi would welcome the opportunity to buy the fifty-gallon drums for use as home reservoirs, which they could keep topped up at their own convenience.

I spread the word out around the factory workers that the oil drums were available for sale at ten shillings each to the public, while the workers themselves could buy them at a bargain five bob. In this way I hoped the word would spread around and the local people would come looking for them. I was right enough. Within a day or two townsfolk and villagers from further afield, were arriving at the factory gates with handcarts, bikes and even prams to carry away the large, prized containers.

When Mr Sloot saw that there was indeed a good chance of getting rid of his embarrassing oil drums, he helped to speed up the process by allowing me two labourers and the use of a forklift to manhandle the goods. Day by day, Mr Sloot's folly shrank away until finally the last of the oil drums was loaded on to a creaking handcart and disappeared along the dusty factory road. Out of more than 2,000 drums, I sold over 1,700 at ten shillings each, 60-odd to the mill workers at half price and the rest I gave away because, for one reason or another, they were too damaged to ask money for. I dare say the locals who got the free leaky ones found some use for them. Less than four weeks after I had spoken to Mr Sloot, the drums were gone.

All good things come to an end, but I think I would have stayed even longer in Ghana if George hadn't been taken seriously ill. He had been complaining about back pains for months, even before I arrived there, he told me. But suddenly the pains became severe and he had to go into hospital. They investigated for all sorts of things before finally discovering that two vertebrae of his spine were crumbling and needed specialist treatment. His employers immediately booked him into the Rowley Bristow Orthopaedic Hospital in Kent and my 'job' in Ghana came to an abrupt end.

George was still able to hobble about and was allowed out of hospital for the week or so before we caught the flight home. By this time we had become good friends and he was a little concerned about my future, mainly because I had told him about my past and he was afraid I would revert to my old ways once I was back home. Of course, he knew all about my success with the oil drums and I had quite impressed him with my business acumen.

It was George who suggested that I use some of the money I had made to buy a selection of woodcarvings and other African craftwork items and have them shipped home for resale. It wasn't a bad idea either. The local wood carvers turned out some excellent work — really attractive and very ornamental carved heads, tribal masks and animals, as well as a wide range of hardwood coffee tables and Ashanti stools. I was offered free transport home for them by one of the shipping companies Gill and Duffus used and the mill workshop would pack and crate them for me. The more I thought about it, the more I liked the idea and I became quite enthusiastic.

The prices seemed ridiculously cheap to me, but the locals were happy enough to sell, so I went ahead and bought up literally hundreds of carvings. The coffee tables and stools were by far the dearest items, but even those were inexpensive. Solid mahogany tables with inlaid palm trees for under a fiver? They had to sell back home.

My African interlude was over, but I was looking forward now to trying my hand at business.

Chapter Seventeen

The Great Train Station Robbery

O nce I got back to Glasgow, I began preparing to run my business. I knew that simply selling the African stuff wouldn't be enough, so I decided to open up a small welding shop where I could produce things like door grilles, gates and railings. That gave me an idea of what to call the business: Crafts & Curios. I rather liked the name. I rented a double-fronted shop in High Street, in the Townhead district of Glasgow as a retail outlet and a workshop in Forbes Street, Bridgeton, to produce the gates and railings.

The Forbes Street workshop was about the size of a four-car garage and had storage and office space above the ground floor. There was a large workbench with vices already fitted and another small office right next to the entrance. With a concrete floor and double sliding doors opening right on to the pavement, it was ideal for wrought-iron work. William, who was working as a welder with a metal fabrication company, introduced me to a first-class blacksmith, Nat Wilson, who jumped at the idea of joining me in setting up a small business, especially as all he had to put into it was his labour and experience.

Three weeks after I had arrived home, I received a letter from the shipping agents telling me that my goods were waiting for collection at Newcastle docks. By this time I had everything prepared in Glasgow. The High Street shop had been freshly painted, the name skilfully written above the frontage, the interior decorated and carpets fitted. All I had to do was stock it out and we were ready for business. I hired a large van and brought my stuff up from Newcastle and the following day approached the labour exchange for a female employee to run the shop.

I started the first woman I interviewed, a Mrs Alice Taylor. She seemed a perfectly capable woman of about forty years of age and I didn't fancy interviewing a string of people. The shop was easy enough to manage so, other than dropping in on her for a few hours every day, I left her to it, while Nat and I carried on in the Forbes Street workshop.

As it turned out, it was the metalwork side of things that proved to be the most successful. There was always a steady demand for gates and railings and the other ornamental ironwork in which we specialised. We even got in the occasional heavier job, such as putting up guard rails or erecting corrugated iron barricades along the roof of a factory to prevent children climbing up. However, although we were doing all right, we were not, by any standard, making a fortune. I found myself now with a full workshop of tools and a small van; it wasn't long before other opportunities arose.

Springburn had at one time been a highly industrialised area with locomotive factories, railway repair sheds and running yards and the large cable manufacturing company in Flemington Street. But by the mid-sixties all these factories were gone and Springburn was an industrial black spot with, statistically speaking, the highest unemployment rate in Scotland, if not the whole of the United Kingdom. A lot of men turned to petty thieving and crime in order to try and sustain some sort of life for themselves and their families. Because of my past I had a reputation of being a bit of a villain and I was always being invited on jobs, or being asked my opinion on one criminal scheme or another. I wasn't really interested but, inevitably, a job came up that was too good to miss and I gave in to it.

One of the lads in the pub had worked on a suburban railway station that did a big trade in weekly and monthly commuter tickets. Most of these tickets were sold on Fridays and the cash was held in the ticket-office safe over the weekend for Monday morning banking. Every week you could expect there to be several hundred pounds in the safe, but on the first weekend of each month, when salaried workers bought their more expensive monthly passes, this money was greatly increased. An acquaintance of mine who I'll call Harry came up with the idea of breaking into the ticket office and forcing open the safe.

The trouble was, Harry didn't know anything about cracking safes. I did, so he asked me if I was interested in trying to open the safe, or if I could advise him on how to open it himself. From his description, I was pretty certain the safe was an old 'ripper', but I wanted to make sure before committing myself. Harry assured me that it could easily be seen from the platform and one afternoon we wandered along to the station to case the joint.

One look through the ticket-office window was enough. I even recognised the make of the safe – a John Tann. And if ever there were safes that could be ripped open, the old John Tanns were market leaders, their solid, almost impregnable-looking construction was really only thin sheet metal riveted on to an internal angle-iron frame. These old safes could easily be torn open by tipping them face down on the floor and forcing any thin, flat-edged tool into the joint or seam on the back to open up a gap. When the gap was wide enough, a heavier jemmy could be pushed in and used to force the metal over the heads of the rivets, ripping the back panel clean off. After the back had been removed, a layer of loose fireproofing material had to be scooped out, exposing a thin inner box that actually held the contents of the safe. This was easily forced open and the contents removed – all pretty routine stuff.

I reckoned the job would take about fifteen minutes and Harry was delighted by my diagnosis. He was even more pleased when

I told him I would take on the job myself and what's more, because it was close to the end of the month, it could be done the following weekend.

I wasn't particularly excited about the forthcoming job – I knew it would be dead easy and put it out of my mind. Preparations would be minimal: I already possessed the few tools we would need and there was my van – or, even better in my opinion, plenty of public transport just a hundred yards from the station. Harry, however, was totally consumed by the job ahead. In the week preceding, it was his constant topic of conversation. I don't know how many times he brought the subject up, anxiously seeking reassurance that I was *definitely* going ahead with it, that I *definitely* had the tools, that the safe was *definitely* a 'ripper', that I could *definitely* open it and a hundred other questions.

Every moment we were alone he would talk about the job, bolstering his confidence with repeated reassurances from me that everything was going to be all right. This lack of confidence and need of reassurance was one of the flaws I was to find with most of the guys I worked with in Glasgow. Whatever they were up to, they all seemed to have an uncontrollable compulsion to talk about it, as if they were actually talking themselves into doing the job.

I managed to keep Harry calm in the last few days before we actually went on the job, then on the Friday night he sprang a surprise on me. Although I had pressed on him the necessity of keeping quiet, I guessed he had told his best pal Brian about our plans. This apparent need to tell someone was and still is, another common flaw among the criminal fraternity in Glasgow. However, because I knew Harry and Brian had been involved in lots of petty crime together, I wasn't too bothered about this lapse. On the Saturday night, about half-an-hour before we were due to leave the pub and go ahead on the job, Harry gave me a shock. Admittedly he was a little embarrassed and avoided my eyes as he told me that he had invited Brian along on the job.

I just shook my head and asked him, 'What for?'

'Well...' he said, staring into his pint, not wanting to look at me. 'He's skint,' he finally muttered. 'And he's my mate.'

'But we don't need an extra man on the job,' I told him. 'What's he going to do?'

'He can cop-watch for us.'

I sighed in exasperation. 'Cop-watch! On a closed railway station on a Saturday night?' In those days, pubs in and around Glasgow closed at half past nine and from then on until the small hours of the morning, every cop on duty was busy either trying to contain running gang fights or attempting to control the Saturday-night domestic violence that was endemic to the city and surrounding areas. A cop watcher on a Saturday-night break-in would be about as much use as binoculars to a blind man. I was annoyed at Harry for issuing his invitation as if the job was some sort of open event, but it was too late to start arguing over it; Brian was officially declared 'in'.

By a quarter past ten that night, the station had closed down, the last train from the town centre having deposited its cargo of Saturday-night revellers and chugged on its way to its next stop. There was nothing to it. A railway station must be one of the easiest places to break into in the world. For all anyone knew, we might just as well have been three drunks who didn't know the train times as we wandered up the drive to the station forecourt. Brian took up position at the end of the small station building, leaving Harry and myself to vault over a low wooden fence directly on to the deserted platform.

I didn't waste any time. The window of the ticket office was, more or less, just the same as a house window. I placed a folded cloth over one of the glass panes and gave it a hard punch, leaving a fist-sized hole with cracks running in every direction. It's a funny thing, but the faster and harder you strike a pane of glass, the less noise it makes when breaking. Pulling out the spiky pieces of broken glass is always dodgy as they can easily fall away and often cause bad cuts to the hand and wrist, but I had no problems and within about two minutes of entering the station, I was climbing into the ticket office.

Harry was a bundle of nerves as he handed in my tool bag and I told him to wait until I had a look at the safe. I went over to see if it was either bricked in, fitted to the floor, or loose and perhaps light enough to be taken away. Sometimes, even though a safe is fairly heavy, it can still be carried or dragged away to a place where it can be worked on under safer conditions. The first thing you do with an unopened safe is to try the door handle – it wouldn't be the first time a safe had been left unlocked. I've never actually been lucky enough to come across this situation myself, but on this occasion I was even luckier: the keys were dangling from the keyhole!

Hardly believing my luck, I opened the safe and immediately saw the leather bank pay-in bag. I grabbed the bag and stuffed it in beside my now superfluous tool kit; then I spent another five minutes or so searching around and opening desk drawers to check their contents – it's surprising what you can sometimes find. Satisfied there was nothing of any value in the office, I made my way back over to the window and began to climb out on to the platform again.

'What's up?' Harry's worried voice hissed at me from the darkness.

'Nothing,' I replied, pushing him out of my way as I stepped through the broken pane. 'I've got the money.'

'What!' His exclamation was loud with surprise. 'You... you've not done the safe already?'

'Aye, it's done. No bother.'

'But... but...' he stuttered, totally stunned at my apparently superhuman performance. 'You were only in there about five minutes.'

By this time I was on the platform and walking towards the fence. 'Come on,' I said. 'I've got the money, let's go.'

Harry stumbled along beside me, still speaking in awed tones. 'You've done it? You opened the safe?'

'Aye,' I told him, truthfully enough, 'I opened it. It was easy.' I had decided by this time not to tell him exactly how easy.

'But, but how?' he stuttered in amazement. 'How did you do it so quickly? You were hardly in the place five minutes.'

IT'S CRIMINAL

I ignored him and clambered over the fence, landing beside the startled Brian. He too was stunned at our sudden reappearance and immediately grew agitated, thinking something had gone wrong. 'It's OK,' I told him, as he anxiously spun this way and that, trying to see the danger. 'Job's done.'

Both Harry and Brian were totally stunned by my seemingly miraculous performance, staring at one another and then back at me with astonished expressions on their faces. They looked so perplexed that I almost gave the game away by laughing out loud, but I kept my face straight and walked off towards the road.

It would be great to be able to say that when we got back to Harry's house and cut open the locked leather bag, a large bundle of notes fell on to the table. The truth of the matter is that when we cut open the bag we found seven one-pound notes, a single ten-shilling note and that was it! So much for all the money from weekly and monthly ticket sales. I was disappointed, but not half as much as Harry and Brian, who were severely downcast at the result. I'm pretty certain there was no police investigation after the station robbery. I think what happened was that either the police had decided not to waste time over such a paltry theft, or the station staff kept quiet about the break-in to save someone getting the sack for negligence. If there had been an investigation the police would have got on to me almost immediately, because there was no way Harry or Brian could keep quiet about what they thought had happened. The first time they showed up in the pub my 'performance' became their main topic of whispered conversation. But naturally they never disclosed the pitiful amount of money stolen; that would have taken the gloss of their story. Instead, they spent their five quid on a couple of rounds of drink, making veiled hints that it had been a 'good wee turn'. My reputation as a safecracker was sealed.

I had discovered that being self-employed made a tremendous difference in my attitude to work. I know that I suited myself as to what time I started in the mornings, but I certainly worked a lot harder and longer hours knowing that whatever money I made off a job was divided between Nat and me.

When things were quiet at Forbes Street, I took to the road and did door-to-door canvassing, finding out in the process that I was a good salesman. I remember leafleting the whole of Bishopbriggs, a large suburb of Glasgow, advertising a locking screw for window catches. Afterwards, I went round and knocked on the doors showing off my sample. I got a lot of orders for our 'anti-burglar' screws, nearly getting arrested a couple of times when suspicious residents thought I was a burglar myself! Later on, Nat would go round drilling the windows and fitting our devices. It was a good little number that we could depend on for an income when things were otherwise slack.

Another series of jobs I drummed up was burning the points off spiked railings. There were always accidents happening with these dangerous spikes that were in widespread use throughout the city's tenements' backyards. Then, inevitably, a child slipped while climbing over them and was killed. The newspapers caused a hue and cry, demanding the removal of all pointed spikes and following the publicity I went round every factory and office in the city offering our immediate services. For weeks afterwards, Nat and I could be seen driving about with our oxyacetylene gear making the spikes safe.

To be honest, I was disappointed in the lack of ambition in most of the Glasgow criminals I met. They all had big reputations, but it's a matter of record that there was very little real villainy – by which I mean money-earning crime – going on in the city. Certainly there were plenty of nutcases who would batter, stab or slash both friend and enemy alike for nothing more than a sideways look, or over the score of a football match, but when it came to earning ability, you were scratching. There were admittedly three or four landmark jobs carried out in Glasgow during the fifties and sixties, but they were really very few and far between. I can only think of a few jobs worthy of mention: the bullion hijack in Bellahouston; Edwards the Jewellers, a quality city-centre shop who had their alarm brilliantly circumvented and lost most of their best stock; Gordon's shoe shop, where the owners kept a large amount of cash hidden in shoeboxes; the Shettleston bank job, where the thieves had obtained keys to the premises and safe inside; the Beauly bank job (outside the city, but carried out by Glasgow men), where they blew open the safe and got away with the cash and one or two other banks done by the same little firm. I can only think of one decent payroll robbery, the City Cleansing Department in Polmadie Road. And once, a lorry load of whisky was hijacked – that made headline news for days!

In terms of big city crime, there was very little serious stuff going on. No one was into blagging, nobody had ever held up a bank and tie-ups were practically unheard of. Most of the Glasgow Police Force's time was spent investigating factory break-ins, household burglaries and countless crimes of mindless violence

There was plenty of information coming my way, but it was nearly always petty stuff of little interest or temptation to me. Now and again, though, something half reasonable would turn up and if I had been skint or desperate for money I would probably have taken them on. But because I had a steady income from Crafts & Curios, I could afford to pick and choose what jobs I did.

Needless to say, out of the many jobs I was approached about, one finally surfaced that sounded good. One of my friends, John Thornwood, came up with a guy who had recently left employment in a large city-centre department store. The important part of the information was that the store banked its takings every day, but because the banks did not open on Saturdays it meant that all the store's takings, from Friday afternoon until closing time on Saturday, were locked in a safe in the cashier's office over the weekend. It was obvious from the informant's description that the safe was fairly new and would not therefore be a 'ripper'. But the key point in this story, if you will forgive the pun, was that a complete set of duplicate keys for the entire premises was kept in an old safe in the manager's office.

Of course, we asked the obvious questions. How did he know the keys were in the safe? The answer to that important question was that if ever a key was lost, or an employee in charge of a key failed to arrive at work, all you had to do was to go to the manager's office and a duplicate key would be produced from the safe. Our man had been in the office several times and seen rows of keys hanging inside the safe. Did he know for certain that duplicate keys for the cashier's safe were kept in the safe? At least our man was honest enough about that and told us that he didn't know for absolute sure, but all the indications were that they *must* be there. After all, there was certainly a duplicate of every other key in the safe.

It sounded all right, but how would we gain entry to the premises? That was really easy. The worker himself was prepared to 'do a sleeper' – hide himself somewhere inside the store until after closing time, then emerge from his hiding place to admit us through a wicket gate in the goods entrance. Once locked inside, we would have the run of the store. It sounded too good to miss and we decided to go ahead.

Everything went as planned. Just before closing time, the informant hid himself inside a wardrobe in the furniture department and at seven o'clock precisely the wicket door opened to let us in. After securing the door, we went straight to the cashier's office to check out the safe. One look was enough: this was no ripper. It was a modern Chubb safe, about six feet high by four feet wide, with two locks on its massive steel door. It's always exciting when you are prying and poking around a safe and it's really frustrating to think that there, just a few inches away from you, is the prize.

Just in case, I tried the handle, but there was nothing doing with this box unless we found the keys. The office was turned upside down on the off-chance that the keys were hidden away somewhere – you'd be surprised at how often they are. But although we found several bags of coins in different drawers, we blanked on the key. Finally we gave up our search and reverted to the original plan, heading downstairs to the manager's office for a look at the safe in there.

It was indeed an old ripper, but the seams on its square edges had been covered by angle iron, making it a very much more difficult proposition to tear open. We had, as a matter of course, brought explosives and detonators with us in case we ran into any difficulty, so rather than take hours sawing out the angle iron, we decided to blow it open.

We tumbled the safe on to its back and dragged it into the carpet department, our enthusiasm growing every time we heard the rattle of keys tumbling about inside. It took us about ten minutes to prepare and pack the keyhole with gelignite and we covered it with so many carpets that we didn't even hear the blast when we closed the circuit with our battery. It took two shots at the old safe before we could open the door and when we did get it open things looked very encouraging.

There were literally dozens of key rings hanging inside the safe, each ring tagged with a number and a location and we felt really confident that the keys we were looking for were there. Although we checked every key in the safe, there was no sign of any duplicates for the cashier's Chubb. Disappointed, we searched the manager's office, looking under the carpet, behind pictures, even moving his desk. It was no good, we never found a thing.

Five minutes later, we were back at the giant Chubb, poking and prodding at the keyholes, trying to figure something out. There was no way we could blow it open. Even after removing the keyhole covers, the keyholes were still too thin to admit a detonator. Besides, most of these modern safes were fitted with anti-explosive devices that jammed the door if any attempt was made to blow it open. It was very frustrating to be so close to the prize yet still be so far away and I was loath to call it quits and go home.

John was all for clearing out the store's gift department; there were loads of watches, lighters, pens, gold chains and cheap jewellery in there, but it was just junk and I wasn't going to settle for that. I had come for money and money I was determined to get. After all, I had a workshop full of tools and we had all weekend to work on the safe. If there is anything strong about my character, it is that I am a very determined person; once I make up my mind and commit myself to a course of action, I will see it through to the end. I decided that we were going to have a go at cutting open the cashier's safe. After all, there were lots of things in our favour. We had a good clean entry and the duplicate keys in the manager's safe would allow us to come and go as we pleased. We had all day Sunday to get the tools into the store and we had until about seven o'clock on Monday morning to get into the safe. It had to be tried.

It was still fairly early when we left the store on Saturday evening and I stuck a strip of Sellotape over the rim of the door so we could tell if anyone had entered during our absence. On the Sunday afternoon, I picked up the burning gear from Forbes Street and later on we slipped back inside the store with our equipment.

The safe was quite close to the windows of the third floor, so we made a huge tent out of carpets to prevent any light from the burning torch drawing attention. I reckon that between muffling the explosions downstairs and damage done by burning we must have ruined thousands of pounds' worth of their carpet stock.

It took only minutes to cut the outer skin from one side of the safe and expose the next layer of protection. The solid material underneath was revealed to be a type of concrete filling and it turned out to be every bit as hard as it looked. About two inches thick, it took hours of patient digging, but eventually we chipped away a section about eighteen inches by twelve. Now we found a layer of cast metal that turned out to be an inch thick and used up almost all of our gas before exposing yet another layer of concrete.

By now it was well into the night, but I knew we were nearly there. This time the concrete fell apart like plaster work – I think the heat of burning the cast metal had destroyed its texture. Within minutes, we had dug it out and I could tap upon the inner box. I knew the gas was on its last legs and I was lucky to cut a hole just large enough to get a hand inside. We got about £2,500 from the safe, but there were other compartments we could not get into and we had to be satisfied.

It was frustrating to read in the papers the following day that we had missed several thousand pounds, but I had to laugh at the headline: BUNGLING ROBBERS MISS MONEY! True, we had missed most of the cash, but then again we had spent a weekend roaming about a city store, blown one safe apart, torched open another and got clean away with the equivalent of over £20,000 in today's terms. Hardly bungling – and there was no mention of bungling city cops wandering about shining their torches hither and thither and arresting innocent drunks while all this serious villainy was going on right under their noses!

Of course we would have been much happier to get all the money, but considering that at one stage we had almost abandoned the job, we thought that we had come out of it quite well. And, just as importantly, I had learned a very valuable lesson: I now knew that any modern safe could be broken into as long as I had the proper tools and time to do the job. All in all, I considered it a fair weekend's work.

Chapter Eighteen

Better Safe, Then Sorry

The cash from the store job, although not a fortune, was enough to give me the taste for extra money again and from then on I began to take a bigger interest in villainy. I still continued to work with Nat in Forbes Street, but I had started another man there and that meant I could spend more time hanging about the High Street shop, or gallivanting about the town with my pals. By this time, I had met most of the crooked element in Springburn, finding out in the process that I was a bit of an odd man out with my ideas on villainy. My repeated enquiries about sorting out a decent payroll robbery raised as much interest among the lads as an invitation to watch a game of cricket.

Being a working villain is a bit like training for a sport: you'll only be as good as the men you work with. As none of my associates seemed to be willing or able to raise their game to serious levels and I had no one else to play with, I found myself falling into their ways. Instead of setting up blags or looking for decent places to screw, I found myself breaking into pubs and licensed grocers to blow or rip open their safes and make off with the stock. But I was beginning to find out why there was so little real villainy going on.

As soon as anyone I worked with got their hands on any money, it was down tools until they were skint again. Not one of them thought about looking ahead and certainly it was unheard of for anyone to keep money back to buy tools or finance the next job. To a man, they would wait until they were skint before deciding to make another effort, then they would be scratching around borrowing tools and stealing some old banger for transport.

The only thing I can say in favour of doing these small pub jobs and the like was that they carried little risk. Entry was nearly always made through the adjoining wall of a toilet, or from a cellar entered from the close next door to the premises. On some luckier occasions, a sleeper could be used, who would gain entrance to false ceilings via the toilets or by lifting the bench-seat upholstery and hiding in the hollow framework underneath. We would signal that the staff had locked up by phoning the pub and letting the phone ring out an agreed number of times. The sleeper then emerged from his hiding place to open the doors. When we had slipped inside with the tools, the doors could be locked again and once safely inside the pub, the safe would be ripped or blown while accomplices stacked the spirit and cigarette stock just inside the doorway. When we were ready to leave, we would carefully unlock the door again, allowing the driver, usually me, to slip out and bring the car or van round to the doorway.

A few frantic moments of loading and we were off, leaving the pub doors loosely pulled over. By the time the tobacco and spirits were sold we could reckon on sharing about £1,500 between us. Not bad money really for a couple of hours' work.

Because I had the tools and transport, it meant that I could pick and choose whom I worked with and what I did. Most of the guys that I did work with were what I would call sporadic operators, only grafting, as I have already mentioned, when they were skint. As a result, I worked more often than anyone else and with several different guys. This meant that I made more money and this, together with my income from Crafts & Curios, meant that I was doing very well indeed.

IT'S CRIMINAL

I was also leading a very active social life at that time. I had two or three girlfriends and shuffled around a lot, trying to entertain them equally. Then I went out and bought a Mk II 3.4 litre Jaguar, causing a great stir among my pals in the pub and making windows rise the first time I parked it in Palermo Street. Yes, Mrs Crosbie's boy was doing very well for himself with his wee factory and fancy shop in the High Street!

I had taken up my cycling again, going out on the regular Tuesday and Thursday evening training runs. After several weeks of getting burned off the back, I started getting fitter and, although I never got really competitive, began staying with the bunch.

I had always enjoyed dancing and started going to the Albert Dance Hall on a regular basis. In those days it was all live big-band music and it was at the Albert that I met my first wife, Margaret Walker of Townhead. I always went to the dancing on my own, preferring to dance with different partners in the course of the evening. Then one night I spotted this lovely, Scandinavian-looking blonde standing among the ladies. She looked really classy and I wasn't sure she would dance with me because, although there was an unwritten rule at the Albert that it was bad manners to refuse a partner, some girls would still shake their heads, leaving you conspicuously embarrassed. But when I approached Margaret and asked her to dance, she smiled and led me on to the floor.

I could hardly believe my luck. This lovely blonde was definitely the best-looking girl in the Albert that night, or any other night for that matter. Things got even better when it turned out she was a good dancer and we spun around the floor like a couple of professionals for several dances. We enjoyed each other's company and stayed together for the rest of the evening, ending up with me driving her home in my impressive Jaguar. Margaret lived in Taylor Street, which was on my way home, but I wouldn't have cared if she had come from the other end of the country. I had met my love.

When Margaret left my car after a chaste kiss or two, I sat there for a long time just thinking about her. I had told her a lot about myself, perhaps exaggerating the size of my business, but the car was flash and I was pretty sure I had made an impression. Margaret had certainly impressed me. She told me that she was a model and worked for a company called Alice Edwards. The name meant nothing to me, but Margaret certainly looked every inch a model with her tall, perfect figure and lovely blonde hair. Later on, when we started going together seriously, she showed me a folio of newspaper photographs where she was modelling dresses and hats. She actually worked from a city-centre showroom in Queen Street, where buyers from the quality dress shops would come to see her modelling new designs. And about four times a year she would travel round Scotland with her boss, modelling new-season creations for the buyers of big stores.

I often wondered why she liked me so much. It wasn't as if I was a great prize to her, even with my business and fancy car. At the time we started going together, Margaret had two or three guys running after her, sending flowers and asking to take her out. One of these guys was Davie Wilson, a Rangers and Scotland football star. Another was a whisky heir who was always sending her huge bunches of roses. I think Margaret could identify better with my background and that's what swung things in my favour.

I seemed to have everything a man needed for happiness. I was fit and healthy, owned my own business, ran a luxury car and had a very beautiful girlfriend. Judging from all normal standards, I had found my rainbow, but my nature being what it was, I still wasn't satisfied. I was still looking for that elusive pot of gold. Frustration began to bother me. These small jobs were all very well and did bring in some money, but I knew I was never going to become rich on them. It was all very well getting a thousand pounds here and there between two or three of us, but getting money in dribs and drabs made it very difficult to actually accumulate a large amount.

My mind kept harping back to my experience with the new Chubb and the knowledge that, given the right tools and time to do the job, I could open any safe. I dreamed about doing a bank and went in and out of numerous branches checking out the possibilities. Certainly I saw plenty of safes that I knew I could open, but they were never in a position where they could be worked on. Every bank kept their safes in plain sight and had a small security light fitted above them so they could be checked at night by looking through the window. It became almost an obsession with me to find and open a safe in a bank. After all, as I said to anyone I worked with, if we wanted booze we would do a pub or a licensed grocers. And if we wanted cigarettes, we would do a tobacconist, wouldn't we? Well, didn't it follow that if we wanted money we should do a bank? To me it was all so obvious.

Then one day I was passing along Riddrie Road, just below Barlinnie Prison as a matter of fact, when I spotted a small branch of the Royal Bank of Scotland sitting on its own like an isolated cottage. Although the bank was on the main road, it stood at the bottom of a hill about a hundred yards further on than the nearest shops or buildings. A further attraction was that a projecting wall blocked the pavement a few yards past the bank's front door, which meant that any passing pedestrians were on the opposite side of the road.

This bank was so temptingly situated that a few years later, when the Glasgow crooks had managed to raise their ideas, it achieved an entry in the *Guinness Book of Records* as the most robbed bank in Britain! When I spotted it in 1965, it was still virgin territory.

When I went into the bank for change, I was surprised to see that, instead of the usual large safe, this bank had two smaller safes sitting one on top of the other. Even placed together like this, the top of the upper safe was well below my eye level. These were the smallest safes I had ever seen in a bank and I immediately decided the place was worth a closer look.

That same night I revisited the bank, climbing over a six-foot gate to gain access to the rear of the premises. Once behind the building, I saw that there was no way I could be seen from the road and a steep embankment protected my rear. It was an ideal situation for working on the rear of the premises.

The more I looked at it, the more interesting this little bank became. Like all the banks I had looked at, there was a security light on above the safes and I knew that it would be impossible to work on them in their present position. But because of their size, I thought it would be possible to topple the top one to the floor then lift it on to a barrow and wheel it out the front door into the back of my van. Instead of having to bring my tools to the safe, I could take the safe to my tools. Well, that was the general idea, but as old Rabbie Burns once said, 'The best laid schemes o' mice and men gang aft agley'.

I estimated I could be in and out of the place with the prize within fifteen minutes at the most. We wouldn't even be in there long enough to worry about the security light. The job looked good to me and with my reputation I had no difficulty in recruiting an accomplice. Indeed, my old pal Jim Thomson was delighted to be asked.

It would be great if all plans worked as easily in deed as they do in idea. But I'm sorry to say that my first big bank job was, in modern criminal parlance, a total bust. The first phase, getting round the back of the bank with the tools and removing the window bars, went well. But within minutes of making the entry we discovered that getting the safe out of the place was impossible. Despite its small size, the safe was just too heavy. I had estimated it to be a couple of hundredweight, but as soon as we tried to pull it away from the wall, we realised that it must have weighed at least two or three times that. We could certainly nudge it to the edge of the safe it was sitting on and let it topple to the floor, but we were equally certain that had we done so the metal cube would have crashed straight through the floorboards, joists and all. And even on the off-chance it didn't plunge through the floorboards, it was obvious that its weight would be far too much for us to lift on to the barrow. It was really very disappointing. My first attempt at real money in Glasgow and we were foiled! We scoured the entire premises desperately hoping to stumble on some money or the keys to the safe, but of course we failed. It was terrible to know we were within inches of a fortune in cash and unable to touch a penny piece of it. The game, as they say in Glasgow, was a bogey!

It so happened that about a couple of hundred yards up Riddrie Road, close to where we had parked the van, there was a post office. From the pavement it was possible to see inside and spot the safe nestling under the counter. It was a type I was familiar with and I knew for sure that between us we could lift it into the van. There was no pavement gate and just two mortise locks secured the shadowed recessed door. Well, there we were, all keyed up and looking for something to compensate us for our earlier failure.

It took about two minutes to wrench the locks open and within another minute we were behind the counter and tumbling the safe towards the door. Leaving Jim in the shop, I hurried off to pick up the van, which was parked just fifty yards away. But unknown to us there must have been an insomniac lying awake in one of the houses across the road who, alerted by the sound of the door being forced open, had dialled 999. I was halfway across Riddrie Road when I spotted a car accelerating up the hill towards me showing no lights at all. I knew immediately what it was and shouted, 'Police! Run!' before sprinting on across the road and up a garden-lined street. I heard the car screech to a halt outside the post office; I put my head down and kept running, expecting at any moment to hear the car racing up behind me, but I found out later that the cops had given chase to Jim.

Riddrie was a suburban area with lots of gardens and hedges to give cover and once out of sight I swerved into garden territory and headed uphill towards the old Monklands canal. I didn't know what had happened to Jim and at that particular time I didn't care; I just wanted to get out of the area. I ran for about ten minutes, cutting through gardens and going straight across any streets in my path until I reached the bank of the canal. I was lucky I didn't burst right on to the towpath, for not more than twenty yards away I caught sight of a torch flashing as a policeman hurried along in my direction. I doubled back through the garden I was in and almost walked into the arms of another uniformed cop coming along the street. He got as big a surprise as me and hesitated just long enough for me to spin round and sprint away. But this cop could run and he was close enough behind for me to see him tear off his waterproof coat so he could run even faster! I could hear his big feet pounding and his loud breathing right up behind me and I flew. The main road rose at this point to bridge the canal and I had to ascend a flight of stairs to reach it, leaping three or four steps at a time to stay ahead of my pursuer.

At the top of the stairs, I turned left over the bridge and the cop was still right behind me. I felt his fingers touch my back and if I had been wearing anything else other than a smooth leather jacket I'm sure he would have grabbed me. Instead, the touch gave me impetus and I drew a few feet clear of him.

Then I heard an engine roaring behind me and I almost gave up, but it was only an early-morning bread van. The cop tried to wave it down, but the driver kept on going and I gained a few more yards. I needed to get off the main road and swung thankfully into the first side street on my left. I had settled into a hard run by now and was very conscious that this fucking cop was keeping up with me.

Right enough, he wasn't gaining, but I wasn't getting away either and I could hear him pounding along behind me like some dreadful nemesis. I was really gasping for breath, but then so was he. Next thing, the sound of his pounding died and I looked over my shoulder to see him staring after me with one knee on the ground. Thank fuck, I thought and stopped, going down on one knee myself, keeping my eye on him.

At a distance of about twenty yards apart, we knelt, staring at one another, both of us gasping like landed fish. I imitated his movements as he slowly rose to his feet. Here we go again, I thought and turned away, breaking into my stride. But I didn't hear his footsteps. What I did hear was the piercing blast of his whistle. Christ, they would all be converging on me now. I knew I had to get off the streets. Once I was out of his line of sight I turned into the gardens again, crashing through hedges, until I found an unlocked garden shed I could duck into.

It grew light at about seven o'clock, but I gave it another hour before I cautiously ventured from my horticultural haven. By this time I could see people moving about in the kitchen of the house, but no one spotted me as I slipped away to the trolley-bus terminus in Provanmill Road. Twenty minutes later, I crept back into my mother's house.

I was a bundle of nerves, knowing it was only a matter of time before the police came for me. I had left the van behind, less than fifty yards from the post office. They had to find it. Tracing the owner was routine and then they would be looking for me. The only possible action I could take was to report the van stolen and hope I could convince the police that I was telling the truth.

I carried on as normal, getting ready for work and leaving the house at my usual time of around half past nine. To back up my story about my van being stolen, I went around a few of my neighbours 'in a panic', asking them if they had seen anyone driving away in my van. Of course, no one had seen anything, but my behaviour was natural under the circumstances and I had witnesses to prove I had been surprised to find my van missing. My next step was to phone the police and report the theft of my vehicle. A bored officer took down my excited report and that was that. But I knew that it wouldn't be long before the police put two and two together. I just had to behave as normally as possible and wait to see what happened.

By this time, I knew that Jim Marshall had been arrested and was in custody at Shettleston police station, but I wasn't worried about that. I knew he wouldn't say anything to incriminate me. At about midday I was in the workshop when a police car drew up outside and the driver asked for James Crosbie. They weren't there to arrest me, but I agreed to accompany them to the police station to assist in certain enquiries. Five minutes later, I was sitting in the CID room at Tobago Street nick talking to Detective Sergeant McGill, a man I was to have far more serious dealings with years later.

Once again I went through the tale of the stolen van, knowing full well McGill didn't believe a word I was saying, but also knowing that there was no evidence to the contrary. I kept my denials up for hours, even after they told me that Marshall had confessed all and told them about my part in the break-ins. But I knew that the police were lying, just the same as I was. The attempt on the bank had been discovered when the premises had opened for business and the police immediately linked the two attempted robberies. I still denied everything. Marshall had probably stolen my van, I suggested. Then I was given my last chance to come clean before they put me on an ID parade.

'Somebody stole my van. That's all I know,' I insisted.

Sometime about the middle of the afternoon, I was paraded along with a bunch of unsavoury-looking characters and who should walk in but the cop who had chased me. Much to my surprise he didn't pick me out. I was amazed at this, taking it for granted that, with him being a cop, he would be told where I was standing in the line-up. But no. He walked up and down the line staring at everyone and never picked me out. In all fairness, I failed to recognise him either, but ever since that experience I have always been suspicious when people complain about their ID parade being 'fixed'.

At half past five, much to my surprise, I walked out of Tobago Street a free man. However, it turned out that my unexpected freedom wasn't to last for very long.

Two weeks later, Detective Sergeant McGill left word for me to call in at Shettleston police station at 9.00 am. Something about the return of my stolen van, he told me. Unsuspecting, I presented myself to McGill at the appointed time and promptly found myself charged with two counts of housebreaking and attempted theft. Apparently the procurator fiscal had checked the evidence and decided to proceed against me. The reason for the nine o'clock appointment became clear when I was handcuffed and driven off to appear in front of the sheriff at ten o'clock, where I pleaded not guilty and was lucky enough to be remanded on bail.

IT'S CRIMINAL

In those days justice was swift; within a month I was standing alongside Jim Marshall at the Sheriff Court on trial for two offences of housebreaking with intent. The case against Marshall was conclusive. He had been seen running away from the premises, was chased and caught. Definitely a case for a guilty plea. Not Jim. He came up with the most ridiculous tale about walking to Ravenscraig steelworks in Motherwell hoping for a day's casual labour. He was about fifteen miles away from the place when he was arrested in Riddrie! Just as he approached the post office in Riddrie Road, a man came running past him being chased by two or three men. He panicked and ran away, but the men caught up with him and must have mistaken him for the man they were really after. He didn't realise they were policemen and had only run away because he was scared. Talk about clutching at straws.

The procurator fiscal even offered to drop charges against me if Marshall would plead guilty. But he persisted with his ridiculous tale and in the end we both went down for eighteen months. If he had taken up the PF's offer he would have received a much shorter sentence by appearing in the dock alone as a first offender. Instead, my previous convictions carried him along with me to a longer term.

The eighteen months was bad enough, but what really hurt me was the knowledge that my behaviour had been unbelievably stupid. I could not condemn myself for the attempt on the bank: that had been a good idea and an excellent effort that just didn't work out. We were never in any danger on the job and once we had decided to scrub it we could have been home and safely in our beds with no one any the wiser about our nocturnal activities. But the attempt on the post office was a different kettle of fish.

Returning to Barlinnie Prison was like entering a time warp. After seven years, nothing had changed in there. Raucous noise was everywhere as doors rattled open or slammed shut to the cadence of shouted names. I was examined by the same doctor, processed by the same screws and given, I'm sure, the same oversized shoes to wear. Passed through to the halls, I heard the same bellowing voices echoing names round the rafters and once again I was banged up behind my door. Déjà vu, indeed.

Chapter Nineteen

Harry Roberts is My Friend, Crosbie Shoots Coppers... Not!

On that first night in the Bar L, I laid my head on my pillow and considered the consequences of breaking into that post office. Crafts & Curios would go, I knew that. Nat was a great craftsman, but never a salesman. When the current work had been completed he would find something else, but I felt very bad about letting him down. Then there was Alice in the High Street. She had a really easy job, more or less acting as a very under-worked secretary now that most of the African stuff was gone. She would be unemployed now and that was upsetting for me. I had no idea what Margaret would make of my conviction and the discovery that I already had a fairly serious criminal record. I would probably lose her too. Then there was my mother. She had been so pleased at seeing me getting on so well. Now she would be disappointed and, being my mother, worry about me. Believe me, lying in bed on your first night in prison going over the consequences of your crime can be a very harrowing experience indeed.

At my reception interview, I tried to bluff my way as a first offender; after all, my previous sentences had been served in

England. But after two days in cushy E Wing, my record caught up with me and I was dragged across to A Wing along with the other incorrigibles. In view of my previous convictions, the allocation board had no hesitation in classifying me as 'untrainable' (their perspicacity is to be admired). Two weeks later I was back in the dog boxes, reversing through reception on my way to Peterhead.

Even if you had never seen a prison in your life before, there could be no mistaking the purpose of Peterhead Prison. The entire structure screamed entombment and servitude and you could imagine passing motorists speeding up to get away from its glowering intimidation. I'm sure the mere sight of Peterhead persuaded many a wavering local into staying on the straight and narrow. But there was no speeding up for our bus and two minutes later the huge, green, wooden gate closed tight behind us.

Margaret had decided to go to America while I was away and, quite honestly, I didn't expect to see her again. But much to my surprise and pleasure, she kept in touch, writing letters and sending photos of her new friends and of places she had visited. Two or three times she mentioned boyfriends, telling me she had been here or there with them and what a nice time she was having. Then when she wrote and told me that she had obtained her green card, I just supposed she had decided to stay there. But two or three weeks before I was due to be released, I got a letter from her telling me she was coming home and would meet me in my mother's house the day I got out. That letter was the nicest thing that happened to me that year and suddenly I became even more impatient to be transferred back to Barlinnie for my release.

I hired a car and took Margaret for a week's holiday in London where I looked up my old pals, letting them know I was out and about again. A lot of things had changed since I was last down there. I found my old mate Albert had declared himself out of villainy and was now a successful plumber living happily in Hanworth. Several other chaps were doing hefty sentences for serious offences and some had simply dropped out of the scene.

Payroll blags had fallen out of favour because of the increased use of security vans and the tide of crime was rapidly turning towards armed robbery. When I had been jailed in 1961 on the conspiracy rap, no one I knew had been interested in using guns. Now their use was commonplace and some of the guys I had worked with in the past were now carrying out armed robberies.

I had always had a reputation for having plenty of bottle and Jack Witney and Harry Roberts, who had one or two jobs lined up, invited me on to their firm, but I didn't want to commit myself. However, I left my phone number with Jack and told him to keep in touch in case anything really sweet turned up. After a pleasant week's socialising with my old pals and visiting the theatre to see *The Black and White Minstrel Show*, we drove back to Glasgow to face my real problem – making a living.

I really didn't know what I was going to do and the idea of actually seeking out a job was never a consideration. Only the fact that I was staying at home with my parents stopped me from immediately seeking out an earner. Then my elder brother Tommy came up with an idea. 'Why don't you take over the shop in Ayr Street?' he asked me.

I had completely forgotten about the small metalwork shop I had opened all those years before. I had handed the business, lock, stock and barrel, including my van, to Tommy when I had been forced to flee Glasgow after that glazing job. And that was the last I heard about it. From that small start, Tommy had prospered and moved into bigger premises; he was now manufacturing Venetian blinds and doing very well too. 'Is it still there?' I asked in surprise. 'I thought you gave that up when you moved into the blinds.'

'No,' he told me. 'The rent was so low that I kept it on in case I ever needed a bit of welding or anything like that done. It's been lying there for a couple of years now. Come on, we'll go and look at it now.'

Everything was there: the welding plant, guillotine, heavy bench, vice and jigs for a variety of tools. I noticed a small paint-spraying plant that was new to me, but otherwise everything was as I had left it. It was a business just dying to start up.

'This is great,' I enthused, knowing that I could make a good living out of it. 'I'll get right into it. I'll go out looking for work tomorrow.'

'Aye,' Tommy said. 'You should be able to make a go of it all right. Now, let me see...' He began pointing out the plant and stock to me. 'There's the welder, the compressor...' One by one he listed the assets. Then he said, 'OK, we'll just call it an even five hundred.'

I looked at him in amazement. 'What?' I asked, a little puzzled. 'Five hundred what?'

'Pounds.' He never even blushed. 'For the tools and stuff. I mean to say... it's practically a going concern. It's worth that much, at least.'

'It's *my fucking shop*!' I yelled at him. 'I started the place up and even sent you my last fiver from jail so you could advertise for work. What the fuck do you mean, £500?'

I saw the realisation in his eyes as he remembered. But still he blustered on. 'Well... well... aye, OK. But that's my compressor and some of the tools are mine.'

'Fuck off!' I told him. 'And where's my van then?' I demanded to know. Then I reminded him of the fact that it was only through doing the wrought-iron work in my shop that he had ended up getting into the Venetian blinds. If it hadn't been for Ayr Street, he'd probably still have been a bus conductor. In the end he had to admit I was right and, grudgingly, he handed over the keys to the shop. I was back in business again.

I called the business Weldart Door Grilles and immediately went into production. There was no shortage of customers: everywhere you looked, huge blocks of multi-storey flats were creating a new, high-rise Glasgow skyline. I didn't particularly like these concrete monstrosities, but there was one feature about them that did please me: the front door of every flat was fitted with a glass panel just crying out for some form of decoration. What better than an attractively designed metal door grille?

Protection *and* decoration in one go! My grilles sold like hot cakes. Things were going so well that by the summer of 1966 Margaret and I had bought a flat in anticipation of our wedding later that year.

One day, it must have been about mid-July, I was in the flat doing a bit of decorating when a telegram arrived. It read: RETURN TO LONDON IMMEDIATELY. URGENT BUSINESS PENDING. It was signed Jack Witney and I knew that a job was on. I admit that I was tempted. I had just about spent all my money on the flat and the wedding preparations were coming up fast; I could certainly have done with more cash. But the wedding was too close and I binned the telegram.

Two or three days later I got another telegram: PHONE CUNNINGHAM 8822. JACK. I was feeling a bit guilty about ignoring the first telegram, so I made the call. It was an offer of work and from the little Jack could disclose on the phone, I knew it was a serious job with guns being carried; but it was too near my wedding and I declined. I couldn't just disappear for two or three days right then. Jack was disappointed – he liked working with me – but he wished me well and said he would be in touch. I hung up with mixed feelings, almost tempted to fly off, but I resisted. It was just too close to my big day and I wasn't in the mood right then. After a few days, the phone call faded from my mind.

About three weeks later, around 3.00 am, I was in my bed in my room at my parents' house when suddenly there was a terrific pounding at the front door. The lock must have burst open just as I leaped out of bed, because I was only halfway across the room when a whole army of cops descended on me and I was battered to the floor and had my hands cuffed behind my back.

Half conscious and in a state of shock, all I could see were huge black shadows looming over me. What the fuck was going on? Practically naked in just my underwear, I was half-carried, half-frogmarched across the hall, past my protesting parents and out the front door. I could hear my mother's voice rising as she shouted at the police. I don't know what it was she said, but I can still hear the copper's reply above the tumult: 'Murder, Mrs, that's what he's done! Bloody murder! He's killed three policemen!'

I can imagine the shock my mother must have felt. Fuck me, I was pretty stunned myself. *Murder! Bloody murder! He's killed three policemen!* What were they on about? My mind went ballistic as I was carried triumphantly downstairs listening to the cops congratulating each other on my capture.

When I was dragged into an interrogation room in the police station, there was a huge reception committee waiting for me. I was still barefoot and in my underpants and feeling very vulnerable.

'What's going on?' I asked.

'Going on? What's going on?' A very angry detective was glaring into my face. 'You're what's going on, you murdering bastard!' I could see he was straining to avoid striking me. 'Fucking police killer!'

But by now I'd had a chance to think and I actually felt a weight lift from me. I knew this was a mistake. There was no way I was connected to a murder, any murder, never mind the murder of three cops. I let my breath go and relaxed. 'What are you talking about?' I asked.

'Don't get smart with me, Crosbie. You're going the whole road for this. Don't you worry about that. The whole fucking road!'

'I don't know what you're talking about,' I said. 'Murder? Three policemen? You must be off your head.' I stood central in the room, focus of a dozen pairs of angry eyes. 'It's madness. I haven't murdered anyone.'

I caught the eye of another policeman who was giving me a calculating look and held out both hands. 'Honest,' I said, 'I don't know what he's talking about.'

It was my demeanour that had caught Detective Inspector Michie's interest; I was too calm for a man who had just been accused of murdering three policemen. 'Where were you yesterday, James?' he asked me.

Where was I? Where the fuck was I? I had to think for a moment. Oh, yes – it came to me. 'I was in Easterhouse [a housing estate in Glasgow]. I was selling door-to-door. I was there all day.'

It was easy to check. Within half an hour my order book, along with a pair of shoes and some clothes for me, were brought from my parents' house and I was identifying a list of yesterday's customers. The police were particularly interested in any calls or sales I had made around midday. By seven in the morning, three worried-looking customers of mine filed into the room. One by one they identified me as the man who had sold them door grilles the day before. There was no question about it: I had been in Easterhouse at the time the three policemen had been shot.

You'd think that the police would have been happy to clear me, perhaps even apologise a little. But no! The air of disappointment was almost palpable as they let me go, a reluctant offer of a lift home coming almost as an afterthought. By eight o'clock I was letting myself back into my parents' house. They had both been up all night, my father so upset that for one of the very few times in his life he had been unable to go to work. My mother was shattered, a complete bundle of nerves and frantic with worry as all sorts of terrible thoughts raced through her mind. Yet here I was, a few hours after being dragged away like a rabid dog, back home as if nothing had happened. It was an experience for everyone.

What had happened was that on 17 August 1966, three men – my old pal Jack Witney, his mate Harry Roberts (an ex-soldier he had teamed up with) and John Duddy, a total stranger to me, had been intercepted by three Flying Squad officers near Wormwood Scrubs. They had resisted arrest, pulled out guns and shot the policemen, leaving them dead in the street. Jack had been traced almost immediately through his car registration number and arrested.

Harry Roberts had disappeared and all the police knew about the third man was that he was 'a Scotsman from Glasgow'. As Jack had been my co-defendant at the Old Bailey in 1960 for conspiracy to rob and I was from Glasgow, the police had put two and two together and got five. But just supposing I had been in London, or having a quiet day to myself somewhere without any witnesses? It's happened before and no doubt it will happen again. John Duddy was arrested at a house in Gallowgate, Glasgow a few weeks later and charged with the murders.

I took time off myself that day, contemplating the telegrams I had received and thanking my lucky stars I had avoided the 'urgent business pending' summons. I don't know what Jack and co had been up to that day, or why the cops had tackled them, but after a trial at the Old Bailey, the three of them were sentenced to life imprisonment, with the judge's recommendation that they serve a minimum of thirty years before being considered for release. John Duddy, the man I had been mistaken for, died in prison of natural causes about ten years later. Jack got out after serving twenty-seven years and was murdered by person or persons unknown after about three months of freedom. Harry Roberts, after thirty-six years, was ready for release and marriage. As recently as May 2002, he was moved from open conditions back to a closed prison for matters of security. He doesn't have a lot of hope.

So it was back to work for me and, although I was completely innocent of the cop killing, I still felt a tremendous sense of relief that I was free to go about my business. And business was good. Not only were the door grilles going well, but I was also doing a brisk trade in stolen goods. Earlier in the year, I had been introduced to a dispatcher at a large British Road Service parcel depot. All this guy had to do was pick a likely package and redirect it to a different address. What I had to do was get large labels printed on gummed paper so that the dispatcher could stick them over the original delivery address. A fresh line was added to the driver's delivery sheet and that was that. The driver knew nothing about the scheme and I would be waiting at the drop to accept delivery. It was as easy as that.

However, there was one slight problem: neither the dispatcher nor I knew for certain what the contents of the redirected package were. He could only make a half-educated guess by seeing where the package was originally addressed. Most of the time it worked out and I got stuff I could easily sell. But quite often I'd open an attractive-looking crate to find a huge amount of useless crap. Once, for example, I took delivery of a huge crate that turned out to hold thousands of worthless (from our point of view) coloured plant-pot holders. The useless stuff still had to be disposed of and I tipped this particular delivery into the Forth and Clyde Canal. I don't know why, but I fully expected them to sink out of sight below the murky waters. But no — instead of sinking, the pot holders gradually spread across the water, filling the canal from bank to bank like a gigantic plantation of brilliantly coloured water lilies. I just stared at the scene and smiled. It certainly brightened up the canal and I knew it would pose another colourful mystery for the Glasgow Police to ponder over.

So, with one thing and another, time slipped past and before I knew it the wedding date came round. We were married in the Barony Church in High Street, the oldest church in Glasgow, on 5 November 1966. The entire day was a success and the party was still going strong when Margaret and I slipped away. We spent our wedding night in a Glasgow hotel and flew out the next morning to enjoy our honeymoon in Ireland.

When we flew back from Dublin at the end of our honeymoon, I had about £7 left in the world and it did not worry me in the least! I had Weldart Door Grilles and I was confident that, even if I was totally skint, I could go out any day or night of the week and come home with cash: I always did well selling door-to-door. So well, in fact, that a few months after my wedding, I moved into much larger premises and began a new line of work.

Chapter Twenty

Twelve-gauge Action

Luxafire Surrounds: that was the new name and fire surrounds were the new game. Open coal fireplaces were on their way out and, with all the new properties having built-in central heating, everyone was buying modern wooden fire surrounds. There was plenty of room for competition and I decided to get into them myself. I had my new, larger workshop in Adamswell Street and I soon got a joiner and another guy in to work for me.

The surrounds turned out to be a good idea and, along with the little bits and bobs of villainy that turned up, the latter end of the sixties were a good time for me. Of course, a lot of the stuff I got involved in then was pretty low key and is now forgotten in the mists of time, but every now and again something really serious would turn up and there's a chance the books have never been closed on them. I don't think it would be very clever of me to say too much about what I got up to then. I was never caught and, with no statute of limitations in this country, some righteous copper might decide to go on a mission against me even now.

As I've mentioned before, I was never impressed by the quality of criminal up here. You would have all these guys perfectly willing to pull out razors, knives and bayonets, prepared to fight to the death and risk years in prison over the result of a football match or a spilled drink; but suggest a bit of real villainy and they would mutter and mumble, even pretend to consider it, until it came to the crunch, the moment of commitment as I call it. It was then that their bottle went and they didn't want to know.

There was one guy, I'll call him John T, who spoke a good line and I took him on a robbery. Everything was going well – we had picked up a car and all we had to do was wait on delivery of the money. As we sat in the stolen car waiting for the money to be delivered, I noticed John getting more and more fidgety, then finally lapsing into an uncharacteristic silence. I put it down to nerves; I sometimes suffered from them myself. Then the security van drove up and the men made the delivery and drove off. The money was there.

'That's it,' I said. 'Let's go.'

At the very last second, just as we were about to enter the premises, this hard case baulked and turned away. I literally had to grab his jacket and pull him into the office with me. Fair enough, once inside he was OK – I only needed him for a minder anyway. I jumped the counter and grabbed the bag and that was that. Afterwards you would have thought we had done the Brinks Mat job, the way he strutted around bragging about his achievement. I never worked with him again.

Then there was the whisky lorry. This guy knew a driver who was willing to let us take his lorry and leave him tied up somewhere. I immediately got on the phone to Les, a pal of mine in London, who I knew could handle the load. 'When can you get it?' he asked me.

'Whenever you want, Les. He's on the same run every day.'

'Sort it out for next Thursday, James. I'll have a lorry and papers for the load ready and up there by then.'

'OK,' says I. 'Next Thursday. Good. I'll be ready.'

IT'S CRIMINAL

I duly passed on this information to the lorry driver and we arranged the 'hijack' for the following Thursday. Everything was looking good. But on Tuesday I was grafting away in the workshop when who should appear but the lorry driver. 'Right,' he says. 'It's outside.' I felt a sinking feeling in my stomach.

'What's outside?' I already knew, but I was hoping for a miracle. Surely he wasn't this stupid?

'The lorry,' he told me, as if I was the one who was daft. 'The whisky.'

'But you're not supposed to be here until Thursday!'

'Ach! Thursday, Friday, Tuesday, what's the difference? If you can sell it on Thursday, you can sell it anytime, surely?'

'Jesus Christ,' I said. 'It's set up for Thursday, not fucking Tuesday! You'll have to carry on to the bond with it.'

'Too late for that, pal,' he told me. 'I'm off my route now and well behind schedule.'

'Well, get back on your route and make an excuse. Say you broke down or something.'

'So you're not taking it then?'

'How the fuck *can* I take it. Where the fuck am I going to *put* it? I told you, it's been set up for Thursday.'

'Ach! All you fucking wide men are the same. Big talk, no action.'

'Go on,' I said. 'Fuck off. Fuck off, you stupid bastard.' I just shook my head in frustration as I watched him drive off out of sight.

That was the sort of criminal mentality I kept running up against in Glasgow. I had to phone Les in London and tell him the deal was off. Naturally he was very pissed off about it. After all, he had put himself about arranging transport and documents to get the whisky down south, no doubt spending a few quid in the process. Now it was all off. I couldn't blame him for being angry. I wasn't too happy myself. If that idiot lorry driver had turned up on time, we would all have had a good earner.

I suppose I should have stuck to full-time legitimate business.

But among all the dross, a diamond occasionally surfaced. That's what happened when George Noble approached me one night in the pub. It took the usual format: a pal of his, a painter, was working temporarily in a travel agent's in the town centre. The painter started work an hour before the agency staff and had a key to let himself in. He was always there when the staff opened up for business and had spotted that there was a lot of money held in the safe behind the foreign-exchange counter. He was suggesting that I go into the place and either steal the safe or blow it open. The tale was interesting and it passed my first test: how do you know that? And it did make sense. Main travel agencies always had a foreign-exchange service and that meant cash on the premises. Yes, it sounded good to me and I decided to speak to his pal.

The painter's tale was good and I liked the way he told it. No glowing exaggerations, no gilding the lily, just a simple description of what he had seen, along with the admission that he didn't know the exact amount of cash held there, but it looked a lot to him. He also told me that the counter was busy all day, changing money and issuing traveller's cheques to a constant stream of customers. Well, he was definitely in a position to know and his story certainly made sense. I decided that it was worth taking a closer look.

I asked the painter to have a duplicate set of keys cut for me and went in one night to check out the safe. As I suspected, it was too modern to blow open but, as I hoped, it was small enough for a couple of men to manhandle on to a barrow and wheel away. I liked the idea and decided the job was on.

The obvious time to hit the place was around eight o'clock on a Saturday morning. The painter, on a five-day week, would be off and at that time in the morning the streets would be busy enough. No one would be likely to pay any attention to a couple of workmen wheeling a barrow across the pavement. Once I explained the set-up, I had no trouble recruiting a willing assistant. All I needed then was a van and a sturdy parcel barrow – both easily obtained items.

IT'S CRIMINAL

In the event, the job was a canter. We weren't even in the place ten minutes before we had the safe loaded on to the barrow and covered under an office rug. As I suspected, no one paid any attention to us as we locked up the shop and wheeled the barrow across the pavement and lifted it, safe and all, straight into the back of our waiting van and drove off. The entire job went sweet. Mind you, opening the safe gave us a bit of a tussle. It was a solid little bastard and it took us a couple of hours with a heavy-duty angle grinder to cut through to the prize.

It turned out that there was about £15,000 in traveller's cheques and foreign currency in the safe, along with just under £3,000 in sterling. Remember, I'm talking about 1968 here and in today's terms it was equal to about £100,000; although it wasn't the biggest job I'd done, I'd certainly describe it as a good wee turn.

I was happy with the result and my helper was delighted to take the sterling and leave me to cash the traveller's cheques and foreign currency for my cut. That was no problem for me: I had contacts in London who would gladly pay me half the face value of everything I had and exchange my goods for a cool £7,500. The painter got £2,500 for his help and information and I pocketed £5,000 for myself – good wages at the time.

That was actually the best earner I'd had in Glasgow up until then and it proved to me that there was good work around if only you could find out about it. So I began looking around with a criminal eye, noting vulnerable premises, checking out security, automatically glancing at my watch if I spotted money being carried across a pavement either into or out of banks or business premises. It gave me a new perspective of Glasgow, like an artist seeing the darker shades and shadows of a chosen subject. Take scaffolding round a building: an ordinary member of the public sees it as a hazard to be negotiated; a criminal sees it as a temporary opportunity to be exploited; a possible means of entry into premises that would otherwise be inaccessible. Without conscious effort we will spot a cashier hiding the high-value notes in a separate drawer, or notice a businessman leaving a bank and putting a heavy bag into the boot or rear-seat area of his car. Make no mistake; our eyes are drawn like magnets to every possible shade of weakness.

Often something will turn up right out of the blue, like the time when I was buying tickets for a European cup final in Milan. I was in a small travel agent's, just picking up the tickets, not a criminal thought in my head, when the girl asked me if I wanted any traveller's cheques. Traveller's cheques? I looked beyond her desk and could see the entire floor area of the open-plan shop: not a safe in sight. Immediately my criminal hat was on. I asked for £50 worth of cheques and watched as she opened an ordinary filing cabinet and produced a thick folder. It was stuffed with traveller's cheques in denominations from £5 to £100 and once our transaction was over, I looked on in amazement as she replaced the folder in the bottom drawer of the cabinet. This was just too good to be true.

Two nights later, around midnight, I had a pal hold his foot against a short ladder as I pushed the louvre fanlight slats above the door into the shop, then followed them in head first. The cabinet wasn't even locked and one minute later, on my pal's all clear, I went out the same way I went in, my hands landing on his shoulders to break my fall. A three-grand quickie! Seconds later, we were just another two pedestrians heading home.

I suppose you could have called me an opportunist villain in those early years after my marriage. I was busy enough with my fire surrounds not to go actively looking for work, but if something really sweet turned up I would be interested. In actual fact you could say that the period after my marriage was, even with the odd job I did pull, the straightest part of my life. If I'm to be honest, it was the happiest and most carefree too. In June 1969, when Margaret gave birth to my son in Rottenrow Maternity, I felt I had it all. I can still remember the first time I saw Gregory, his little face all scrunched up and two huge bruises on his cheeks where he had been dragged into the world. I made up my mind that I would stick to legitimate business from then on and I really meant it at the time.

IT'S CRIMINAL

By the end of 1969 I had bought my workshop outright and moved up a gear in production, totally phasing out the grilles and turning my attention to fire surrounds and also fitted bedroom furniture. Business was so good that, less than twelve months after Gregory was born, we left tenement life behind and moved into a nice semi in a leafy suburb of Glasgow.

Leaving Springburn was a dynamic change for us and I remember how proud I felt standing outside our new house in Bishopbriggs on the day we moved in. I remember looking up and down the street. It was quiet, clean and respectable. Yes, I thought to myself, I'll be living the quiet life from now on. And yet it wasn't long before I was dabbling again.

I found myself in a halfway world. I was doing well in business, yet all my pals were petty criminals and, like it or not, I kept getting involved in their schemes. It was one of the penalties of having a workshop full of tools and good transport. My pals were all on the dole and forever trying to scratch those extra few pounds that made a difference to them. I couldn't refuse them the odd loan of tools or the use of my van when the need arose and I was always politely invited on every 'wee bit of business', whatever it was. Some of the stuff was so ridiculous it was hard not to laugh. I was asked for a hacksaw to cut down a ship's bell mounted on the fourth tee at a local golf course. 'It's pure bronze,' I was earnestly assured. 'Worth a right few quid, so it is.' Well, they could have the saw but they certainly couldn't have me for that one. Another time they spent an entire weekend digging an enormous crater under an old electricity pylon on a quest for some mythical copper earthing block. Whatever it was supposed to be, they must have shifted several tons of earth and they still came up empty-handed. I told them that if they were prepared to work half as hard for Wimpey the builders, they could earn a fortune!

The crime scene in Glasgow had taken a dramatic change in the late sixties and early seventies with the first reports of bank robberies leaping from the front pages of the press. I read the newspaper reports of these armed robberies with great interest, noting that there was nothing subtle or difficult about them. In fact, I didn't even consider them real 'armed' robberies. It was simply a case of three or four men piling into a bank brandishing pickaxe handles, throwing a bag at a teller with instructions to fill it up and dashing out again. The entire job would be over in a matter of seconds. But it was all very exciting and I admit I was impressed by the boldness of this little firm. The only thing I didn't like about it was the money they were getting: three or four thousand pounds a time certainly didn't seem good value to me for the risk and effort involved in these robberies. It seemed obvious that you had to get behind the business side of the counter and help yourself if you wanted to get your hands on real money.

There was no doubt in my mind that the key to success in robbing a bank lay in getting total control, which to me meant proper tools. If I was going to commit an armed robbery it was going to be a real armed robbery and that meant using guns, not big sticks! I soon got my hands on a suitable weapon – a twelve-gauge automatic shotgun – and from then on it became a question of when, rather than where. There was no shortage of targets: there was a bank on practically every street corner in those days. I only had to sort one out.

There were a few limitations I had decided on when picking a target. I didn't want a building to overlook the bank's windows, I didn't want a bus stop right outside it and I wanted a good maze of side streets in the immediate area. That still left a good choice of targets and I selected a bank opposite a swing park in the south side of the city.

I've often been asked how you rob a bank. The answer is that there is no instruction book. The fact is you never know what will happen when you step through the door of a bank and declare yourself. You can, however, work hard on the preparations: have everything organised from vehicles to weapons and set out the getaway. If you don't feel totally confident and completely in control, don't do it. You must be 100 per cent certain of your abilities, be totally committed to the job and be prepared to do whatever is required to pull it off and escape from the scene.

Everything was prepared and I was ready to go ahead. All I needed now was a partner and I approached an old pal of mine – I'll call him Andy Wilson, seeing as he has never been done or suspected of anything in his life. Andy had helped me out on the odd occasion before and I knew that he was reliable. I also knew that he was in desperate straits and would agree to anything I suggested in order to earn some money. Once I explained my plans, he leaped at the idea.

I put the first robbery down as a partial success, maybe even a good learning experience. The fact is I relied too heavily on Andy carrying out his part of the robbery. It was agreed that I would control any customers and staff while he leaped the counter and emptied the cash drawers. Everything was set up, getaway car on the corner, changeover car in place and Andy's escape route sorted out. All we had to do was perform.

The bank appeared very quiet, with nobody coming or going for over five minutes. So in we went. There must have been some sort of hold-up (no pun intended) with the tellers because it looked as if there was a queue a mile long. About a dozen customers stood there gaping at us as we crashed in through the front door.

'Don't move!' I shouted. 'Stand still!'

I was waving the shotgun about, wondering where all these people had sprung from. Then one man started to panic, clutching a heavy canvas bag to his stomach and spinning round looking for a way out. He was infecting the others and looked likely to be a problem. I fired the shotgun into the ceiling, blasting a cloud of plaster all over the place. Everyone stood stock still, even Andy. 'Get over!' I shouted at him. 'Get over the fucking counter!'

With all the noise, billowing plasterwork and gaping crowd, Andy obviously felt safer on his own side of the counter. Instead of going over the top, he threw the bag at the teller. 'Fill it up!' he screamed.

The teller scrambled a few bundles of notes into the bag, tossed it back to Andy and ducked down behind his counter again. I knew it wasn't enough, but we had to leave. Time was tight and the gunshot would have attracted attention. Sure enough, outside on the pavement people were staring at the entrance of the bank and I heard a gasp when I walked out with the smoking shotgun in my hands. I got my eye on a middle-aged man in a hat and raincoat who looked a bit iffy. I thought he was a cop for a moment, but he gave me a wink and a grin when I eyeballed him. Then we were round the corner, into the getaway car and away.

I dropped Andy off as soon as we were out of sight – he would get home on public transport – and carried on to park beside a short footpath, cutting through it to get to my own car parked at the other end. I was half a mile away before I saw the first police jeep racing towards the scene. I smiled as they careered past, klaxon screaming, on their way to the scene of the crime. What the fuck were they going to the bank for? The deed was done and we were gone.

As I suspected, it turned out that the teller had only stuffed about three grand in the bag – the average take from the other robberies that had been going on. Andy was happy enough; his share of the money got him out of immediate cash problems and all he had done was turn up on the day. But I was disappointed. With all the time and money I had spent in preparation, I had been expecting more than a paltry three grand.

Still, we had pulled off an armed robbery and got clean away with the loot. And importantly, irrespective of the amount of money we had taken, I was aware that I had felt comfortable throughout the entire operation. I did hesitate for a second or two when we were confronted by the unexpected queue, but that hesitation went the moment I pulled the trigger. Control had been instantaneous and I knew that, given the right amount of time, the bank could have been cleaned out. If I decided to rob another bank, I would have to make sure that I got that time.

IT'S CRIMINAL

It didn't take me long to decide. Within a month of that first robbery I started looking at other banks, trying to pick out one that fitted my requirements regarding location. I had no idea at the time that fate had already taken that task off my hands.

Chapter Twenty-one

A Bit of Business with Bob

Bob Ross was my next-door neighbour. He was a friendly, chatty guy, always ready with a smile and a quick quip across the garden fence. We soon became friends and often went out for a drink together at the weekend. One Sunday evening we were heading along the canal bank at Bishopbriggs on our way to Torrance village for a pint. Normally a very cheery, outgoing bloke with plenty to say for himself, Bob was uncharacteristically quiet as we strolled along.

'What's up, Bob?' I asked. 'You're a bit quiet tonight.'

'Aye,' he answered, making a face. 'I've got money problems. The wife's nagging about her motor – says it's clapped out. The house needs painting and she's going on about a holiday. I don't know what I'm going to do.'

'But I thought you had a good job,' I said. 'I mean, I see you going out every morning in a suit and tie. What is it you do anyway?'

He seemed to hesitate a little. 'I've been told not to talk about my work,' he said. 'Company rules.'

'How's that? Is it a secret or something?' I was joking with him, but he seemed to take it seriously and I saw him turning it over in his mind.

'No,' he finally said. 'It's not a secret. But they say that you never know who you're talking to.'

'Well, you know me,' I said, getting a little curious now. 'Surely you can tell me?'

'Aye, I suppose so.'

'Well?' I prompted him.

'I'm a bullion guard with the Clydesdale Bank,' he finally told me. 'I deliver money to the bank's branches every day.' I felt a quiver rattle the entire length of my spine and took a deep breath. 'And do you know something,' Bob continued talking, 'I wish I knew someone who would rob a fucking bank.'

'You know what, Bob,' I told him, 'they were right.' He gave me a puzzled look and I put my arm around his shoulder. 'You never know who you're talking to.'

'What's that supposed to mean?' He stopped walking and looked at me.

'I'm your man, Bob,' I told him. 'I'd rob a bank.'

He burst out laughing. 'Aye, right! You'd rob a bank! That's a good one.' At least he'd snapped out of his depression. 'You?' He laughed again. 'You couldn't rob a bank.'

It was obvious he found the idea a huge joke. His quiet next-door neighbour rob a bank? I laughed along with him, knowing he wasn't taking me seriously. 'Aye, OK,' I finally said. 'But if you *were* going to rob a bank, which one would you rob?'

'That's easy,' he said, still chortling. 'The Hillington branch. It's in the middle of an industrial estate, no shops or anything near it and the place is wide open.'

'And when do you deliver the money?' I asked, while he was still willing to talk.

'Tuesday. Every Tuesday morning. That's their day.'

'About what time?'

'Late on,' he told me. 'It's our last drop after the Whiteinch branch, then we head back to the main office.'

'And that's the one you would go for yourself?'

'Oh, definitely. Everyone on the van says that.' Then he went quiet and put a hand on my arm. 'You're not serious, are you?' He suddenly looked a little worried.

'C'mon, Bob.' I gave him a smile. 'You just said you had money troubles. Ten per cent of a wee bank robbery would straighten you out, wouldn't it?'

'Ach! You're kidding! You'd never rob a bank.' He dismissed the idea with a wave and began walking again. 'Come on, I'm dying for a pint.'

Well, I had the main details: the time and the place. I dropped the subject and we continued on towards Torrance. I was looking forward to a pint myself now.

Within a week of talking to Bob, I was out looking at the Hillington branch of the Clydesdale Bank and immediately liked what I saw. The building itself looked like a small family bungalow, almost incongruous among the factory buildings surrounding it. Set well back from the road and slightly elevated on a small grassy knoll, it was impossible to see into the bank from pavement level. Perfect. I knew as soon as I saw it that I was going to rob this bank and immediately began setting things up.

Finding a partner was no bother, Andy being the obvious choice. His money from the first job was long gone and I knew he had the taste for more. And putting the equipment together was easy: I already had my sawn-off and transport was never a problem. The smother – or clothes – would be no bother either: a visit to Paddy's Market would easily produce suitable untraceable clothing. A long trench coat for me to hide the shotgun, a boiler suit and pull-down woolly hat for Andy and a couple of pairs of gloves were what we needed. We also needed a plan.

I've never been one for long drawn-out scenarios, but the Hillington job appeared to have a problem regarding the getaway. Being situated in an industrial estate on the outskirts of the city certainly had its advantages in as much as the area was quiet and out of the way. But this very isolation raised a serious problem.

Theoretically our getaway would have us speeding directly towards the anonymity of the city, but it would also have us heading straight into the arms of the swiftly converging police response units. I say theoretically because, although that seemed the obvious route and I gambled the police would think the same, I had a different plan. I would be heading in the opposite direction.

Three miles away along the nearby M8 motorway lay Glasgow Airport and, while the police were racing to the bank and sealing off routes into the city, I would be heading there. At first sight this escape route appears almost suicidal: a dead-end, or at best a traffic-jamming bottleneck. If the cops put two and two together fast enough and sussed we were heading there, we could find ourselves in serious trouble. We couldn't take the chance of checking in and taking a flight off into the blue. The nearby robbery would have sparked off an immediate alert and every passenger would be getting well checked out. It would also be too dangerous to do the classic car swap and drive out again – we would just be heading back into the area of police activity. Still, I considered the airport to be our best option and I had a plan. The Hillington bank job was on.

On the day of the robbery my accomplice John, who was also my gopher on the job, met us in a stolen car, a ringer already fitted with false plates. We loaded our gear into it – in this case my gun, our smother and two good suitcases. John then drove the car to a prearranged spot near the bank and parked it. A minute or two later we drove up and parked round the corner before transferring to the ringer, leaving my own car to be picked up by John and driven back to my workshop. This placed us only a short distance from the bank, leaving us with minimum time on offer.

It took us just seconds to move the suitcases on to the rear seat of the car and change into our smother. Andy wore worker's overalls with a woolly pull-down hat, completely hiding a neat business suit, collar and tie. I wore a Paddy's Market trench coat and scarf topped off by a wild wig. Less than two minutes later and exactly two minutes before closing time, I pulled up outside the bank. It was all very quiet and peaceful.

Four tellers gasped at me as I leaped the counter brandishing a wicked-looking shotgun, yelling at them to stand still. Behind me, Andy was closing the front door, a Yale lock making it easy for him to secure it.

By the time he appeared inside the bank, I was already herding the terrified tellers towards the door of a walk-in document vault. As I pushed the door over, I deliberately placed a thick floor mat inside the gap so they could see they wouldn't be locked in. I didn't want anyone getting hysterical or having a heart attack on me.

The huge standing safe was open and I began filling my bag with wads of money. Here I learned a lesson: when you take a bag on a robbery, make sure it has other bags inside it! Within seconds my sports bag was full and there was still loads of money left in the safe. What to do? I looked around and spotted a hessian rubbish bag, grabbed it and tipped its contents on to the floor. In the meantime Andy was ripping out the phones, checking the side office and toilets. The hessian bag was great. It took all the remaining cash, including a small tobacco tin I had spotted among the notes. I rattled it against my ear. A nice chunky sound – diamonds or gold coins. It sounded valuable and into the bag it went. The safe was soon cleaned out of notes and I was not interested in coins, so we were done. Or nearly done. I went back to the vault door and taped an empty Duraglit tin across the small opening I had left.

'It's a bomb,' I warned the wide-eyed clerks. 'Open this door and you'll blow yourselves up!' I hoped my little trick would gain us a few valuable minutes. I grabbed the sack and lifted the counter flap to leave and my heart suddenly skipped a beat. There on the counter was a little metronome gadget flashing red and green lights as it swung from left to right. I found out later that it was only a warning light in case someone got locked inside the vault, but at the time it only meant only one thing to us: an alarm direct to the police. For all we knew the cops were probably on their way already.

And so much for my 'bomb' warning! We were hardly settled into the car when one of the clerks poked his head out of the bank's doorway. He stared directly at the car but bolted back inside when Andy levelled the shotgun at him. Then the engine kicked in and we took off. I drove fast, but not madly. I still thought the cops were on their way and I knew the clerk had clocked the car. I wanted to be on the M8 before the word went out and the car became a target.

I hit the motorway in about twenty seconds and slipped into the fast-flowing traffic. As I was driving Andy turned in his seat and flipped open the lid of the top suitcase. He stuffed the sports bag and sack into the case along with my shotgun and zipped it shut before pulling it forward to drop into the space behind our seats.

His overalls came off to reveal his suit and he flipped the second suitcase open. All his smother went into the case, followed by my wig and scarf which he grabbed from me while I wriggled about getting out of the trench coat at eighty miles per hour. Job done and cases closed, we swooped down the long curve off the motorway and into the airport area.

The huge car park was busy, but I soon found a slot and pulled up. Andy got out right away, grabbed both cases and headed directly for the terminal building to deposit them at the airport hotel luggage reception desk. Two days earlier, he had booked a room in the hotel under a false name, giving an arrival flight number that suited our timing.

The hotel porter service would take care of the cases now and see that they got to his room. Andy then strolled back across the road to check in and pick up his room key. The plan was clicking away nicely.

I left the car park, now a smart businessman in my suit and tie, but with one important addition: some years earlier I had joined the Glasgow Flying Club and finally realised my flying ambitions by obtaining my Private Pilot's Licence (PPL), and now my lapel displayed a Glasgow Airport police identity card, issued to all flying-club members. Unchallenged, I strolled through a restricted area to the flying-club building hidden behind the huge Loganair service hangar in the far corner of the airport. It was good, sitting safe and comfortable while the world went mad not very far away. I even thought about putting in some flying time, but all the planes were booked.

Within half an hour, the place was buzzing. 'The airport's been shut down.' 'Bank robbers have dumped a car.' 'They've taken hostages.' 'They're trying to get out of the country.' The gossip ranged wide and wild as 'information' trickled in. I gave it a couple of hours, then got a lift back to the main terminal from one of the club members. I immediately spotted our getaway car. It wasn't difficult, highlighted as it was by a ring of police and their colourful motor vehicles.

I must admit that my stomach lurched at the intensity of the police activity, more so when I entered the terminal concourse. There were policemen everywhere. Uniformed officers and CID were swarming like angry bees around innocent travellers, questioning, searching, tipping out the contents of bags and suitcases. Even the luggage deposit boxes were sealed off as another squad of cops master-keyed them open in a frenzy of expectation. If the cops ever deserved the nickname 'busies', they certainly deserved it that day. Their job wasn't made any easier by the presence of a huge crowd of increasingly belligerent fanatical Glasgow Rangers supporters who should already have been halfway to Germany. Their team was playing Bayern Munich in an important European Cup tie and, bank robbery or not, they intended to be there. Things could easily take a nasty turn if the flights were delayed much longer. I had to smile though when a raucous voice roared out above the general tumult, 'I bet the fucking robbers were Catholics!' It seemed to me that the irate Ranger supporters had more of an idea of who had done it than the police!

I strolled through the bedlam unmolested, my security ID enveloping me in a protective cocoon of righteous respectability as I threaded my way through the crowd to the upstairs cafeteria. From there, surrounded by nosey cops and angry travellers, I checked the airport's exit ramp. The barriers were gone and traffic was moving smoothly on to the motorway again. Just a bit of fine-tuning to the plan and it would be time for me to leave.

After a soothing cup of tea, I phoned the airport hotel and booked a room before boarding the airport shuttle bus into the city. An hour later, I picked up my car at my workshop and headed home for dinner.

I checked into the hotel around eight o'clock and, as luck would have it, my room was on the same floor as Andy's. I gave it ten minutes before joining him in his room. Real life isn't like the movies or TV. There was no wild celebration, no tossing wads of money into the air accompanied by shouts and dancing through a storm of fluttering banknotes. The suitcases were still zipped up and they stayed zipped up even after I arrived.

We already knew how much there was: it was splashed all over the evening papers in large, glaring headlines: BANK ROBBERS GRAB £67,500! BIGGEST BANK ROBBERY EVER! DARING BANDITS ESCAPE WITH HUGE SUM! Take your pick, it all made lurid reading. According to the press, the police were closing in on the raiders and their arrest was imminent. I got up and put the 'Do Not Disturb' sign on the door – that should stop them!

Andy's window overlooked the car park where we had left the car and he told me the biggest fright he got was when the police had turned up with a dog team. Dogs were something we hadn't thought of. Sure enough, the hounds were sent into the car on a long leash and started sniffing and snorting around. But his fears proved unfounded as he watched the dogs tear away in the opposite direction across the car park, under the motorway and off across a field. So much for the bloodhounds! They had even less idea where we had disappeared to than the police.

Andy and I swapped suitcases. I took his to my room and left him with the one I had brought with me for appearances' sake. It was just a precaution in case a smart cop realised the significance of the car park and its proximity to the hotel and decided on the off-chance to check afternoon arrivals.

Of course they didn't – but they just might have. Andy checked out before me the following morning after making arrangements to meet up later on. I took a taxi into town and was amused when the driver handed me a police questionnaire directed at anyone who had used the airport yesterday and who may have vital clues in their memory banks. 'Sorry,' I told him. 'I arrived last night after the excitement was over.' But I kept the questionnaire. Maybe Andy could help them.

The money was spread all over a single bed in a flat we had borrowed. With no notes over a fiver and more than half the total in cash in ones, it made a spectacular sight. And I had kept the tobacco tin till the end, feeling in my bones that this was the real prize.

I called Andy over and with a loud fanfare ceremoniously spilled the tin's contents across the surface of a coffee table. I should have blown a raspberry. No diamonds and no gold coins, just a few coppers and several pieces of paper. I picked up one of the bits of paper and read it: an IOU for 10p; another promissory note for 15p upped the ante. 'One coffee and one tea,' I read. It seemed I had inadvertently stolen the tea float. And they complained about it too: 'They even took the tea money!' a newspaper reported. Yeah, big deal!

Still, job done and another mystery for the hard-pressed Glasgow Police. 'An arrest is imminent,' they said. They could say what they wanted as far as we were concerned. With nearly thirty grand a piece after we weighed in Bob Ross and John the gopher, we were laughing all the way from the bank.

Bob Ross made me smile. When I arrived home with the money, I spotted him peeking at me through the slats of his Venetian blind. I gave him a wave, but the slats snapped shut. That evening, I jumped the fence with a carrier bag in my hands.

'You… you robbed that bank,' he stuttered, clearly still shocked.

'I told you I would,' I said. 'And here's your share of the money.' I tried to hand him the bag. 'There's £6,700 in there. Ten per cent, just like I said.'

'I don't want it. I don't want any of it,' he panicked. 'I want nothing to do with it.'

'Bob,' I said. 'There's £6,700 in here.' Remember, he could have bought his house for less than that in those days. 'It's yours. I said I would give you ten per cent and here it is. Fuck me, you said you were desperate, didn't you? The wife's motor … a holiday. This will straighten you out.'

'Well,' he hesitated. 'Nobody got hurt or anything. And the police have no idea who did it.'

'Bob, nobody knows anything. The job was sweet. You just take the money and nobody will know anything about it.'

'Right enough,' he said and nodded. 'It's all a big mystery.'

'So you can take the money,' I told him again. 'Just be a bit careful and you'll be all right.'

'Look … look …' he was stammering again with excitement. 'I'll take a thousand pounds. That's all I need anyway. £6,700 is too much for me. Just … just give me a thousand and that'll be that.'

'OK,' I said, handing him a grand. 'But I've still got £5,700 here for you. I'll put it away and whenever you want it, you just have to ask.'

'No,' he told me. 'That's definitely all I want.' He pushed the money under a cushion and ushered me towards the door. 'I don't want any more. Oh and James …' He began to look a bit embarrassed. 'If you don't mind, I really don't want to be seen with you just now. You know … just in case.'

'OK, Bob,' I told him. 'Don't worry about it. I understand. But don't forget, I still owe you £5,700.' I held up the bag. 'I'll keep it for you.' By now he was practically pushing me out of the door.

For over a month Bob studiously avoided me. If I went out into the garden and he was there, he would go indoors. He wouldn't even meet me in the eye. But one day he finally waved to me and that night I jumped the fence.

'Hello, Bob,' I greeted him. 'You all right now?'

'Aye,' he said. 'Everything's fine. Nobody's said a word.'

'So what did you do with the money?' I asked.

IT'S CRIMINAL

'It was no bother,' he told me. 'I bought a couple of suits and the wife's got a better motor. We've even booked a holiday.'

'Well, there you are then,' I said. 'See. Just be a bit careful and the money's no problem. And don't forget,' I reminded him, 'I still owe you £5,000.'

'What!' He stood back and looked at me indignantly. 'What do you mean, £5,000? It's £5,700 you owe me!'

And he took it, too – all at once this time and without even a blush.

Chapter Twenty-two

Blagger on a Bike

The efficiency of the job, followed by the successful getaway, had the city in an uproar. Both crooks and cops vied with one another in their efforts to discover who had pulled the job. All over the city, eyes and ears from both sides of the fence watched and listened for any clue that would help to identify the missing miscreants.

Nothing surfaced. After an initial week of unsuccessful dawn raids, car stops and sudden searches of increasingly disgruntled Glasgow faces, the investigators began a war of attrition, gradually nit-picking their way through a long list of possibles. It was all they had and their hearts weren't even in it. The total lack of evidence – no clues, no signs of sudden wealth among the criminal fraternity, no unexpected disappearances, not even a decent rumour to go on – left them distinctly disheartened. But I knew they would eventually get round to me; my name would definitely be somewhere on their list. Sure enough, two weeks after the robbery the police phoned my house. It was the Serious Crime Squad. They wanted 'a wee word' with me.

'Could we call round to your house at about seven?' they asked. Of course, I had to act puzzled. I mean, what on earth could the Serious Crime Squad be wanting with me? I had a bit of tightness in my stomach when they arrived, but the interview went well. My story regarding my whereabouts on Tuesday, 15 May was unadorned. Nothing particularly memorable – a normal day in and around my workshop, dinner and tea breaks in the local café covering the crucial times.

Detective Inspector McGill and his underlings were satisfied. I was only a possible anyway, and my tale was good. Not too precise, but precise enough to rule me out.

The day after that interview, I left on holiday with Margaret and Gregory: two weeks in Porec, Yugoslavia. It was lovely to get away and finally totally relax.

I honestly don't know what it is about me. I come from a respectable working-class background; no one else in my immediate family, going back two generations, has ever become involved in anything criminal. I cannot even think of anyone who has even been remotely adventurous, apart from a second cousin who became a Salesian brother and disappeared into the South American jungle for years.

Me, I just don't seem to be able to sit still for ten minutes. Just two weeks after returning from Yugoslavia, I talked Andy into coming with me to sunny Cyprus, having made up a story for our respective spouses that we were looking at timber yards around the UK. The holiday was great. Even now, thirty years later, I can look back and laugh at the memories of it. We took the Sandy Beach Hotel in Famagusta by storm! Room service fought to answer our calls to supply the ongoing party with food and drink.

One day on the beach, I picked up an airmail edition of the *Daily Express* and started reading a front-page article that had caught my eye. I had to read it through twice to check I wasn't making any mistake. No, the article was quite clear and well up to normal tabloid reporting standards.

'Hey, Andy,' I gushed with a wide smile. 'Do you know where we are?'

'Course I know,' he said, looking at me funny. 'What are you getting at?'

'Come on,' I asked again. 'Where are we? I mean, right now. Where are we?'

'Fuck me,' he retorted. 'OK, we're in the Sandy Beach Hotel in Famagusta, Cyprus.'

'That's what you think,' I told him. 'According to this' – I crackled the newspaper – 'we're living in some place called Fear.'

I read the article out. The headline was THE MEN WHO LIVE IN FEAR:

Somewhere in the city of Glasgow, two men are living in fear. Several weeks ago these men robbed a bank and instead of the usual three or four thousand pounds they were expecting, they stumbled across the huge sum of £67,000. Now they live in fear, crouched in some dingy basement, afraid to spend even a penny of this money. They know that the police are hunting them and, even worse, they know the underworld is also scouring the city in a desperate search for them too. Their fate is in the balance. If the criminals find them first they will break their legs, torture them, or even worse, to get their hands on their loot. The best thing these men can do is hand themselves in to the police and return the money. This way, they will at least be safe from their criminal counterparts and no longer have to live in fear.

I lifted my beer to Andy. 'Here's to living in Fear! Come on, race you to the speedboats ...'

Back in Glasgow, the furore over the bank robbery had died away, although I did hear from several criminal sources that the police were pulling their hair out over their lack of success. They just could not figure out why none of the money had surfaced, why there were no wild parties, celebrations or big spending by any of the local criminal element. And no matter what outrageous offers they made to informers, no one could tell them a thing. As far as the Glasgow Police were concerned, the job was a complete mystery. Eventually they decided it must have been a mob from the Smoke that had carried it out and, as far as I know, they concentrated their investigation down there.

I carried on as normal with my work, producing furniture at Adamswell Street, generally doing well and enjoying life. Margaret and I had several luxury holidays and I began travelling about a bit more on my own. They say that travel broadens the mind – well, I certainly found out a few interesting things: in Italy, for instance, you could go into a gun shop and buy an automatic pistol over the counter.

I liked that and decided that it would be handy for me to own a decent handgun rather than the huge automatic twelve-bore shotgun I had hidden away. However, I also found out that you needed to produce your passport when you purchased a gun in Italy and its number was entered on a triplicate receipt, a copy of which was sent to the local *carabineri*. I didn't know why they did this and I was worried in case the Italian Police used it to inform the UK authorities via Interpol that a British passport holder had purchased a gun. With my record, I couldn't take a chance on this and it was a bit of a problem until I was introduced to a young guy who was a serving soldier in the Royal Scots Fusiliers.

This young guy, Kenny, had previously served two tours of duty in Belfast and it was this that gave me an idea. I put it to him. 'Come to Italy with me and buy a gun using your own passport for ID. If the police there refer back to Scotland Yard and the cops come to ask you about it, you tell them that you have been threatened by the IRA because of your service in Ireland.' I reasoned that as he was a serving soldier with no previous convictions, the cops would just give him a slap on the wrist. After all, he carried a big fucking gun to his work every day, didn't he?

IT'S CRIMINAL

Kenny was over the moon with my suggestion and delighted at my offer of a free holiday in Italy with a chance to earn a few quid. A couple of days later we flew to Turin and he bought a nice 7.65 Beretta pistol along with a box of shells. Gun secured, we enjoyed a few days' driving about in a hired car before taking, for safety's sake, the train and cross-channel ferry back to the UK. I let Kenny carry the gun – after all, it was legally his anyway – and during the trip he told me that he was sick of the army and wanted out. Later, back in Scotland, I drove him through to Redford Barracks near Edinburgh and wrote out a cheque for his freedom. Kenny was delighted. He had been a well-paid mule, had enjoyed a nice trip to Italy and now he was out of the army.

I was busy enough in my workshop, but the quality of the material I was buying was continuing to deteriorate and I was getting annoyed at having to spend more and more time checking every board for flaws before assembling the furniture. Eventually things got so bad that I decided to stop making furniture myself and instead buy it in from the big manufacturers and simply retail it. After all, the other furniture shops in the city seemed to be doing well. And it appeared simple enough: order up, take delivery and sell. I could do that.

But it turned out that it wasn't as simple as all that. I found myself having to source out furniture from as far afield as Germany. I had been to Hamburg a couple of times and noticed the style and quality of the furniture in the shops there; it was far superior and much better value than anything I could get here. Delivery was no problem – ten days. Ten days from Deutschland, against three months from England. It was no contest.

I went over to Germany and visited a few manufacturers to compare their products. I finally settled on Rauch of Freudenberg, a company that specialised in bedroom furniture, and started buying directly from them, arranging my own transport and paying cash with my order. But fitting out the shop and paying cash for the large stock cost a lot of money, so to give myself a little financial cushion I decided it was time I robbed another bank.

There was no problem in sorting one out – I already had a bank in mind from my conversations with Bob Ross nearly two years before. The only real problem I had was in finding a partner to work with. I decided that Andy was out of it: he had invested in a small engineering company and I was quite sure he wouldn't be interested. There was no point in asking him about it only to receive a refusal. I never did see any reason to let anyone who was not directly involved know my business, especially the serious stuff.

But there was one man: John, the guy I used as a gopher on the Hillington robbery. I knew he had pulled off a couple of jobs himself fairly recently – nothing big, just a couple of small wage snatches – but he had assisted me before and kept his mouth shut afterwards. On top of that, he had recently been on at me to let him into something decent. Yes, I thought, John will do nicely.

Sure enough, he was up for it. John had even bought himself a .410 shotgun and kept it in storage for just such an occasion. I showed him the target: the Whiteinch branch of the Clydesdale Bank on the corner of Dumbarton Road, just yards from the Clyde tunnel exit. It was a fairly quiet, run-down area with no big shops to attract pedestrians and half the tenements under demolition.

The location was good, but I checked the job out just to be certain. Even though it had been two years since Bob Ross had told me about it, the routine and timing were just the same – Tuesday mornings around eleven o'clock. Yes, this was the one all right.

When you've got a few quid behind you, it's easy to set things up. As far as I could see, our only problem would be the getaway. Whiteinch is a Clydeside district, with the river making any escape route southwards impossible. This effectively cut our escape options in half, which meant that the police could concentrate their efforts over a much smaller area and quickly seal off our getaway. Roadblocks were a very definite danger for us on this job. Of course, we could put the boot down and try to beat the cops to the canyon, but you have to realise that the high-speed getaway is mostly film fiction. The fact is, unless the cops are right on top of you, the last thing bank robbers want to do is draw attention to themselves by barging through traffic and screeching round corners on two wheels. But in this case it seemed that only speed would get us clear of the area before the police could close us down. So we had a choice: drive fast to beat the roadblocks, or drive carefully and hope to bluff our way through if we were stopped.

Then again, maybe there was another way ...

All my life, ever since I could ride, it was routine for me to jump on my bike if I was going somewhere. And what could be a more innocuous form of transport than a bike? The more I thought about it, the more I liked it. A bank robber fleeing the scene on a bike? Even the cops wouldn't go for that.

John was a bit iffy about the idea when I put it to him, but then he wasn't a cyclist. However, when I told him that he wouldn't need to ride a bike himself and explained how he would get away on his own, he became more interested and eventually agreed to my plan. Finally everything was set up and we were ready to go.

On the day, we met up in my shop and drove to a garage near Whiteinch where the ringer was stashed. All our gear was already in the car: John's .410 and his balaclava, along with a wild wig and an old coat and scarf I had bought at Paddy's Market for myself. Oh and my bike.

I let John do the driving, as much to steady his nerves as anything else and directed him to a block of flats just off the main road about 400 yards from the bank. I went into the building and up to the first half-landing of the emergency stairs where I chained my bike to the banister – you just can't trust anyone these days! Putting the bike in place was the last of our preparations and once back in the car I checked my watch. We were well ahead of time. This was good because I knew the bullion van made a delivery at the Clydesdale branch in Partick, the district before Whiteinch, before carrying on to our bank. The time cushion allowed us to drive the short distance to Partick and we parked up in sight of the bank and waited for the van to turn up. As soon as it appeared, we headed off for Whiteinch in the sure knowledge it would be along just five minutes behind us. This leapfrog tactic meant our timing was precise and we would not have to hang about too long near the bank we were going to rob.

The five minutes gave us just enough time to get into our smother and when the bullion van pulled up outside the bank I kept my eye on the delivery as I applied a thin smear of Evostick glue to my cheek – the stuff really does have a thousand uses. From our vantage point, we watched the crew carry a large silver bullion box and several sacks of coins into the bank. Things were looking good. It took them a few minutes to complete the delivery and I was just pinching the flesh of my cheeks together to form an evil-looking scar when the van pulled away.

'That's it,' I ordered. 'We're on!'

There were no customers in the bank and none of the tellers as much as looked up when I entered. In about two strides, I jumped up on the counter and straddled the low screen, one foot landing right next to the counting fingers of a teller.

'On the floor!' I barked. 'Quick, now! On the floor!'

There was a stunned silence as wide-eyed faces gaped up at me.

'On the fucking floor!' I shouted with hostility in my voice. This time the clerks began to move. I was conscious of a teller's fingers flicking through a pile of banknotes right next to my foot. The guy seemed hypnotised, as if ignoring me would make this nightmare disappear. Flick, flick, flick, his fingers continued to rustle the notes. I tapped him on the head.

'You too!' I instructed. 'On the floor.'

I was actually on the other side of the counter before John appeared round the door from the street, white as a sheet and obviously a bundle of nerves. However, he strengthened up when he saw I had everything under control and he did all I needed him to do, which was look threatening while I collected the dosh.

The silver box was lying open on a table with half its contents already spread out beside it. I picked up one of the bundles of notes to put it back into the box, but I had a gun in my hand with my finger through its trigger guard. As I picked up the notes, my finger squeezed the trigger and, as much to my surprise as anyone else's, the fucking gun went off. *Bang*! Bollocks, I thought. I can do without this. *Bang*! Again. Behind me I heard a nervous gasp from one of the clerks; they must have thought I was firing at them. In fact, the only person in danger of being shot was me, as my back was turned to the staff and the bullets were going straight into the money.

I looked over at John to see him confronting a customer who had entered the bank. He handled the situation well and I told him to march the man behind the counter and get him to lie down with the others before we left. Being on the floor would discourage them from getting up too quickly, hopefully allowing us to drive off without anyone seeing the motor. When we hit the pavement, there was a small crowd gathered outside staring anxiously at the bank's doorway, no doubt alerted by the sound of the gun going off. There was a collective gasp when we burst out of the door, but no one seemed inclined to interfere, simply staring open mouthed as we rushed past, scrambled into the car and disappeared in a cloud of burning rubber.

It took us less than a minute to reach the flats where I had stashed my bike and, once off the road and out of sight in the shelter of the flats, I stuffed all the money into a large rucksack along with my handgun and John's now dismantled .410.

Once out of the car, I made my way to the half-landing; my wig, coat and scarf went down the rubbish chute; I unlocked my bike and pedalled off. John was already gone, simply walking away from the ringer to the nearest bus stop, just another citizen going about his business.

I didn't even feel the weight of the heavily money- and gun-laden rucksack on my back as I rode away to the sound of police sirens closing in. Sure enough, within minutes I was approaching a police roadblock and I looked ahead to see how conscientiously they were handling it. I had a choice at this point: I could either ride straight up to the roadblock and gamble on being waved through; or I could cut off into the side streets and try to bypass it. The pros and cons were clear: the police on the roadblock were looking for a getaway car and with so many vehicles on the road they would probably ignore a cyclist. On the other hand, police cars would almost certainly be cruising the side streets hoping to luck on to the changeover motor or any suspicious vehicle. Even a lone cyclist, especially one carrying a large rucksack, might just make them look twice.

I had to make my mind up quickly before I passed the last turn-off. Go with the traffic, or stand out alone? The traffic won. I always did favour the bold option and I had already seen that the car searches were perfunctory – a word with the driver followed by a quick lift of the boot. It looked good to me. It was also obvious that they were paying more attention to cars with two occupants, so I adjusted my speed and fell in behind a car with a passenger in it. Sure enough, up went the copper's hand and the car stopped. I pushed on as the cop rounded the bonnet to stand right in front of me.

'Come on, come on.' He pressed against the side of the car and urgently waved me through. 'Fucking pest!' I heard him mutter under his breath as I shot past.

Out of the saddle, three pushes of the pedals and I was through. Yes! I felt the exultation as I continued up the road and fifteen minutes later I was in my shop in Springburn, out of breath but safely home and dry.

It came to £87,000, a fortune in 1974 and once again the biggest bank robbery in Scotland.

Needless to say, the cops were outraged and pulled out all the stops to make an early arrest. The story front-paged for a couple of days, moved on to the inside pages for another few days, then dropped out altogether. The robbery became a mystery, with the cops left sucking their thumbs.

John and I split up the cash, less the money I took off the top for expenses and a cut for Bob Ross. I hadn't actually told Bob that I was going to hit the Whiteinch Bank, but I had used the memory of our two-year-old conversation and he was still entitled to his ten per cent. Of course, he guessed it was me that had pulled off the job, but he was pleased with the money and he certainly had no qualms about taking it this time. I left him with a happy smile and settled down to normal life again.

Chapter Twenty-three

The Most Dangerous Man in Scotland

I hadn't been skint when I went on the Whiteinch job, but I had spent a lot of money re-laying the workshop floor and having storage racks installed to turn the Adamswell Street place into a small warehouse. Then there had been the expense of stripping and fitting out my new retail premises on Springburn Road. All this, along with my policy of paying up front for my stock, had used up most of my cash in hand and I hated standing about in my shop praying a customer would come in and buy something. It always seemed to me that the more you needed money, the harder it was to come by. But when you had a few quid behind you and weren't totally dependent on sales, things definitely seemed to run more smoothly. Suddenly everything was good: instead of taking money out of banks, I was depositing money from my business into the bank every week; but I still had a bag full of cash, about £40,000 stashed away.

I was beginning to live a more or less straight life, but I began to worry about this money. How should the incriminating cash be safely put away? In the end, I broached the subject with my accountant, telling him that I had been accumulating profits for years and just stashing the money, but now it was bothering me. He was surprised at the amount, but he agreed to handle it for me and I made arrangements to bring it down to his office.

The following day, bag in hand, I telephoned his office just to make sure he was in. I admit that I was feeling a bit self-important. After all, I was going to hand this guy £40,000 and he would be getting a good fee out of it, as well as a share in any profit. I thought he was getting a good deal. 'I've got that money,' I told him. 'I'm just checking that you're in right now.'

His reply was offhand to say the least. 'Oh, I'm a bit busy right now,' he said. 'Could you bring it down tomorrow?'

Jesus, I thought. I'm telling this guy I'm on my way with forty grand, giving him the chance of a really good earner and he's telling me to come round tomorrow! Who does he think he is? 'Tomorrow?' I managed to squeeze the word out. 'You want me to come round tomorrow?'

'Yes,' he said. 'Tomorrow. I'm a bit tied up today. Just you bring it in tomorrow and we'll deal with it then.'

Fuck you, I thought. I'll give you tomorrow! I'll make you sweat over this – mugging me off like some second-rate punter. But now he had given me a problem. For the first time in months, I had taken my money from its safe stash and now I was in a bit of a dilemma: should I take it back to the stash, or should I just keep it handy so I could get to it quickly, after I had made Mr Smart-ass Accountant sweat over his commission for a couple of days?

I had a pal, Alec McNeil, who lived nearby and decided to leave it with him. Alec suffered badly from spondylitis and rarely went out, so I felt my bag would be safe at his place. Of course, Murphy's Law raised its pernicious head.

Because my money was there, I made a point of spending more time than usual with Alec. Normally he stayed at home, but with me there and having a car handy, we decided to go out. In our absence, a visitor to the house, a seventeen-year-old girl who was a friend of Alec's daughter Lesley, was rooting about in a cupboard and came across my bag.

There were a lot of stories in the press about a gang of

youngsters finding the money and throwing wild parties at the house, but that was just tabloid journalism trying to make a story out of it. What actually happened was that Margaret Ann Keenan, Lesley's pal, was suspicious about me hanging about so much and thought I was up to something. Maybe she had seen me looking in the cupboard and found the bag. I don't know. But as soon as she got the chance, Margaret Ann gave the cupboard a spin and found it. She filled up a vanity case with £27,000 in fivers and rushed down to her nineteen-year-old boyfriend – I don't even know his name – and presented him with the money. This guy came from Possil, a run-down, dole-dependent district in North Glasgow that could compete comfortably with Liverpool's Toxteth or Manchester's Mosside in the deprivation stakes. There is no doubt that 999 out of 1,000 guys in Possil would have fallen to their knees, thanked God and hugged Margaret Ann to death in gratitude for this miraculous windfall. But not this stupid prick. Maybe his name was Murphy; if it wasn't it certainly should have been. Instead of expressing his undying love, taking the cash and changing his impoverished lifestyle, this nutcase grabbed Margaret Ann, marched her round to the nearest police station and stuck her in! The cops couldn't believe it and even now, nearly thirty years later, I still can't believe it myself. But that is what he did and that's what got me caught.

At first, Margaret Ann was going to be charged with stealing the money, but when my name came up, old memories stirred and the CID sprang into action. Of course, by this time I had missed the money and realised something had gone badly wrong. I immediately moved the remaining cash and, late that night, when I was sitting in Alec's house trying to get to the bottom of things, the front door crashed in. The CID had arrived.

The cops had no idea who had robbed the banks and even at this stage they weren't certain it was me. But backtracking made things easy for them. The fact that Bob Ross was my next-door neighbour soon came to light and started alarm bells ringing. Bob, of course, stood up to interrogation for about two minutes before collapsing. I had told him several times, 'Bob, if I ever get arrested for these bank jobs, the police will definitely come for you. All you have to say is: "I don't know what you are talking about. I never told James Crosbie anything. He's just my neighbour." Nothing more than that and stick to your story no matter what they say.'

Pointing out to him that there was dozens of Clydesdale Bank employees living around us and any one of them could have passed out the same information, I gave him a full rundown on police techniques and impressed upon him that whatever happened, I would never mention his name. I warned him not to get into any dialogue or offer any explanation. All he had to do was deny, deny and deny.

That's what I was doing myself. I claimed the money was from my business and that Margaret Ann had stolen it – well, she had, irrespective of where the money had originally come from. But the cops weren't buying it. They had found receipts for deposits in several building societies and then they turned up my gun. All this, along with Bob Ross's confession, gave them enough to charge me with the Whiteinch bank job, attempted murder and possession of a loaded firearm. I was remanded in custody and carted off to Barlinnie.

Needless to say, the first person I made a point of seeing was Bob Ross. He was in a terrible state, weeping and feeling depressed and almost suicidal. I felt really sorry for him. 'Come on, Bob,' I said. 'What happened? How did you end up in here?'

'It was you,' he sobbed. 'You told the police all about me. You even said that I was the leader, that the whole idea was mine.'

'Bob, Bob,' I pointed out. 'I'm pleading not guilty.'

He looked at me, not really understanding the implication of my words. 'You're blaming me,' he said. 'That's what the police told me.'

I spoke slowly. 'Bob, think about it. If I'm pleading not guilty, I'm saying I never done it. So why would I tell them you gave me the information? That would be sticking myself in.' I could see the realisation dawning on his face.

'But … but … the police told me you were blaming me.'

'I told you all about that, Bob. I warned you they would say things like that. There is not one bit of evidence against you. They've only got what you've told them yourself.'

I was still very upset about Bob being nicked, but it was his own fault. It was too late now. The deed was done and he had put himself inside. I settled down to my remand, desperately trying to conjure up some kind of defence.

Three days later, I was astonished to see a familiar face on the exercise yard: young Kenny, the soldier boy I had taken to Italy for the gun. 'What the fuck are you doing in here? What are you in for?'

'Same as you,' he replied. 'Armed robbery, attempted murder and possession of a gun.'

'Jesus Christ!' I was shocked. 'When did you get into that?'

'I didn't,' he told me. 'I've been charged with exactly the same as you. The police think I am the other guy that was on the robbery.'

I was stunned by this information. Kenny had nothing to with the robbery and both he and I knew that.

'So what happened?' I asked. 'How come they charged you?'

It was the police backtracking again. They had sifted my bank accounts and come across the cheque that I had paid to buy Kenny out of the army. An identity parade was promptly set up and you can imagine their delight when Kenny was picked out by several of the witnesses both inside and outside the bank. He was in deep trouble and promptly got himself charged with the offences.

'OK,' I said. 'But you weren't there, so why don't you tell them where you really were and get yourself out of this?'

'Plenty of time,' he said. 'I'll give it another couple of days, then tell them. The cops have left word with the governor that I can send for them any time and they'll come up right away to see me. I should be out by the end of the week.'

Yeah, I smiled to myself, knowing exactly what he was up to.

Two days later, Kenny spoke to the governor and said he had

evidence for the police. Within the hour they had rushed up to the Bar L and were speaking to him, but the interview didn't go the way they were hoping.

'Right. What have you got to tell us, Kenny?' They were all smiles, no doubt thinking he was going to produce vital evidence against me, maybe even turn Queen's. But their smiles soon faded when Kenny told them that he was completely innocent of the bank robbery. In fact, he had actually been at his job of work driving an Edinburgh city bus all that day.

Wow! What an alibi. What's more, it was true and there were literally hundreds of witnesses to prove it. The police were snookered. After rushing through their checks, there was no gainsaying the evidence. No matter how desperate they were and despite the fact that he had been positively identified at the ID parade, Kenny was not their man.

However, instead of being man enough to apologise for their mistake and immediately releasing him, the police in their infinite convoluted wisdom took Kenny down to the Sheriff Court and released him on bail. And that was when Joe Beltrami, Glasgow's top criminal lawyer and acting for me, stepped in.

Joe had heard that my co-defendant was appearing in court and as soon as Kenny had been granted bail, he made application to the same sheriff for bail on my behalf. The procurator fiscal almost laughed out loud at the idea. But Joe Beltrami knew his sheriff and explained to him that he had already granted bail to my co-defendant, who was charged with exactly the same as his client and argued that I should be treated no differently. He was chancing his arm, but Joe Beltrami could argue better than most. To the PF's confusion, the sheriff agreed with Mr Beltrami and I was granted bail.

I was lying on my cell bed when I heard the shout from the desk. 'On the threes. Three twenty-eight, Crosbie.' There was a definite pause, then the magic word rang out: 'Bail.' I was up, pillowcase packed and standing by the door, before the landing screw unlocked my door. Fifteen minutes later, Joe Beltrami himself was driving me away from the prison.

IT'S CRIMINAL

Apparently the cops missed me by the skin of their teeth. We must have passed them as they were arriving at the prison to charge me with the Hillington robbery. 'Crosbie,' the inspector said to gate control. 'We're here to see Crosbie.'

'You've just missed him,' he was told. 'Crosbie was released on bail a couple of minutes ago.'

'Aye, right!' The inspector laughed at him. 'Pull the other one. Come on. Open up. We haven't got all day.'

The gatekeeper had to show the inspector the book before the truth finally sank in. I was gone! By six o'clock it was on the television news and I was a wanted man. The police were raging about my release, questioning the sanity of the sheriff who had granted me bail on such serious charges as armed robbery, attempted murder and possession of an automatic pistol. But it was all their own fault. Once the cops realised that Kenny was a honest, hard-working man with an airtight alibi, clearly in no way involved in the robbery, they should have apologised and released him immediately. Instead of that, they gave him bail and opened the door for me.

But what about the much-vaunted Glasgow CID? You'd think that even a rookie cop might just have wondered why a young guy would choose to spend a week in the dire conditions of Bar L? Obviously no one did. Ah well, that's the highly trained CID for you.

Anyway, I was out and I was off. Mr Beltrami had warned me not to go home; he knew the score. The police would be out in droves looking for me. So I made a few phone calls from a friend's house to arrange some clothes and money and, as the papers said at the time, vanished. Gone! Disappeared in a cloud of exhaust fumes! The facts are much more mundane: I actually took a bus to Falkirk and checked into a small boarding house in Orchard Street.

First of all, I had to be able to get about. With only a few hundred pounds in cash, I had to do something. Every cop in the country was looking out for me, so how could I get away without wearing a mask? Then I spotted a motorcyclist zipping past wearing a helmet and I twigged. Bikers wore masks – masks that you could wear up and down any old road without anyone batting an eyelid. That would do for me. I searched through the Falkirk local paper small ads and I bought a wee Honda motorbike, along with a full-face, dark-glass helmet and got myself mobile. It was time to go to work again, but first I needed some equipment.

There was one pal I wanted to look up: Tam Carrick, whom I guessed would be able to help me. Tam wasn't one of my really close friends, so I felt safe in approaching him. I knew he had recently moved from Springburn to Kirkintilloch, a small country town five miles north of Glasgow and just over ten miles from my temporary base in Falkirk. It took me fifteen minutes to get to Kirky on my motorbike and just ten more minutes to locate my pal. Tam was good. He was pleased to see me and offered to do anything he could to help. My request was simple: 'Get me a gun, Tam.'

Tam came through for me. I couldn't even afford to pay full price for it, but Tam got hold of one of his country friends and came up with an old .410. Not ideal, but needs must when the devil drives. It would have to do. But there was a bonus from Tam as well: a driving licence along with some pieces of matching ID material that would enable me to hire a car. My only problem now was sorting out a bank and this was where my wee Honda and helmet came in handy. I liked the idea of scooting past right under the noses of the cops.

My favourite place for a bank was Glasgow and I travelled through there from Falkirk for a good look round. There were one or two banks I fancied, but I felt a little more vulnerable riding about than I had anticipated. This vulnerability was emphasised when I spotted one of my neighbours at a bus stop. Traffic was slow and he definitely did a double take as I rode past. I kept my eye on my mirror and saw him step out a little and stare after me. It made me cringe and I imagined him phoning the police. I decided that Glasgow was out.

Edinburgh seemed the next logical choice. I spent a couple of days nipping in and out from Falkirk trying to sort out a suitable bank to rob. I ended up with a choice of two, both on the west side of the city. One was on an industrial estate on the outskirts, the other in Gorgie Road, not too far from the city centre.

Having narrowed the field, I now had to make some vital preparations, the first being to find a place to hide immediately afterwards and not too far away from it either. During my scouting around, I had already spotted plenty of empty shop premises with estate agents' boards hanging outside. One of them in particular suited me and the easily obtained 'keys to view' were quickly re-cut before being handed back to the estate agent, solving my bolthole problem.

All I really needed now was transport. I didn't fancy the motorbike for a getaway. The Honda was the first motorbike I had ever ridden and I knew I wouldn't have felt comfortable trying to ride it hard if I got involved in a chase, especially if I was balancing a big bag of cash and a shotgun across my chest. I preferred a car and Tam's welcome gift of a driving licence and ID were all I needed for a hire company to supply that. Everything was turning out fine. There was just one little extra touch I threw in to give the cops a bit of misdirection and leave them something to think about.

A day or two before the robbery, I shot through to the city of Dundee and took a ride on a local city bus, carefully tucking the ticket into my hip pocket. I had a special use for it later on. The next morning back in Falkirk, I packed my bag, paid my bill and gave my Honda to the teenage son of the boarding-house owner; mind you, he did wonder why I kept the helmet. An hour or so later, I picked up a car at Waverly station, Edinburgh, deposited my gear in the shop and got ready to go to work.

In those days, banks closed at 3.30 pm. At exactly 3.25 pm, I parked the car on the other side of a pedestrian underpass that led to Sighthill Industrial Estate. I had decided on this bank because of the quiet pavements – just like Hillington. At bang on 3.28 pm, I put on my helmet and turned into the short footpath leading up to the door of the single-storey bank, the .410 hidden under the folds of a sack I had picked up from outside a fruit shop.

JAMES CROSBIE

Two paces to go and I braced myself for my entrance. Then a bank clerk suddenly appeared, flicked the Yale lock open and pushed the door closed in my face. I had my eyes on him, but he never looked up at me, avoiding eye contact by keeping his head down as he slammed the door so he wouldn't have to admit a late customer.

Shit! I was really wound up: confusion, frustration and disappointment all at once. I got into the car and drove off in a worse state than if I had actually done the job. But I've always been philosophical about things and once I had cooled down I reminded myself that tomorrow was another day – and another bank!

I spent an uncomfortable night in the shop. The next morning I had changed my target to the Gorgie Road branch of the Royal Bank of Scotland; it was nearer my bolthole anyway and just after ten o'clock I was parked up in a side street from where I could monitor its entrance. Things were quiet. In twenty minutes or so, I counted just four customers enter and leave the bank. It certainly looked good to me and I got myself ready. No last-minute appearances this time.

There were three elderly housewives huddled outside the doorway, so engrossed in gossip that I was totally ignored when I squeezed by them and entered the bank. It was a long bank inside, almost twenty feet to the counter and I could see three tellers, an elderly woman, a guy in a leather jacket and a young girl staring at me as I approached. The woman was first in line and I threw my sack over the counter at her.

'Fill it up!' I demanded – a trifle optimistic, right enough, considering the size of the sack. But the woman froze and just stared blankly at me like a dummy in shock. I grabbed back my sack and moved to the middle teller, the guy in the leather jacket. My sack sailed over the counter again, followed by the same instructions to fill it up. I could see the sneer on his face as the teller chipped a small wad of notes into the wide mouth of the sack and lobbed it contemptuously back at my head.

Fuck it! I wasn't here for that. I leaped up on the counter to

256

persuade him to be more co-operative, spotting, as I did so, that the young girl in the last position had a box full of blue fivers in front of her. 'Here,' I threw the sack down to her. 'Put that money' in there,' I instructed, before turning my attention back to the guy in the leather jacket. But he had capitulated and backed into a corner, offering no resistance. Then I spotted a staircase behind him that obviously led to a basement of some kind.

'Right! Everyone downstairs,' I yelled. 'Come on, down the stairs right now!'

While I was giving my orders, I noticed a door off to my right marked 'Manager'. Jesus! For all I knew he was already on the phone to the coppers. I burst into the office and caught him behind his desk, apparently having heard absolutely nothing.

'On your feet,' I roared, pointing the .410 at him. 'Come on, up!'

He looked at me with a half-grin on his face, definitely thinking I was kidding. 'Up!' I yelled. I could see realisation dawn on his face as he slowly got up from behind his desk. And up and up. He was a fucking giant! With his shiny bald head and wearing a hairy orange sports jacket with huge leather elbow pads, he looked like an ogre rising up from his den to eat me.

Wow, I thought. I hope he doesn't take this gun off me and beat me to death with the wooden end. 'Come on! Down the stairs!'

I had to keep it up; after all, I was a bank robber, not a mouse.

Thank God he was sensible and did what he was told, getting up and following the others down into the basement. I checked the young girl's position, saw half the money was still in the box and quickly transferred it into my bag.

The main safe was lying open and I looked across at it, but I had already been in the place too long – someone could enter at any time. I knew that I was beginning to chance my arm and that discretion was called for. Caution overcame greed and I put my helmet into the sack along with the money and left, squeezing past the still-chattering housewives. They would have something to gossip about now, all right.

Two minutes later and less than half a mile from the bank, I was stashing the money in the shop before driving on into the city centre to dump the car. The five-minute drive to get rid of the car was pretty hair-raising. I was driving straight into the face of responding police vehicles. At one point I thought I had run into a roadblock and almost jumped ship, but it was only a snarl-up where two police cars had shot the traffic lights and collided with one another.

It was a full nerve-wracking minute before I got across the junction and found a parking slot right in the centre of town. The last thing I did was drop my Dundee bus ticket into the car's footwell before locking up and abandoning the vehicle.

After leaving the car, I crossed the road to a large department store on the corner of Princess Street and bought myself a backpack and a kind of Australian bush hat. I had the idea that the backpack and hat, along with my sunglasses, would provide the perfect cover for me to mingle with the hordes of festival fans and make my way safely out of Edinburgh.

I felt really relieved when I finally locked the shop door behind me and collapsed into a chair. The adrenaline rush of the robbery, sustained by the getaway and the need to get rid of the car, then the hurried walk back to the shop, knowing I was heading in the direction of the bank again, had all taken their toll and I was utterly frazzled.

I must have sat in that chair for over an hour just watching the scene outside, smiling every time a police car raced past on its way to or from the bank. And I had something else to smile about: when I finally got the energy to count the cash, I discovered I had netted almost £20,000 – a lot of money in 1974 and the most money taken by anyone on a single-handed hold-up in Scotland.

By mid-afternoon I was fully relaxed and I planned on slipping out of town the following day using local buses, leapfrogging south until I felt safe enough or far away enough to catch a train. My idea was to get myself to Southend Airport, where I knew I could obtain a 72-hour, single-use passport on production of a driving licence as identification. This would at least get me out of the country and remove the danger of being recognised on the streets and I didn't foresee any difficulty in travelling through France into Spain and onwards to the Costa del Sol. I already knew some people there and with the money I had I would have no problem settling down. I spent another uncomfortable night trying to sleep in the shop, although thinking about my prospects certainly made it easier to bear. I was pleased to see daylight coming through the window the following morning.

After smartening myself up, I was satisfied with my appearance – even my mother would have walked past me in this gear – and just after nine o'clock I hit the pavement. My first thought was breakfast and I made my way a couple of hundred yards down the road to a workman's café at the junction outside Haymarket station. It was lovely to get into warm surroundings again and I ordered a big mug of tea right away, with another to follow along with a full breakfast.

I don't usually suffer from headaches, but the night in the shop must have brought this one on. I tried to ignore it at first, but it was really becoming too much for me. Then, halfway through my mug of tea, I spotted a box of aspirin tablets on a shelf behind the counter and asked the girl for a packet of them. She reached up and felt inside the box, before lifting it down only to discover it was empty. 'Sorry,' she said. 'But if you really need them, we buy them from that shop over there.' She pointed to a large newsagent's directly across the road.

I got up from my seat and, leaving my rucksack, hat and even my sunglasses behind, headed across the road to the shop. Traffic was heavy and I dodged across the busy lanes, dived into the shop and bought myself the life-saving aspirin. Unfortunately I never got the chance to take them, because on the way out of the shop I was hit by the ubiquitous Murphy's Law in the form of two Glasgow CID officers who just happened to be driving back from the High Court in Edinburgh when they spotted me crossing the road in front of them. They leaped on me, stuffed me into the rear seat of their car and hightailed it for police headquarters. I was captured.

Edinburgh Police Headquarters was disturbed by the sound of my chauffeur as he drove into the car park madly pumping his horn. Heads popped out from everywhere and in two minutes I was being frogmarched upstairs and directly into the chief superintendent's office. He was almost beside himself with joy and hands were being shaken all round – except mine, of course!

I was shoved down into a chair and became the object of intense curiosity as almost everyone in the building seemed to make a point of looking in to check on me. The circus went on for ten minutes or so before anyone actually decided to speak to me. 'Right. Shoes off. Empty your pockets.'

I did as I was told, having thrown in the towel by this time. My meagre possessions lay exposed on the chief super's desk – very few items and just about £25 in notes. The chief super poked the money about for a second or two, then looked at me.

'We're looking for a lot more than this,' he shouted, throwing the notes into my face. 'Where's the rest of it?' I looked up at him. Did he actually think I had twenty grand hidden about my body? 'Come on!' he screamed at me. 'Where's the rest of it?'

As I said, I had chucked it in by now. I was fucked mentally and just didn't feel like putting up a fight or being awkward. 'I left it in the café,' I muttered.

'Café? Café? What … what do you mean you left it in a café? What bloody café?'

'Across the road where I was picked up,' I told him. 'I was in there having breakfast when I went out to the shop.'

Faces paled and there was a mad scramble for the door as my words sank in.

'The café! He's left the money in the café!'

'What café? Where?' I could hear them shouting at one another as they scrambled downstairs. I could only describe it as a mélée as they thundered downstairs in a mad race to find the money, leaving just me and the chief super staring at each other. I've often wondered what would have happened if I'd got up and ran out along with them. Looking back, I think that there's every chance I would have got away with it.

'You left it in the café!' The chief super muttered the words almost to himself as I sat staring at him.

Once the initial excitement of my capture had faded, I found myself locked up in a holding cell waiting for an identity parade to be organised. Although I had already admitted carrying out the raid in Gorgie Road, the police still wanted to gather evidence against me in case I reneged on my statement.

Sometime in the early evening, I was opened up and taken to an interview room. The troops had arrived from Glasgow and Paisley, all of them anxious to speak to me. But I had very little to say. I told them I had thrown in the towel and would be pleading guilty to all charges. Of course, that brought a smile to their faces and you'd have thought it would satisfy them. But the next thing I know, Chief Inspector McGill from Glasgow gets out a blank statement sheet, puts my name on it and gets ready with his pen.

'OK, James,' he says (they're all very friendly when they want something), 'that's good. So if you'll just tell me when you first got the idea to rob a bank?' He prepared himself to scribble.

'Hold it! Hold it!' I said. 'I've just told you, I'll be pleading guilty.'

'Aye,' he says, 'I know that and that's good. But you'll have to tell us where the money is [he actually thought the Whiteinch money was still around!] and explain how you planned the robberies, where you got the guns, where you left the car, where you went after the robbery and, of course, we'll need to know the name of your accomplice.'

'I'm not telling you,' I said, plain and simple. 'I've already told you, I'm pleading guilty. What more do you want?'

'That's the point,' McGill said. 'If you are pleading guilty, you've got nothing to lose by explaining things. I only want to dot the Is and cross the Ts. You know, fill in the details. And it will definitely go good for you if you give us back the money and tell us the name of your partner.'

'Look, Mr McGill,' I told him. 'You've got me and you've got a result, but you're not going to get anyone else or any money back through me. I'm pleading guilty and that's all I've got to say.'

'Look, James,' he coerced, 'you're done and you're going to jail. What harm can it do now if you tell us everything you know. Remember, we're in a position to help you if you help us.' He gave me a wink. 'Know what I mean? All I'm asking is a bit of co-operation from you.'

'Co-operation?' I was getting fed up with his cajoling. 'I've already told you.' I emphasised my words. '*I'm pleading guilty.* Full stop. And as far as I am concerned, that's cooperation.'

'You do realise, James,' he said, sitting back and trying to look confident, 'that what I'm doing here is giving you a chance to show you are willing to help. You see, we actually know everything anyway. We know all about it, the whole shebang.' He leaned into my face to drop what he obviously thought was a bombshell of information. 'We even know about the Dundee connection!'

I looked at him for a couple of seconds. I had momentarily forgotten about my bus ticket ruse. Then the penny dropped and I suddenly burst out laughing. It hurt him. I could see his eyes squint in frustration.

'You … you...' he stuttered with rage. 'Listen, Crosbie, if you don't help us out here, I'll see you get twenty fucking years for this. You'll be an old man by the time you get out.'

I just couldn't help it. The Dundee connection! I was still laughing. Jesus, it had worked! McGill gave up on me after that, stomping away with his face a picture of frustration.

After that the others took turns talking to me and talking at me, always trying to sound so reasonable. 'What have you got to lose?' 'You could only do yourself a favour.' 'Why should you take the rap on your own?' I listened to what they had to say and simply reiterated my position: 'You've got me and I'm pleading guilty, so think yourself lucky with that.'

During one of the lighter intervals, I remember one of them shaking his head and saying to me, 'A bike! Imagine getting away from a bank robbery on a fucking bike! Aye, you had us there, son. But tell me, what gave you the idea to use a bike?'

IT'S CRIMINAL

I just couldn't resist it, but I kept a straight face when I replied, 'You know my record, don't you?'

'Aye, we know that all right. But what has your record got to do with you getting away on a bike?' He looked really puzzled.

'It's obvious,' I told him, my face as straight as a die. 'My last offence was drunk driving. I'm under a year's driving ban.'

I saw him look puzzled for an instant, then my answer sank in and he lashed out, slapping me across the face – frustration, I suppose. 'You … you … fucking Glasgow Keelie!'

It was about the only bright spot of my day, finally convincing them that it was no use trying to make me talk. They gave up after that and headed back to Glasgow, leaving me to my thoughts.

The following morning, the sheriff remanded me (no bail!) to Saughton prison, where I waited three dismal months before being called to perform a starring role in the trumpet-blowing, fancy-dress panoply of the long-running Edinburgh High Court pantomime. You would think that they would be happy with my guilty plea. You know, saving the cost of a trial and all that. But instead of getting a little consideration, maybe even a slight discount on my sentence, all I got was a severe tongue-lashing from a stern-faced Lord Robertson for my failure to co-operate with the police in naming my accomplices or returning any of the money stolen from the Whiteinch and Hillington bank raids. 'James Crosbie,' he said, 'you are nothing more than a cold, calculating scoundrel, whom I consider to be the most dangerous man in Scotland and, indeed, a threat to the very fabric of our society.' (I was beginning to think that he was talking to someone else at one stage of his diatribe). 'And as such I have no hesitation in sentencing you to twenty years' imprisonment. Take him away!' And that was that.

Twenty years! Twenty years tossed out as if it was nothing by a judge who later sentenced a multiple rapist to five years, then gave eight years to a paedophile who kidnapped, sexually abused, burned and tortured a three-year-old and left her for dead. Yet this same judge gave me twenty years for stealing money, with no one physically hurt or injured in any way. Lord

Robertson's message was clear and simple: people, even children, don't matter – money does.

What could I do about it? Not a lot, that was for sure. Only one thing was certain: I was going to have to get on with it. The Chinese have an old saying: even the longest journey begins with the first step. Well, even the longest sentence begins with the first second and I had just started. I remember lying on my bunk that night, on strict security with my clothes outside my door, light on all night and my cell-door spyhole being rattled every fifteen minutes. Twenty years? How many days is that? How many hours? How many seconds? I couldn't work it out, not even the days.

But one thing I did know for sure; I was on my way to Peterhead Prison. PH. The Napper. All names for Scotland's very own Alcatraz. A place full of nutcases and psychopaths and I was booked on the very next bus.

Chapter Twenty-four

Papillon of Peterhead

The road to Peterhead and by this I mean the metalled road, not the metaphorical road paved by a wayward lifestyle, started for me at the gates of Saughton Prison. There were about eight of us on the fortnightly draft to the penal outpost and the journey began in an almost carnival atmosphere: cons were cheerfully passing round precious tobacco and sharing treasured sweets as they cracked jokes and made outrageous observations about the passing world beyond the confines of their bus. But the carefree convict carry-on and false bravado did not last for many miles. We were handcuffed two-by-two; the darkened windows were barred; the doors were securely chained; there was a sawdust-filled bucket for a toilet; and we were guarded by six surly, uncommunicative screws who soon destroyed the fleeting illusion of freedom. It wasn't a bus we were on, it was a travelling jailhouse.

Gradually we withdrew into a quiet, introspective silence as the bus drove us steadily northwards, pausing first at Perth Prison and then advancing to Aberdeen. Soon enough I was back at Peterhead and I did not like it at all. It was very depressing sitting on a concrete stool in a cold cell of the punishment block, waiting for my name to be called out, then hearing the tramp, tramp, tramp of approaching feet and the rattle of keys as a screw unlocked the door and led me through to the reception desk.

'Crosbie?' The reception screw looked up from his papers and spoke down at me as I stood in front of his high, schoolmaster's desk.

'Yes.' I had long since learned to be economical with answers in jail.

The screw studied me for a moment or two, a slight questioning look on his face. 'Crosbie, James.' He gave me my full name in reverse and continued his query. 'Twenty years?' He sounded sceptical, as if he had made a mistake

'That's right,' I said.

'You're Crosbie?' He looked me up and down and there was no doubting the surprise in his voice. By now I was beginning to think that maybe there had been some mistake.

'That's me,' I confirmed.

'Huh!' His snort was very definitely disparaging and he had a distinctly disappointed look as he began to process me. I didn't realise it then, but I later found out that my appearance had been most disappointing to him. He had obviously been aware that I was arriving and had conjured up an image of some huge, thick-necked, brawny, bald-headed bank robber well worth slapping with a twenty-year sentence. But it was only me. And there I stood in front of him as threatening as a high-street handbag snatcher. He was not impressed.

And it appeared that the resident gangsters had also seriously misjudged me, obviously equating the size of the man to the size of the jobs he had done, a fact that became clear when I was handed a cardboard box containing my prison issue clothing. In anticipation of my arrival, the gangsters of PH had had my uniform and shirts specially made up for me in the prison's tailor's shop. The clothes would have fitted John Wayne, with the shirt sleeves dangling from my wrists like two flapping sheets and a jacket that would have looked loose on Mike Tyson.

IT'S CRIMINAL

I was very definitely a disappointment to the welcoming committee of known Glasgow faces. I even caught one of them looking at me in shock, his face screwed up in consternation and mouthing to his pal in tones of amazement, 'Is that him?' Yes, I'm afraid it is, pal, I thought to myself as I was escorted up to my security cell on the third floor of A Hall.

The day after my arrival, as the final part of the reception procedure, I was marched in front of the governor – a kindly old soul (for up there anyway) called Angus – and officially 'welcomed' to Peterhead. You often hear of people being described as a fatherly figure and that was exactly what old Angus was. He never ranted and raved, was never vindictive, did his daily rounds of the workshops with a tolerant smile on his face and accepted the misbehaviour of his charges with a reproachful look and sad shake of his head as he imposed his inevitable penalties on them.

But like all prison governors, Angus was merely a figurehead. The real power in any prison in those days was the Chief Officer. It still is, but they have different titles nowadays and wear suits instead of uniforms. But, a rose by any other name ... So it was Gibbering Gibby who took it upon himself to put me in my place.

'You! You, Crosbie! You're the one that robbed all those banks. Aye, well, there will be no bank robbing here [he wasn't called Gibbering Gibby for nothing]. You'll behave yourself in this place, I'll see to that. Tailor's shop for you, m'laddie. Security party, that's where you're going. And mind, I'll be keeping my eye on you!'

And that was that. My reception was complete. I was in the jail and in my place, all sorted out in a matter of minutes.

On my first working day in Peterhead I lined up with the other security men and off I marched to the tailor's shop. I was witness to everything in that workshop, from near fatal stabbings to practical jokes and crazy killers telling crazier tales. It would be impossible to report on all of the players who starred in the continuous workshop soap opera that was the PH security party.

The very fact that each individual had ended up there meant in itself that every one of them had a unique, often bizarre story to tell. And, just to give you a taste of the really bizarre, I'll tell you about Hadgey.

With a forehead that sloped downward at almost forty-five degrees, ending up in a thick thatch of eyebrow fur that shadowed the deep hollows of his sunken eyes, Hadgey could easily have been mistaken for a walking, talking Piltdown man. Huge in the shoulder and strong as an ox, this modern-day Neanderthal worked on the sewing machine next to mine and naturally we talked about our cases. It didn't matter that everything had been widely reported in the press and although every word had been minutely pored over and discussed in detail, other cons still thirsted for the inside story. And Hadgey's story would make even a Hammer Horror scriptwriter recoil.

How do you start a conversation with a madman? The trick is, you've got to pretend both to him and yourself that he's not mad. You've got to learn to treat these nutcases with kid gloves and talk to them in a perfectly normal conversational manner. You must listen to them as if their story is simply part and parcel of normal daily life. Usually these sorts of conversations begin with the simple question: 'How long are you doing, then?' But this is merely a ploy to pave the way for the next question: 'What did you get that for?' It doesn't really matter that nine times out of ten you already know the answers to these questions, it is just a polite opening gambit to get the guy to tell his tale. Hadgey's story takes the top prize. Well, there was another guy who butchered most of his family, including the dog – but for now I'll just tell you Hadgey's tale.

'Life!' You always had to inject a little note of surprise when your first question was answered. 'What did you get that for?'

'Strangled a fucking dwarf.'

Not exactly monosyllabic, but without any elaboration of any kind it sounded rather stark to say the least. And you mustn't recoil or look in any way shocked at this bald statement of fact. It is, after all, just a normal conversation – for Peterhead, that is.

'Oh, aye. And what did you do that for, Hadgey?'

'Caught the wee bastard shagging my bird.'

'Oh, did you? So, what happened then?' Meantime, we are stitching and sewing away at our prison task.

'I told you! I caught him at it with her and strangled him.'

'He was dead?'

'Aye, he was dead all right. I told you. I strangled the wee bastard.'

'Aye, well, so that was him dead. Then what did you do?'

At this, Hadgey stopped work to explain how he coped with this unusual inconvenience. 'Well, he was dead, so I decided I had to get rid of the body.' I nodded encouragingly, showing keen interest. 'I decided to cut him up.'

'Aye, right enough,' I said, trying to keep things conversational. 'You would need to do that, all right.' Hadgey leaned towards me and spoke earnestly, as if sharing a secret.

'But I knew if I cut him up, he would bleed all over the place.'

'Yes.' I could only sympathise with his predicament. 'So what did you do?'

'I got hold of a Black and Decker electric drill and bored a hole right on the top of his head. Right through his skull I went. But see, when I went to pour his blood down the sink ...'

'Aye?' I admit I was a little puzzled at this, but I tried to look serious as he continued his lurid tale.

'See, when I tipped him over the sink and tried to empty out the blood, you know something?'

'What?' I dared to ask.

'It never came out. The blood just stayed there, stuck in his body.'

'Did it?' I didn't really have to feign surprise. Obviously the workings of the human body were a complete mystery to the intellectually challenged Hadgey.

'Nothing,' he explained with a mystified shake of his head. 'Not a drop.'

'So what did you do then?' I asked. This was better than fiction.

'I had an old hacksaw in the house, so I got him on to the

kitchen table and cut his head off. Then I got his hands and arms off, but the blade broke when I was cutting through his thigh.'

'Did it now!' I tut-tutted in disapproval at the failing quality of the British hacksaw blade.

'So that was me fucked.' Hadgey nodded regretfully at the memory.

'How?' I queried. 'You could always have got another blade.'

'No,' he replied, tapping the side of his nose in a knowing way. 'I'm too wide for that. Right out of character that would have been. A dead giveaway.'

'Aye, well, right enough.' Hadgey's logic was definitely giving me problems. 'So what *did* you do?'

'I got a big fire going in the grate and decided to burn him.'

'Aye?'

'I stuck the feet in first and they were burning away fine, but there was a helluva smell and I had to stop.'

I looked at him and nodded sympathetically. 'So?'

'So I phoned up my lawyer and asked him to come round to the house. I told him it was a big case.'

'Did he come?' I asked

'Aye, he came all right,' the bold Hadgey told me. 'When he saw the head on the sideboard and a couple of hands lying about, he took a right flaky: ran out the house and got the police. And he was supposed to be my fucking lawyer!'

'The bastard!' I loudly condemned the treachery of the man. 'He got you jailed!'

'Ah well,' Hadgey waxed philosophical. 'I would have been done anyway. You see, my bird had run away and told her pal about me strangling the fucking midget and the word was out. When the police came I just admitted it and got a lifer.'

He looked over at me and accepted my sympathetic mutterings as his due and without a pause continued speaking. 'Here, pass me over the quick pick a minute, pal, I've just got a couple of extra stitches here.' He snipped away delicately for a few seconds. 'And by the way, do you know what my psychiatrist said to me?'

'No.' I shook my head and waited for his next revelation.

'He said,' Hadgey began, nodding knowingly. 'He said that I was one of the cleverest murderers he had ever met. And do you know why he said that?'

'No I don't,' I told him. 'Why did he say that, Hadgey?'

'Because I tried to get rid of the body.'

And that was just one of the guys in the tailor's shop.

As time passed I settled into life in Peterhead, becoming part of the place and getting on with my sentence. All in all I fitted in quite well with my criminal contemporaries.

I've always liked words and phrases and especially like collective nouns. My favourite word is 'serendipity' (look it up yourself!) and my favourite collective noun is 'a murder of crows'. But I hadn't ever heard of a good collective noun for convicts, so I made one up: 'a conglomeration of convicts'. I think that description is apt because that's exactly what they are: a mixed bunch of humanity struggling to survive in the hostile society of a prison. There are leaders and followers, the weak and the strong, extrovert and introvert and, even in Peterhead, guys and dolls. The only group of society missing from the population of Peterhead was intellectuals, probably because anyone with more than half a brain knew how to avoid the place. With such a diverse conglomeration of humanity, it is no wonder there are many stories to tell. But where to begin? Nicknames: that's as good a start as anything.

It always surprised me how aptly nicknames fitted individuals in Peterhead and this went for both screws and cons alike. I've already mentioned Gibbering Gibby, and you don't need much of an imagination to picture the screw Jellybuttocks waddling along the landing, fat face red with exertion and neck squeezed tight in his collar. His claim to fame was that he stuck Jimmy Boyle's head in a bucket of water and tried to drown him down in the punishment block.

Then there was Cement Head, a product of an inbred fishing village community. He had earned his name on two separate counts. Firstly, he originally appeared in Peterhead making regular deliveries as the driver of a cement-delivery lorry. After making deliveries for some weeks, he realised that the uniformed prison officers he saw there did not appear to do very much in the way of actual physical exertion. The second reason Cement Head acquired his sobriquet was blindingly obvious: the idiot was as thick as two short planks. One of his more memorable blunders was when he approached a fellow officer and reported that he had got rid of a certain prisoner's pigeons.

Now pigeons were a big thing with some of the men in PH and with so little else to do they often became an obsession. Men would spend hours letting them fly from their cell windows and catering for their every need. Some of the men had even nurtured their pigeons up from eggs laid in their cupboards by birds they already owned. The authorities turned a blind eye to the practice of keeping pigeons; it was a harmless pastime and it did keep the men out of mischief. But somehow or other one of the men had fallen foul of Cement Head, leaving himself open to attack and revenge was swift and brutal.

'Aye, that's that,' Cement Head announced one day to his shift partner, the Fairy Queen. 'I soon got rid of his pigeons,'

'Aye, man.' The Fairy Queen nodded approval. 'And how did you do that?'

'I put them out the window. They flew away.'

'Och, don't be daft, man,' the Fairy Queen retorted. 'That's no good. They're bloody homing pigeons. They'll be back by now.' Not wanting his colleague to be cheated out of his revenge, he unselfishly offered to help out. 'Come on,' he said. 'I'll show you what to do with them.' And with that they both marched back to the prisoner's cell.

The pigeons, as the Fairy Queen had rightly predicted, had already returned and were cooing away on their perches on the window ledge. Quite calmly, the Fairy Queen took one of them down and callously wrung its neck. 'There, that's the way to get rid of them, man,' he informed his appreciative audience. 'Just wring their bloody necks. They'll do no more flying then.'

IT'S CRIMINAL

Nodding enthusiastic agreement, Cement Head followed the Fairy Queen's example, a few quick twists of his wrists promptly dispatching the rest of the innocent birds off to that great pigeon coop in the sky. Both officers were seen leaving the cell looking pleased with themselves, four dead pigeons on the prisoner's table clear evidence of their foul deed.

Talk about a furore! The con went ballistic and even some of the screws temporarily shelved their usual solidarity to voice objections at their colleagues' barbaric behaviour. However, and you had to give him credit for this, although the con knew who was responsible for killing his pigeons, he remained sensible enough to keep his hands to himself as he ranted and raved at the assassin. He did, however, decide to take what we all thought was the sensible course, hoping that Cement Head would at least suffer some penalty for his crime. A letter reporting the incident was despatched to the RSPB and we all sat back waiting for retribution to descend on the ignorant, pigeon-killing Cement Head. He received the following letter in reply:

> The Society regrets the incident regarding the killing of your pigeons. However, we can only act if the behaviour of the individual concerned led to the birds suffering cruelty or undue pain and suffering. Furthermore, as pigeons are regarded as vermin, such a method of dispatch is considered to be humane and in this case we can take no action against the individual concerned. End of story.

The pigeons were the man's pets, his friends and companions during the lonely hours in his cell. We were all disgusted and Cement Head continued to stand guard on the landing with a self-satisfied smirk on his face.

Red Alert was a screw who got his name from a sudden, ill-advised action he undertook one day in the tailor's shop. New to the service he had yet to make his mark and up until the day of his official christening he was known, for obvious reasons, as

Baby Face. His introduction to guard duty in the tailor's shop, just a few short weeks after joining the service, was well out of order. He was thrown in at the deep end by his fellow officers who resented the senior status he enjoyed, which had been carried forward from his previous job in the local taxation office.

To say he was a bundle of nerves would be an understatement. Primed by exaggerated reports from his fellow screws of the dangers from the unpredictable top-security prisoners, Baby Face stood nervously against the rear wall of the shop anxiously counting and recounting his charges. Resplendent in his shiny new peaked cap, he braced himself against a radiator, careful not to catch anyone's eye and so avoid a confrontation with any of these dangerous prisoners.

Two men, Billy Mac and Tony T, both lifers, sat directly in front of him in the back row of machines and recognised immediately that Baby Face was a total nervous wreck. It so happened that outside, within sight of the window, a con was working away at the prison incinerator and was at that very moment digging a small pit. Billy Mac gave Tony a wink and nodded out of the window.

'How's the tunnel getting on?' he asked in a hoarse stage whisper.

Tony pretended to look surreptitiously out towards the incinerator where he could clearly see the con digging lustily with his spade. 'It's going well,' he answered in a low voice that just carried to Baby Face. 'Must have dug a good bit out by now.'

Baby Face nearly keeled over as, leaning at an angle of almost forty-five degrees, he eavesdropped on the 'escape plot' unfolding before him.

'Has he got the rope and the hook organised yet?' Mac whispered.

'No problem. It's all been well stashed. We'll be ready to go any day now.'

Obviously not even stopping to consider what use a rope and hook would be in a tunnel, Baby Face launched himself into action and, in doing so, earned himself the sobriquet that would henceforth follow him throughout his service life. 'Red alert! Red alert!' He screamed the words at the top of his voice as he raced down the shop to expose the infamy. 'Red alert, Mr Noble!' He burst into the office and yelled at the senior officer. 'They're digging a tunnel and ... and ...' He stuttered to a halt as Noble looked at him and slowly shook his head.

'And how do you know about this?' Noble asked, totally unperturbed at the alarming news.

'I heard them,' Red Alert blurted out. 'Those two at the back, they were talking about it and if you look out of the window you'll see they've got someone digging a tunnel!'

'Oh, a tunnel, is it?' Noble dragged Red Alert back up to his station to confront the grinning Billy Mac and Tony T. 'You two stop fucking about now,' he told them. 'And as for you, you fucking idiot,' he said and cuffed the red-faced rookie on the back of his head in time with his words. 'Don't you be so fucking stupid. Red alert?' He shook his head. 'You fucking idiot!'

For a prison work party, it has to be said that the tailor's shop in PH was never a dull place. As well as the usual subversive activities of sabotaging the machines, destroying material and setting elaborate incendiary devices, there were always games to be played and stories to be told. And even some of the screws got into the story-telling action.

Hank the Yank was a screw who had apparently spent some time in the USA. No one really knew if he had ever actually been to America, but Hank the Yank continuously boasted of his life there in an obviously desperate attempt to impress the cons. The thing is, we never ever got the stories at first hand from Hank. It wasn't the done thing for an officer to converse with prisoners and give out information about his private life, past or present, so Hank developed a technique that allowed him to impart his information at second hand.

Hank would stand against his radiator at the head of the stairs and engage his opposite number in conversation across the width of the workshop floor, loudly relating stories of his past life in Vegas. He made constant references to Frank, Dino, Sammy, Gina and other well-known names, as if they were familiar boozing buddies of his. According to Hank, he practically ran Vegas. Eventually the PO in charge of the party got sick of him and his tales and one day, in front of everyone, took Hank to task.

'So you know all the famous people in Las Vegas?' he challenged.

But Hank did not even seem disturbed at the disbelieving tone adopted by the PO. 'They were all my pals,' he boldly confirmed.

'Well you tell me,' the PO demanded. 'If you were doing so well in Las Vegas and were pals with Frank, Dino and all those others you talk about, what the fuck are you doing working here as a screw in Peterhead?'

Not a bit nonplussed by the PO's scathing attack, Hank looked him straight in the eye. 'Ah, well, that's for me to know and for you to wonder about,' he said, leaning against the wall, looking confidently back at his interrogator.

'No, I don't need to wonder,' the PO replied, poking Hank in the chest with his finger. 'You see, I know. I know what you're doing here.'

Hank's eyes narrowed at this. 'What then?' he said. 'What do you think I'm doing here?'

'You're on the run from the Mafia,' the PO triumphantly announced, obviously enjoying the pantomime as much as the cons. 'You're hiding from the Mob.' He looked at Hank and shook his head. 'Well, you're fucked now, because I'm going to phone them up and tell them where you are!' And with that he turned round and headed determinedly for his office.

But Hank the Yank, a diehard to the end, still kept his end up. 'Aye,' he shouted. 'That's just the sort of dirty trick you would pull. You're nothing but a fucking grass!'

You couldn't make it up, could you?

There were some serious assaults and stabbings that took place during my time in the tailor's shop, but to my knowledge there was only one occasion when anyone ever got charged. This was when a serious escape attempt was made from the shop and an officer was stabbed in the back with a large pair of cutting shears.

The escape bid failed when the cutting-room screw managed to press the alarm bell to summon the riot squad. I can still remember having to take an extra long step to jump the huge pool of blood on the shop floor when we were all marched away. Larry L, along with three others, was charged with attempted murder, but he was the only one found guilty and was sentenced to another fifteen years on top of his lifer. The other guys got off because as soon as Larry struck the first blow, the other screws dived for cover and didn't see anything after that. It's maybe worth noting here that another screw was christened that day with a nickname: Shitty Breeks. I'll leave the reader to guess why.

Extra searches were all part and parcel of being in the security party and we could expect snap searches at any time. Most of the screws kept things at a reasonable level – a daily cell search and a once-a-week strip search. After all, we were also searched twice every day on return from work and, apart from pieces of cloth and home-made denims, there was little opportunity to build up a tool kit or arsenal.

But there was one screw who took his job more seriously than the others – Andy Bunnet, so called because his uniform cap was several sizes too big. The Bunnet took his job really seriously. A narrow-minded Highland bumpkin, it seemed his sole mission in life was to torment and irritate prisoners. No one got away with anything when he was on duty and you could expect him at your door at any time, ready to annoy you with a strip search.

Eventually one of the guys, Walter E, got so fed up with Andy Bunnet's constant strip searches that he penned an official letter of complaint – a petition – to the Secretary of State for Scotland.

Dear Sir

I would like to complain about the constant strip searches I have to undergo here in Peterhead Prison. Most of the time they are pretty normal and do not give me any cause for concern. However, there is one particular turnkey [Walter insisted on calling all screws turnkeys] who is disturbing me with his zeal when carrying out these searches. At least once or twice a week this turnkey, Andy Bunnet, insists on coming to my cell and giving me a strip search. Now I realise that he is allowed to do this and I am not complaining about his seemingly insatiable desire to see me in the nude. But this Andy Bunnet always makes me strip down to my vest, then gets me to pirouette around my cell like a demented ballerina so he can freely inspect my bare buttocks and my other dangly bits.

It is obvious to me that Andy Bunnet is a pervert; I can tell by the way his eyes pop open and his breathing sounds funny when he is inspecting me. However, if he gets his kicks out of watching me spinning around in my vest with my private parts merrily jiggling up and down, that is entirely up to him. In fact I am not complaining about his perversion. What I am complaining about is that I am beginning to get to like it!

Yours faithfully

Walter E

These petitions were a constant source of amusement for us cons but, of course, not all of them were funny. Sometimes a con would have what he considered a real grievance and getting nowhere through the local complaints procedure would resort to writing a petition. But it was a last resort – do you think for one minute that the Secretary of State for Scotland ever clapped his eyes on a petition from a convict? Besides, it didn't matter what you wrote or who answered it, the reply was invariably the same: 'Please inform the prisoner that he has no grounds for complaint.'

There was one guy, Pokey Turner, who got so frustrated by this repetitive reply that he decided to really put the process to the test. He wrote a petition in utter gibberish, along the lines of:

IT'S CRIMINAL

Yjr kgpt yr dommy dllyp;y fisyylh dkdky rldsylyy iy y
nn syss snf yi ld I hr.

Yours sincerely

W Turner

Six weeks later, Pokey was called up in front of the governor to
receive his reply. The governor opened the envelope and
prepared to read it out. He studied it for a few moments, slowly
shaking his head, before finally passing it to the waiting Pokey.

'Here, Turner,' he said. 'You better read this for yourself.'

Pokey stared at the paper for several seconds before bellowing
out, 'What the fuck's this? I can't read this shite!'

The governor took the paper back and looked at the writing
again. It went something like this: 'Okeadt ubgtin yhr ptidonrt
yhsy hr hsd no htounfd gto vompl.'

'Well, it's quite plain to me, Turner,' the governor told the
puzzled Pokey. 'The answer quite clearly states: "Please inform
the prisoner that he has no grounds for complaint."'

Pokey's baffled expression told its own tale to the waiting
prisoners. Fucked again! The moral here was clear: you will
never beat the system.

Sojer (Soldier) Thompson's nickname was a mystery. He was
certainly never in the army, because with a wonky foot and the
beginnings of a hump on his back there would have to have been
a state of national desperation declared before Sojer was ever
called to the colours. Sojer and his pal had taken it upon
themselves to mug an elderly female cheque collector and steal
her money. His accomplice was arrested shortly afterwards, but
Sojer managed to avoid arrest. Later, at the High Court in
Edinburgh, the woman was asked if the man in the dock was one
of the men who had robbed her. The lady confirmed that the
accused was, indeed, one of her attackers.

'And what about the other man,' the prosecutor continued.
'Would you recognise him if you saw him again?'

'Oh, yes,' said the woman. 'I would know him anywhere. He was ugly. In fact, he had a face like a monkey.'

'Who are you calling a fucking monkey?' Sojer's voice rang out loud and clear as he leaped from his seat in the rear of the public benches. This ill-advised action resulted in his immediate arrest, followed by a sentence of four years in jail.

'Nobody's going to call me a fucking monkey and get away with it,' Sojer stoutly defended his action whenever he was questioned about his foolhardy outburst.

Mind you, it wasn't all laughs in Peterhead. Tempers were always on a short fuse and even a casual, offhand remark could spark an immediate outraged reaction. Many a con has been beaten up or stabbed over an ill-advised comment on the result of a football match or some other innocuous subject. Even if hands are shaken and apologies made at the time, loss of face makes a comeback almost inevitable.

One such case was when Jimmy H asked Walter E for a small piece of marquetry veneer. On his request being refused, Jimmy picked up a scrubbing brush and belted Walter across the side of his head and hastily departed. Walter did nothing about it at the time and it looked as if he was taking a back seat. With Walter being on security due to a twenty-one-year sentence for armed robbery, while Jimmy worked out a seven-stretch in the mat shop, their paths actually seldom crossed. Added to that was the fact that Walter *never* left his cell to engage in any so-called recreational activities in the hall, reducing the chances of them running into one another even more. So as the months passed it seemed that the incident with the scrubbing brush had faded from memory.

Six months or so later, Jimmy, along with Mick K, was sitting in Howard W's cell enjoying a chat and a cup of tea. There was a polite knock at the door and Walter appeared carrying a large basin of boiling water straight out of the immersion heater. Naturally he totally ignored Jimmy and spoke directly to Howard about the return of some magazine or other. Agreement reached, he turned to leave and unfortunately 'tripped' over the edge of Howard's carpet. Needless to say, Walter lost his balance and lunged forward, 'accidentally' throwing the scalding water straight into the face of an unsuspecting Jimmy.

Jimmy's face peeled like a banana and he collapsed, screaming in agonising pain. Walter was distraught, running for help, demanding an ambulance and wringing his hands in worry as Jimmy was stretchered off to an outside hospital.

I was one of the few people Walter talked to at any length but, even to me, no mention of the 'accident' was ever made.

Around this madness, life still went on in Peterhead. After all, the jail held over three hundred prisoners and they weren't all crazy. Most of the men just wanted to put their heads down and get on with doing their time. And you could do that too if you wanted. No one forced you to join a gang. If you didn't want to get mixed up in jail politics, all you had to do was keep yourself to yourself and mostly you would be left alone to get on with it. I was proof of that.

Escape had been uppermost in my mind during that first long year of my sentence, so much so that in my dreams I escaped every single night. However, I did more than just dream about it. At one stage I got myself a hacksaw blade – smuggled up from Edinburgh in the sole of a training shoe – and began the long slow task of cutting through my window bars. It's a big job when you have to cut through six sections of cast metal before tackling the horizontal steel bars outside. I made a small frame that would hold half a blade and grip it steady enough for use. Then, with a pal called Jimmy K keeping watch for me, I began my task. In all, I would need six cuts in the frame and four cuts in the outside steel bars. A formidable job, even if you had the best of equipment and the freedom to use it openly; but a hopeless task for my puny tool working under the close supervision of the screws.

Is it some kind of blind optimism, or maybe sheer stupidity, that spurs on people like me to try the impossible? Whatever it is, I was having a go. My optimism had even led me to prepare a rope to get over the wall. It wasn't a thick rope, but it was strong, made from heavy fishing-net material woven into four or five ply, with pieces of wood tied into it to provide grips for my hands and feet. I tested it by tying it up in my cell and standing my full weight on it and it worked OK.

After a week of surreptitious sawing, I had managed to cut through two sections of the cast-iron frame and visions of freedom loomed ahead. Then one night I was carried away by the noise of a North Sea storm that should also have carried away the sound of my enthusiastic sawing. A patrolling screw crept round the corner of the cell block and heard the sound of the saw. Jimmy K should have been sacked! The screw immediately alerted his colleagues inside who rushed my door and I was caught bang to rights, hand on saw, saw biting into metal.

Captured! Again! Fuck it!

The charge laid against me when I was marched in front of the governor for adjudication was attempt to escape. There would appear to be no defence – after all, I was caught with the saw in my hands halfway through the third bar on my cell window. Not so. You are forgetting the devious criminal mind with which I was endowed. Remember, it takes a clever man to act the fool.

'Not guilty, sir,' I replied to the charge. 'I had no intention of trying to escape.'

'What do you mean, not guilty, Crosbie? What were you doing with the hacksaw then, engaging in a bit of fretwork? Trying out some sort of new cell hobby perhaps?'

'No, sir. I cut my cell bars as a protest.'

'What do you mean a protest, Crosbie? What were you protesting about?'

'I was protesting about being held illegally on security.' I tried to be indignant. 'I'm fed up with being treated like an escapee when, in actual fact, I have never tried to escape. So I sawed my bars to justify being treated as an escapee.'

The governor exchanged a long-suffering look with his Chief Officer and shook his head. 'Wait a minute, Crosbie,' he said.

'Are you trying to tell me that you cut your bars because you think you should not have been on security?'

'That's right, sir,' I replied. 'But now that I *have* cut my bars, you are definitely fully entitled to put me on security. I knew I would be caught, but at least now I don't have to worry about being treated unfairly any more.'

The governor looked at me, then round the other staff in the orderly room, as if seeking help. Then he fidgeted with his hands, obviously at a loss at what to do. 'A protest?' He stared hard at me, his eyes crinkled in confusion.

'That is correct, sir,' I assured him. 'I never had the slightest intention of trying to escape.'

Finally he shook his head in total exasperation. 'Right, Crosbie,' he made up his mind. 'I intended to treat this as a serious escape attempt and remand you until the Visiting Committee could deal with you. However, in view of what you have just said, I have decided to deal with the matter myself and punish you to the limit of my powers.'

I felt a wave of relief. I knew the governor's limit was measured in days, whereas the Visiting Committee could take months of remission from me. Dodging the VC was a victory and I listened happily to the governor's admonishing voice as he told me off before handing out his punishment. I got twenty-eight days all round for my antics with the saw. That means twenty-eight days' loss of remission, twenty-eight days' solitary and twenty-eight days' loss of earnings. And that was getting off light.

The Chief Officer marched me off to the cells.

Chapter Twenty-five

Poofery at Peterhead

My twenty-eight days in the cells had seen no change in PH. Christ, twenty-eight years had seen no change in that place. Still, there was gossip to catch up with. On top of that it was good to enjoy some human company again and I was glad to sit in with Walter E to be brought up to date with what had been going on in my absence.

Nothing out of the usual: half-a-dozen transfers in and out. Scruffy S had gone to Bar L for accumulated visits. Mac the Knife had returned on a life-licence recall. There was a rumour that we were going to get lamb chops in a couple of weeks' time. The new three-month film list was up and looked pretty crap. And, of course, there had been a couple of stabbings – one over the use of the tea urn, the other because of a false accusation about some sort of poofery.

It was a rare occurrence in Peterhead, the poofery I mean; in all the years I spent there, I can only think of maybe half-a-dozen occasions where incidents of blatant, outright homosexuality came to light. In the normal course of events, it was statistically inevitable that every now and again one or two of the more extrovert gender benders would turn up at Peterhead and unashamedly strut their stuff, taking full advantage of the child-in-the-sweetie-shop syndrome to enjoy several clandestine affairs. But one thing was sure: if anyone did have an affair, it was all kept behind closed doors. Well it would be, wouldn't it?

Image and reputation were everything in Peterhead, especially among the hard men and the gangsters. Any hint of weakness or fallibility of character could destroy a man and make his life a misery. That was why comebacks were made and justified, on the slightest of provocation. A man had to show he could not be bammed up – made to look stupid or weak – without some form or retribution, usually violent, being sought. But there was one memorable occasion when one of the big names, perhaps in a moment of recklessness, chose to be bold about things.

Mandy, one of the more outrageous poofs, came upstairs to the security party in the tailor's shop one day and made a point of speaking familiarly to Boulder Head, a known hard man. Conscious of the many witnesses and keen to maintain his standing in the macho community of Peterhead, Boulder Head's response was predicable to most of us, but obviously came as a shock to Mandy himself. 'Fuck off!' he was told in no uncertain terms. 'Don't you come trying to talk to me, you fucking wee poof!'

But the suspicions of the workforce were already aroused. Why would the flouncing Mandy be so bold as to openly approach Boulder Head and try to engage him in chit-chat? What made him think such a liberty could be taken with impunity? We all looked at one another. Surely not! The unspoken question hung in the air.

Slowly Mandy backed away, sensible enough to curtail his attempt at conversation with the scowling Boulder Head, at least at close quarters. Visibly hurt, he edged back towards the safety of the stairs before uttering his damning words. 'Oh!' he announced, his voice trembling with emotion. 'So now I'm just a wee fucking poof. Well, it wasn't that last night when you were shagging the arse off me, was it?'

There was a stunned silence at the accusation and all eyes swung to Boulder Head, expecting some sort of immediate retaliation, violent, verbal or both. Well, we got one, but it wasn't the one we were expecting. It would seem that Boulder Head had decided to apply reverse psychology. Mandy wouldn't embarrass him; he would embarrass Mandy.

'Aye!' He looked round the shop with a stupid grin on his face and yelled at his accuser. 'I was right up you last night! And you fucking loved it, you wee cow!' He stood up and made violent pumping motions with his hips. 'You fucking loved it!'

'Oh, aye,' Mandy replied. 'You were up me all right,' he repeated, positioning himself at the head of the stairs in preparation for a speedy retreat. 'But why don't you tell your pals that while you were up me, you were giving me a wank!'

'You fucking wee bastard!' Boulder Head leaped to his feet, ready to do murder. But Mandy was too far away and too quick for him, bolting for the safety of the downstairs workshop to the sound of our raucous laughter.

There was another occasion when an 'accident' occurred that led to the unexpected disclosure of a face as a closet homosexual. A young guy arrived in the hall, a round, glowing-faced, bespectacled little fellow with a very definite effeminate air about him. Now this little guy, I don't recall his name, was small even to me and I'm barely five foot eight, so to the towering six-foot-three Big Wullie D he must have seemed a veritable midget.

Apparently, Big Wullie had managed to sneak the little guy into his cell where, in the unlit shadows, he proceeded to have his hitherto-unsuspected wicked way. It so happened that a young, inexperienced screw was supervising that evening and was patrolling the landing when he heard strange grunts and heavy breathing emanating from Big Wullie's cell. An older, more experienced screw would have minded his own business and just walked on by, but not this guy. He just had to stick his nose in and upon opening the door he discovered two naked men locked in what could only be described as a homosexual embrace. Or, as the screw later informally described it, Big Wullie was buried to the balls in the wee guy's behind.

It must be reported here that Big Wullie's presence of mind upon being caught in this compromising situation was admirable. 'Help! Help!' His voice rang round the landing. For a moment, some of us thought there had been an incident, perhaps an ambush – a common occurrence in PH. But when the little guy appeared from the darkness of Wullie's cell, shirt over his arm and still pulling up his strides, all became clear.

Help, help? No chance! No one was having any of that.

The situation was viewed so seriously by his associates that I was called in to arbitrate on the matter so they could decide whether or not Big Wullie should be expelled from the gang. I like to think that I was quite open-minded in my appreciation of the situation. What I said was: 'What harm has Big Wullie actually done? He's still the same guy and it's really nobody's business what he gets up to behind closed doors. If Wullie enjoys a bit of bum, so what? It doesn't mean he wouldn't stand by you.'

'Aye, and you can fuck off too!' I was collectively informed after delivering my considered opinion.

There was one regular in Peterhead, however, who made no bones about his sexual behaviour. Nellie Drummond was, strangely enough for a person of his inclinations, well liked and on good terms with most of the known villains and jailbirds of Scotland. In fact, many of them knew him outside and had even worked with him on occasion. However, although during his spells in the free world Nellie kept his homosexuality well in the closet, once in jail he became quite brazen.

Nellie also got on well with the screws whenever he was in Peterhead and on admission to B Hall, his usual residence, he would be put in charge of the stores, the cleaning and the hot plate, all of which he organised with the efficiency of a first-class maitre d'. As well as this, he would immediately take over the jail bookmaking business, to which he applied the same dedication and efficiency as his daily work, even accepting cash bets from several of the screws.

IT'S CRIMINAL

There are a lot of stories about big Nellie and the things he got up to in Peterhead and there's no doubt in my mind that Ronnie Barker's Fletch could have learned a thing or two from him. Along with the usual tobacco trade, he trafficked in chocolate bars – three for two on a weekly basis – as well as trading in banknotes (25p in the £1 commission) smuggled in from visits. I always thought that if Nellie had applied himself on the outside half as much as he did when he was inside, he would have been a millionaire in no time. Needless to say, stories about big Nellie are legendary in the Scottish prison system, especially among the older cons, but I have always considered the two I am about to relate here as among the best.

The first story concerns Nellie's bookmaking dealings. In the 'good old days', before drugs became the pre-eminent trading commodity in prison, every jail had a bookie and prisoners would bet with tobacco, receiving their winnings in kind. But prisons, harbouring the sort of people they do, meant that the bookie was a target, with nearly everyone trying to put one over on him. One desperado spent hours perfecting the insertion of bread into an empty tobacco packet, boldly presenting the finished product to Nellie as his stake on a horse that duly obliged at odds of 3–1.

'Oh aye,' says Nellie when the trickster appeared. 'You had that bet on the 3–1 shot, didn't you?'

'Aye,' the confident conman held out his hand. 'Makes a change to pick a winner, eh?'

Unperturbed, Nellie looked the man straight in the eye and repeated, '3–1, wasn't it?' before turning away to open his cupboard. 'Right then, I'll just get you your winnings.'

The beaming gambler could hardly contain himself, no doubt already dreaming of an entire weekend puffing away on unlimited roll-ups, probably thinking about swapping a half-ounce for a few bars of chocolate to round off his celebrations.

'There you are, that's your stake back,' Nellie handed over the original doctored tobacco packet, then, with his face straight as a die, he counted out three thick slices of bread into the shattered prisoner's outstretched hand. 'And at 3–1, that's your winnings.'

The other story that went the rounds of PH was that a newcomer, a naive young prisoner, made the mistake of going into Nellie's cell to borrow a couple of LPs. 'Oh, aye, sure, son,' Nellie said, as he invited the young chap into his cell. 'You'll find a box of them under the bed. Take a look and see if there's anything you like.'

Then, as the unsuspecting young man bent low to look under the bed, Nellie suddenly grabbed him round the neck in a half-nelson, at the same time ripping off the unfortunate chap's trousers. Now everyone had heard stories about Nellie having a massive member and personally I can only go on hearsay, but rumours were rife – Nellie was *big*! The story goes that as Nellie forced himself upon the attractive young man, holding him tightly in his favoured half-nelson grip while thrusting away at his rear, the lad was heard to scream, 'Stop it! Stop it! You're hurting my neck!'

Strangely enough, after that incident it was seldom anyone in PH ever had the nerve to complain about having a sore neck ...

Chapter Twenty-six

The Coodgie Gang

B oring' is probably the most common adjective used in prison, because that's what it is. It was the stories the cons told about themselves, myself included, that gave us the best entertainment. A laugh is always welcome in jail. One old storyteller, Michael John Burnside, a well-liked prisoner of traveller stock and the last man to be declared an outlaw in Scotland, was, for the umpteenth time, relating some of the adventures he had while prowling and plundering the Highlands of Scotland.

Hyperbole would be a word unknown to Mick, but it was certainly no stranger to the structure of his stories. 'Aye,' he spoke in hushed tones as he related one of his many adventures, 'I had just done the safe in the Oban bus depot and was heading for the hills, but someone must have seen me and phoned the police. Och, there must have been a thousand of them out looking for me that night. But I wasn't worried because once I get into the countryside that's it. I'm off! No one can find me once I reach the hills. You see,' he would say and nod a knowing head, 'I know every blade of grass, every rock, tree, bush and burn in the Highlands. It wouldn't matter if there was a million people out looking for me, once I hit the hills I'm safe.'

'You're talking a lot of shite!' announced Walter E, a man well known for his direct, outspoken opinions. Now normally this sort of outright, embarrassing accusation, especially in front of witnesses, would be deemed a serious insult and be met with an immediate violent reaction. But Walter was an old prison friend of Mick's, so the insult was tolerated to the extent that an explanation was required before any action would be considered.

'Oh, a load of shite, is it?' Mick demanded. 'And how do you make that out?'

'You just told us that you know every blade of grass, every rock, tree, bush and burn in the Highlands, didn't you?' He repeated him word for word, leaving no room for error about what Mick had said.

'Aye, that's right! That's what I said. And it's a fact, too. I know every inch of the Highlands, so I do.'

Everyone sat back and listened in. Walter's wit was well known and we all knew he was going to say something that would devastate Mick's outrageous claim. Walter looked at Mick and nodded, as if considering his choice of words. 'Well,' he finally said in the deadpan voice he adopted when putting someone down, 'if you know every inch of the Highlands, how come you were up to your neck in a swamp when the cops found you?'

One look at Mick's face told a tale on its own. Guilty as charged!

I spoke to Mick a few minutes later and asked him about it. 'Aye,' he said, ruefully shaking his head. 'He's fucking right enough. He knows everything, that bastard.'

'So what happened?' I asked.

'I was getting away,' he told me, 'when I jumped over this dyke, landed in a bog and sunk right up to my neck. No kidding, I thought I was going under and I let out a roar that the police would have heard ten miles away. The fucking cops came and pulled me out and the story got into the bloody papers. That's how that bastard knew about it.'

Violent behaviour was commonplace in Peterhead and I was

witness myself to several assaults, many of them serious and resulting in outside charges being made. One man was even charged and found guilty of murder, receiving the mandatory lifer for his trouble. At one stage, things got so bad in the tailor's shop that our large cutting shears were taken from us and we were issued with tiny, blunt little snips we could hardly get our fingers through to use properly. It came to the point when a fight hardly caused anyone to lift their heads from their machines. Even these days, years later, I have found myself sitting in a pub when a fight has broken out with people all around me scrambling wildly to get out of the way, while I just sit there in the midst of it all trying not to spill my pint.

The loss of our big scissors, however, cost us an amusing and highly competitive pastime. These scissors were about a foot long, their large handles giving them, if you used your imagination, a pistol grip. With the ruler pocket down the right leg of our overalls as a holster, we had all we needed for fast-draw competitions. You could almost hear the Clint Eastwood music as the 'gunfighters' faced each other down the length of the passage between sewing machines, eyes fixed, fingers quivering over their weapons.

It was serious stuff and prestige was at stake. The signal was given and hands blurred into motion as both went for their guns. Bang! Kapow! Then the arguments began, like kids playing cowboys and Indians.

'Got you!'

'Bollocks, you were well beat!'

'Fuck you, you're dead!'

'No I'm not, I got you first!'

'You're fucking dead, you cunt!'

'Who are you calling a cunt?'

Suddenly the 'guns' became knives or bludgeons and the cons would be rolling about the floor, hacking and stabbing at each other to settle the argument. Then the riot squad would arrive to cart them off, usually via the treatment room, to the punishment cells. It wasn't really surprising that our 'shooters' were eventually taken from us – they were causing almost as much damage as the real thing.

Another pastime, and this applied to any workshop, was sabotage, burning out the sewing-machine motors being the most common form of action in the tailor shop. All you had to do was press hard on the foot pedal while preventing the wheel from turning with your hand. This overheated the motor and, in a few minutes, its copper windings would heat up and burn off their insulating varnish, sending acrid-smelling smoke belching from the machine. Another burn out! Although it didn't take long for a replacement motor to be fitted, it caused disruption and the perpetrator would enjoy an hour or so sitting back with a self-satisfied grin on his face.

Arson, too, was attempted at every opportunity. Simple incendiary devices like home-made candles would be hidden away in storerooms or remote corners in the hope that they would burn down and set fire to the workshop a few hours after it had closed for the night, giving the flames time to inflict maximum damage. There had been some success at this in earlier years, but gradually the cons had run out of hiding places and all they could count on now was a temporary flare-up and some superficial damage. But any conflagration, however small, was seen as a moral victory and greeted by cheers from the cons. They knew they were annoying the screws and keeping them, quite literally, on their knees with daily searches for hidden time bombs.

And this war against time didn't just end in the workshop. The cell blocks had more than their fair share of incidents to keep life interesting. Many seagulls – and they're big bastards up there – have been captured by a string snare laid out on a window ledge and stowed away in someone's cell cupboard. In the darkness of the cupboard, surrounded by alien sounds, the frightened seagull would sit dead quiet. After nine o'clock, by which time we were all locked up and everything had quietened down, the seagull would start to move around a little, gradually making more and more noise until finally the con would rise to investigate the source of the strange sounds. You can imagine his surprise when, on opening the cupboard door, a huge seagull leaped out at him, screeching loudly and frantically flapping its five-foot wingspan in the confines of the cell. We could all tell when this happened because the hysterical screeches and screams emanating from the cell were loud enough to wake the dead, causing the rest of us to convulse in fits of laughter!

There was one gang in Peterhead that I cannot fail to mention and, believe me, at least half the prisoners in PH were fully paid-up members. What's more, the tentacles of this particular gang spread insidiously across the entire prison estate both in this country and abroad. In the UK, they are known as the Coodgie (could you) Gang and many a hardened con has been spotted ducking furtively aside to avoid the approach of a known member.

Prerequisites for admission to the gang are simple: an eagle eye, well-honed stalking skills and the ability to make a perfectly timed swoop on an unsuspecting mark are basic requirements. These, along with a brass neck and an ingratiating smile, topped off by a whining, 'poor me' voice and you have all the necessary attributes for membership of the Coodgie Gang.

You might think you are alone and unobserved as you sneak your snout tin out to grab a fly smoke. But it is a known fact that at least one member of the Coodgie Gang will mysteriously materialise by your side and you will hear the dreaded words: 'Coodgie give us a wee puff of that, pal?' For him, it's a *fait accompli*; for you, it's a roll-up and Coodgied again.

Every demand is always delivered in an appropriately obsequious tone and manner: Coodgie give us a biscuit? Coodgie give us a magazine? Coodgie give us some sugar, some milk, some tea, some coffee? Whatever you possessed, a Coodgie man desired.

There was one member of the Coogies, Tam 'the Tapper' L, who was well known for his scrounging proclivities and he had no shame about it either. In fact, Tam thought it was an admirable accomplishment to be able to scrounge his way through his time. And I am forced to admit that I was a victim of his constant tapping myself. I know it would have been easy to say no, but I have my own little set of standards I work to and one of them is that I don't mind sharing things like sugar and teabags and such like. I don't smoke and always had enough cash to buy things like that from the canteen. So if someone asks me for a spot of sugar and I have some in my cell I will not refuse them, even if they do, like Tam the Tapper, take advantage and come every day.

It must have gone on for months, so much so that it simply became another part of the daily routine. Every day, just before lock-up, Tam's outstretched cup-carrying hand would appear through my doorway, followed by his head and shoulders bearing the most ingratiating grimace I have ever seen, before or since.

'Aye, Tam?' I would greet him as if it had never happened before.

'Aye, Bing,' he would reply, his face almost ingratiating itself to death. 'Coodgie spare me a wee drop of sugar?'

'Aye, help yourself, Tam.' I gave him free rein to my sugar and to be fair he only ever took enough for the one cup. Now I honestly didn't mind giving Tam some sugar every day; in fact, I found the daily pantomime amusing. Still, I found myself wishing that one day Tam would turn up and I could honestly tell him that I didn't have any sugar.

Then, one day, it happened. I forget the reason why I had no sugar that particular time – maybe I had more guests in than usual that week and my sugar had just run out a bit earlier. Whatever the cause, I had no sugar and I couldn't wait for Tam to appear to tell him so. Sure enough, dead on time, he appeared at my door.

'Aye, Bing,' the show began. 'Coodgie spare me a wee drop of sugar?'

'Sorry, Tam,' I replied, trying to keep the delight out of my voice. 'There's none left.'

'None left!' The bold Tam's voice expressed disappointment and there was a brief flash of confusion in his eyes. 'Aw fuck it!' he finally said. Then, without even a blush, he looked me in the eye and asked, 'Coodgie just give us a wee teabag instead, then?'

I could only shake my head. Coodgied again! I had to admit it: the guy was a genius.

IT'S CRIMINAL

Although they were a nuisance, there is no doubt that the Coodgie gang added a certain colour to life in drab Peterhead. Their insidious presence forced you to learn new skills in avoidance techniques and diversionary tactics, almost like living outside, in the struggle to repel their advances without causing offence. The 'two tobacco tins' ploy came into being because of them – an empty tin was produced as evidence of poverty, while your real tin remained out of sight in your pocket. It is the same now with phone cards, a wise man showing an almost used card to fend off any would-be tappers. You learned to keep items like teabags, coffee, sugar, milk and biscuits hidden away in a cupboard, only to be taken out once your door was safely closed to acquisitive eyes. Another tactic was to anticipate an approaching Coodgie and get your own request in first. Then, recognised as a fellow Coodgie, the rest would leave you alone and you might get a bit of peace. The only trouble with that particular move was that you could gain an unwanted reputation yourself – but it was all part and parcel of surviving in jail.

Steering a safe, neutral passage through Peterhead wasn't always easy for a lot of the guys. I didn't have things too bad myself because everybody knew me and knew what I was in for. And although I had committed serious offences I didn't offer, and was never perceived as, a threat to the current kingpins of the jail. On top of that I had the reputation, among the guys in Peterhead anyway, of being quite brainy. I was always being asked to settle arguments and help guys out with their lawyers' letters, write petitions and prepare parole submissions. On the whole, I got on very well with everyone as time marched slowly by.

Riots came and riots went. Hunger strikes were a regular occurrence and outright rebellion was never far away in Peterhead. One time, Big Hosie, Stein, John O'Boy S and a few others fought a pitched battle in the yard with the screws, won and climbed on to the roof of reception and the punishment block wearing captured riot gear – shields, helmets and long white batons. For the rest of the day, they marched about the rooftop, chanting aloud like gleeful children, 'We won the war! We won the war!' Two or three days later, after a visit from a Scottish Office official, a truce was declared. The rioters agreed to come down from the roof by one o'clock. Then, at about half past twelve, smoke began belching out from the reception office windows as the rioters broke in and set fire to the clothes and clothing records of the inmates, all to the frustration of authority and loud cheers from those cons who could see it from their windows.

The fire brigade had been standing by but, although the flames were soon doused, nothing was saved. What hadn't been destroyed by fire was damaged by smoke and the hoses of the fire department had completed the destruction. Not to worry though – the jail was insured.

About three weeks after the fire, the insurance assessors arrived and every prisoner was interviewed regarding their loss. Naturally, with the clothing records gone, every con made the most of their claim. Guys who had been arrested in T-shirts, jeans and trainers were claiming for Chester Barrie suits, Ben Sherman shirts and Gucci shoes. Everyone, except the insurance company, of course, had a field day. One guy even had the nerve to claim for a suitcase full of expensive clothing, plus the case as well. There was no argument – it was all paid out in full. Word later filtered back that the insurance company considered the cons of Peterhead to be the best-dressed criminals in the UK!

A postscript to that particular story was that the screw in charge of prisoners' private cash was run off his feet as the grateful cons spent their windfall on the newly permitted possession of tape decks and record players. With each claim averaging around £200 there was a total of around £70,000 floating about the prisoners' coffers. Manna from heaven there to be spent and spend it they did.

For weeks afterwards deliveries to the jail were made on a daily basis, every delivery requiring prisoners' private cash cards to be altered and the cash signed off. Then the purchase had to be recorded, in triplicate of course, and sent down to reception to be signed on to the prisoner's property card. The lucky buyer was then marched down to the reception to sign for receipt of his purchase, sign it on to his property card, then sign it out again as 'in use' – all typical bureaucratic prison rigmarole. With so much work being generated, the screws should have been grateful for the overtime, so in a sense, you might say the fire benefited everybody in one way or another.

The cons in Peterhead never did anything by halves. Even the governor was known to take things to extremes at times. Perhaps it was the ambience of the place, the underlying tension, the short tempers and routine violence in Peterhead that caused people to behave irrationally at times – I suppose there must be some sort of psychological explanation. I do know that the screws there got an extra environmental allowance because of the alleged contaminating effect of constant association with low-life cons affecting their own moral standards and personal lives.

With so many incidents and diversions, time slipped away in Peterhead and after four or five years I came off high security and started attending education classes. I soon found myself involved in O-level examinations. I must admit that I found no difficulty with any of my subjects and quickly moved on to ONC and HNC courses in Business Studies, all of which I passed, several of them with distinction.

Then I was offered an Open University place, which I declined as the only course left with spaces that year was mathematics, a subject I was never very good at and had never studied beyond secondary level. By this time, however, I had developed a serious interest in writing, spurred on by the success of John C, a guy in PH who had written a play that had won first prize in the annual Arthur Koestler Awards Scheme, a writing competition open to all prisoners in the UK.

The following year, I spent most of my spare time writing, producing among other things a 90,000-word crime novel and a stage play about bent coppers. I entered these two items in the Koestler Competition and was very pleased and surprised to win first prize in both categories. My success, along with the prize money, gave me the incentive to buy a typewriter and I immersed myself in writing from then on.

Of course, I still had work to do, but after nearly seven years I had progressed to a job in the prison stores department and things were a lot more relaxed. For one thing, I no longer had to line up in the yard every morning to be counted off, a small perk, but it made a difference to the start of each day. I had also progressed to C Hall, the so-called 'privileged' wing and thirty years on I am still trying to figure out just exactly what these privileges were supposed to have been.

However, the main point in being moved to C Hall was that you were now considered trainable and were listed for possible upgrading to a less secure establishment. In the meantime, things stayed much the same as before: the same old faces surrounded you and the same old jail business just kept rolling along.

Eventually, after eight years or so, I was told that I was to be upgraded and transferred to Saughton, the prison where my sentence had begun. My goodbyes were few and casual at that. I had always taken care not to establish any enduring friendships and the three or four long-termers I had mostly associated with were equally offhand. We exchanged addresses and phone numbers; maybe we would get in touch or run into one another again, maybe not. Two or three days after being told of my move, I was sitting in reception smelling stale from stored clothes, waiting for the bus to take me away.

Peterhead certainly held a lot of memories for me, both good and bad; and I was glad to be moving on, but I couldn't help looking back at the place as the prison bus drove off. I remember craning my neck to catch a last glimpse of the workshop chimney, my first sight of the jail and now, hopefully, my last. When the chimney finally disappeared behind the shoulder of a hill for the last time I thought, almost aloud, Well, that's that. But I continued to stare in its direction for another few seconds, as if to make sure it really had gone.

Chapter Twenty-seven

Blagger on the Box

When I arrived in Saughton, I only had about four or five years to do. *Only!* That's what I mean about time being different in jail. We say 'only' to periods of time that would see a student through an entire university course that would qualify them in one of the professions. There was one drawback to arriving in Saughton from Peterhead: we had such a bad reputation that every screw in the place was determined to show the Peterhead gangsters, as they called us, that we were nobody special and they could keep us in our place. Almost every screw in the place made a point of picking on us, mostly just to show their colleagues that they were not going to be intimidated. In fact, more than half the cons upgraded from Peterhead actually asked to be sent back, saying that at least they knew where they stood in PH.

I was lucky. I had my writing to keep me busy and the fact that I had been successful in the Koestler competition for the past couple of years gave me a bit of leverage in getting extra time at the education classes. I justified this time by writing a novel called *Ashanti Gold*, which won the Outstanding Award prize in the Koestler the following year.

There was no doubt that facilities at Saughton were better than Peterhead. There was better access to the gym, drama classes, Alcoholics Anonymous, a chess club and even the Prison Christian Fellowship to go to in the evenings. With plenty to do, I had no problem passing the time and, when I wasn't attending some meeting, I worked away at my writing.

On one occasion, I thought my writing had got me into some serious trouble. It was well known among the guys that I had a typewriter in my cell, which meant that I was always being asked to write letters for someone or other. One evening this con, a Moroccan milkman who lived in Edinburgh and was serving life for murdering his wife, came into my cell with a piece of paper in his hand.

'Sshhh, sshhh,' he said and put his fingers to his lips, looking furtively around, as if he suspected someone was following him. 'Is secret,' he whispered. 'Please, you don't tell anyone?'

'Come on, come on,' I said, impatiently holding out my hand for his note. 'Just give me the fucking letter and I'll type it out for you.' I didn't have time to muck about with all this secret-service stuff.

'Is secret,' he said again. 'You keep secret?'

'For fuck's sake, pal,' I told him. 'Just give me the bloody letter.' I just wanted the job done and Abdul out of the way. 'Come on, letter!'

'OK,' he says. 'You write for me, please.'

This letter went along the lines of:

Dear Governor and Chaplain

I am sorry. I kill my wife and now she is in heaven. I feel bad about this and I want to be with her again. I go to be with her now. No blame for you or anyone. I just want to be with my wife.

Abdul

What a load of shite, I said to myself, dashing it off and handing the finished letter back to him. 'There you go, Abdul. That do you?'

'Thank you, thank you. You good man. I remember you in heaven.'

Aye right, fucking idiot, I thought to myself. I went back to my own work, totally dismissing the incident from my mind. Then a few days later, around two in the morning, I was awakened from my sleep by noise and flashing blue lights outside my window. When I got up to look at the commotion, I saw an ambulance with paramedics unloading oxygen equipment from it.

Jesus Christ, I thought to myself. He's only gone and done it! Then a terrible thought struck me: the note. The bloody suicide note. I was the only con in the jail with a typewriter. 'Oh fuck!' I said aloud, with no thought for the demented Moroccan. 'They'll take my typewriter away.' I listened at my door to the sounds in the hall, feet pounding upstairs, keys rattling, doors opening, then a stretcher rushing past and the ambulance taking off.

At morning slop-out, I emerged from my cell waiting to be pounced on and hustled away to the cells. Then I spotted the Moroccan, large as life and emptying out his piss-pot. What a relief! It wasn't him and my machine was safe.

It later transpired that one of the men in a two-man cell had assaulted his cell mate with a metal chair so severely that he had caused permanent brain damage. Prison black humour raised its head and the story went round that the injured guy had been reading one of my stories out aloud and his cellmate hit him with the chair to shut him up. A pack of lies, of course! But I made up my mind about one thing: no more suicide notes from me!

Shortly after that, the governor sent for me and asked if I would be willing to appear on a BBC2 television programme called *Bookmark* and be interviewed about my writing. Of course, I was delighted. As a result of this, I was moved on to the semi-open conditions of Dungavel Prison out in the sticks near Strathaven in Lanarkshire, a cynical move to make things look good for the television people.

When I got to Dungavel, I found that the governor was a pompous, self-important, fat little prat. He loved the idea of the cameras in his prison, but he didn't like a con being the star of the show. And it really bugged him that because of the forthcoming TV appearance he had to be seen to be encouraging me in my writing. In actual fact, the fat little bastard was as awkward as he could be, telling me that he didn't consider my writing to be work and insisting that I scrub a flight of stairs every day before he would allow me to 'play', as he put it, with my typewriter.

On top of that I taught myself to type Braille and did lots of bits and pieces like knitting patterns, instructions booklets and even a restaurant menu for the local blind – all good PR stuff for the jail. Then, to top it off and prove my work had value, I won another Koestler Award with a crime thriller – *The Golden Stool* – an action-packed sequel to *Ashanti Gold*. So I earned and justified my time spent on writing. And that little prat hated every minute of it.

Some months later, the BBC team appeared at Dungavel and I did my stuff. They filmed me scrubbing the stairs, eating my dinner, working out in the gym and jogging, all wonderful PR for the Scottish Prison Department. Finally, they had me typing away in my 'office', a converted toilet, as I informed the presenter. Apparently I made a good subject and they were pleased with the show. The show's presenter, the literary critic Ian Hamilton, made the comment, 'Crosbie's writing is as good as and shows at least as much ingenuity as the average crime writer today.' High praise indeed from Mr Hamilton.

I was actually naive enough to expect a rush of offers after the show was broadcast, but nothing developed. All I ended up with was a bit of publicity, two large bars of chocolate and £25 for my co-operation. But I really enjoyed making the show and when it was screened the whole jail turned out to watch it on TV. What they were actually looking for was to see whether or not I was a creep, handing out thanks to the jail and the governor and all the staff for their help. But I didn't let the chaps down, getting laughs and cheers when I brought out the fact that the governor had made me work in a toilet and more when I reported that I received no help at all from the prison, having to scrub stairs to earn time to write and even buy my own writing paper. The show went down well with everyone, except the governor who stayed out of the jail in a huff for the two days it took them to make the programme.

If I got nothing else out of the television programme, it at least got me away from closed conditions and into a semi-open nick. I spent the next couple of years in Dungavel before finally being offered a place in the Training for Freedom (TFF) hostel attached to Perth Prison. I quite liked the idea of that and packed my kit for the move, heading north again. Fat Prat had another last dig at me by sending me to Perth under escort in the back of the laundry van. Normally any prisoner moving on to TFF gets an automatic six-day home leave and reports directly back to the TFF hostel. But that guy definitely held a personal grudge against me – and he's the only member of prison staff I've ever said that about.

So, after about twelve years, I was on the last leg of my twenty and starting my Training for Freedom. Sure it sounds great, but in reality all it means is that you get turfed out of the hostel at half past seven every morning with a packed lunch of cheese sandwiches and orders to report to some menial job, where you are expected to know your place and be grateful for the opportunity. I didn't like it very much. In theory, it sounds great; in practice, it is not for real long-termers, guys who have served periods of ten or twelve years inside and have forgotten what it is to work properly. It's impossible to simply shake off the lethargy of doing time and leap overnight into a normal work routine. The first day or so, maybe even the first week, is a bit of a novelty, but then you begin to notice that the week seems to be going on forever. Then you realise that your late morning start, with its long, lazy tea break, exercise period and two-hour lunch, has been swapped for what seems a straight eight-hour shift of hard graft.

Every day seems like a week and a month is just too long to

think about. It's like looking at time through the wrong end of a telescope, the exact opposite of doing time inside where your days are compressed and broken up into short periods of activity. Believe me, it's a struggle both mentally and physically to get through TFF.

And time isn't the only problem facing a prospective long-term release. Things that a normal person takes for granted caused me unexpected embarrassing moments, like handling cash and getting confused over decimal currency. I remember going into a cake shop on my way back to the jail after my first day of work on TFF, very conscious of the fact that this would be my first cash purchase for over twelve years.

I remember trying to be casual, offhand even, as I rapped out my order: two chocolate éclairs, two pineapple cakes, a couple of empire biscuits and an apple tart. I handed the lady behind the counter a pound note, confidently expecting change back. I flushed red with embarrassment when she asked for more money and suddenly felt everyone in the shop was staring at me and knew exactly who and what I was as I stuttered back at the shop assistant and changed my order to a packet of chocolate biscuits.

There was this one particular guy who put things into perspective: the ubiquitous Walter E. Now Walter had just served a full fourteen years out of a twenty-one-year sentence for armed robbery and barely three months after his release found himself back in the High Court again on a similar charge. Found guilty, he was asked by the judge if he had anything to say in mitigation before sentence was handed down. Indeed, Walter had plenty to say.

He told the judge that he had been released after fourteen years in Peterhead Prison without so much as one day's preparation for the outside world. He said that he had never received any trade training and in all that time he hadn't seen a tree or a dog or a child. The whole world had moved on; even the district where he lived had been rebuilt and, when he had asked the governor to supply him with a map, his request was denied. He was released after fourteen years with just a travel warrant and one week's social-security money with which to begin a new life.

Once on the outside, he had felt totally disorientated and completely out of touch. Decimal currency was a complete mystery to him, traffic a total hazard. And when he ran after a corporation bus and tried to jump on board, he bounced off the back because they had moved the doors to the front. In an alien world, unemployed and unemployable, he had simply drifted back into crime and now found himself in front of the court again.

The judge was rather sceptical about these allegations and told Walter that he had intended handing down a severe sentence. However, having listened to him speak, he decided to defer sentence until he had looked into the matter. On Walter's return to court a few days later, the judge told him that he had been shocked to discover that everything he had said was true. After announcing his disapproval of the Prison Service and deploring its total lack of any pre-release training for Walter, the judge, almost apologetically, sentenced him to a minimum term of three years.

I was out on the exercise yard in Saughton the day Walter returned from court. Everyone had tipped him for a twelve, a ten at the very least, but there he was smiling all over his face and shouting out the window at me, 'Got a three, Bing. I'll be out before you!' And so he was. But I had the last laugh, because unfortunately Walter later got a twelve-year sentence and I was actually out before him.

The TFF did have certain perks: six hours a week free time to be taken in the evenings or over the weekend and the luxury of a full weekend home leave once a month. That was probably the only thing that made TFF bearable for the likes of myself. But it was a double-edged sword: returning to the hostel after a weekend leave once a month was like getting captured all over again – sheer torture.

I had long since been divorced and my ex-wife was staying in my house in Bishopbriggs. I found myself spending my weekends with Mum. Fifty years of age and back at Mum's! Thank God for her and God bless her too, because I really don't know how I would have managed if she hadn't been there for me.

But it was nice to get out now and relax at home again, knowing that it would soon all be over.

I was eventually given eight months' parole, getting liberated from Perth TFF hostel one bright morning as casually as a man who had just paid a fine. With around £20 in my pocket, plus the discharge grant of £38, I was set to face the world again, hoping that I wouldn't bounce off any buses along the way.

Did the TFF work? Well, that's another story.

Afterword

Iceland Can Wait

So there I was, a free man. I had worked my way through the system and now my hope was of new horizons. While in prison, I had sent a book out to a publishing company. Now, some five years later, my life story is published – not the typescript I originally sent and not by the publisher I sent that first typescript to, but published nevertheless.

After being released, I married my loyal girlfriend Marlene in 1999. And now, I'm back behind bars, doing an eight-stretch. How did it all happen? Where did it all go wrong? A rather bizarre set of circumstances sees me writing this from behind the bars of HMP Castle Huntly near Dundee. I must be the first man to be charged with attempting to smuggle drugs out of Scotland, or even the whole of Britain.

In 2000, while waiting on the west coast of Scotland to board a ship bound for Iceland, I was arrested by HM Customs. They found me wearing a corset of cannabis wrapped around my body, I must rather embarrassingly say. Not my preferred *modus operandi* and not my forte as far as crime goes, but it happened.

After starting my sentence, I was moved on through the Scottish prison system. After a failed appeal bid, I managed to pull myself back from the brink of depression and started writing again.

Although I remained in constant communication with Stephen Richards, the man behind the first publishing company I approached, I just couldn't get back into the stride of things. But thanks to his prompting me on, I found a renewed vigour in the writing stakes. I've ditched my crime-ridden days and now look forward to a career in writing. And my heartfelt thanks are due to my wife Marlene, for her loyalty and support during this last stint behind bars. Iceland can wait.